Tear Down the Walls

Tear Down the Walls

White Radicalism and Black Power in 1960s Rock

PATRICK BURKE

The University of Chicago Press
Chicago and London

The University of Chicago Press, Chicago 60637
The University of Chicago Press, Ltd., London
© 2021 by The University of Chicago
All rights reserved. No part of this book may be used or reproduced in any manner
whatsoever without written permission, except in the case of brief quotations in
critical articles and reviews. For more information, contact the University of Chicago
Press, 1427 E. 60th St., Chicago, IL 60637.
Published 2021
Printed in the United States of America

30 29 28 27 26 25 24 23 22 21   1 2 3 4 5

ISBN-13: 978-0-226-76818-2 (cloth)
ISBN-13: 978-0-226-76821-2 (paper)
ISBN-13: 978-0-226-76835-9 (e-book)
DOI: https://doi.org/10.7208/chicago/9780226768359.001.0001

Library of Congress Cataloging-in-Publication Data

Names: Burke, Patrick, 1975– author.
Title: Tear down the walls : white radicalism and black power in 1960s rock /
    Patrick Burke.
Description: Chicago : University of Chicago Press, 2021. | Includes bibliographical
    references and index.
Identifiers: LCCN 2020043576 | ISBN 9780226768182 (cloth) | ISBN 9780226768212
    (paperback) | ISBN 9780226768359 (e-book)
Subjects: LCSH: Rock music—United States—Social aspects—History—20th
    century. | Rock music—United States—1961–1970—History and criticism. | Black
    power—United States—History—20th century. | Music and race—United States—
    History—20th century.
Classification: LCC ML3917.U6.B87 2021 | DDC 782.42166/1592—dc23
LC record available at https://lccn.loc.gov/2020043576

♾ This paper meets the requirements of ANSI/NISO Z39.48-1992 (Permanence of
Paper).

For my parents

Contents

Introduction

For instance, what is a white person who walks into a James Brown or Sam and Dave song? How would he function? What would be the social metaphor for his existence in that world? What would he be doing?

LEROI JONES [AMIRI BARAKA], 1966[1]

Why Do Whites Sing Black?

ALBERT GOLDMAN, 1969[2]

Brothers, it's time to testify and I want to know: Are you ready to testify? Are you ready?

J. C. CRAWFORD, 1968[3]

Tear down the walls! Won't you try?

JEFFERSON AIRPLANE, 1969[4]

This book begins with some difficult but tantalizing questions about a practice fundamental to American (and thus global) popular music—white fascination with, and imitation of, Black performance. The questions that musicians and critics ask about this practice, as well as the answers they propose, depend on their beliefs about the cultural, social, and economic relationships among white and Black musicians and audiences. One observer, perhaps (but not necessarily) white, seeking to demonstrate the possibility of interracial respect and collaboration, might answer with such words as "borrowing," "influence," "imitation," or "homage." Another observer, perhaps (but not necessarily) Black, invested in protecting African Americans' cultural property, might choose more pointed terms such as "appropriation" or "theft." And the answers always raise more questions. From Frederick Douglass's 1848 critique of blackface minstrelsy to Brittney Cooper's 2014 takedown of white rapper Iggy Azalea, the conversation has shown no sign of winding down.[5]

This book examines these questions in a particular context: white US and British rock musicians' engagement with Black Power politics and African American music during the late 1960s. This was a moment when many musicians and critics raised serious questions about white uses and understandings of Black music. The Black poet and critic Amiri Baraka, then known as LeRoi Jones, asks rhetorical questions that answer themselves. His hypothetical white person simply cannot function meaningfully in the world of James Brown and Sam and Dave. For Baraka, Black music is rooted in a "racial memory" encoded into an embodied history.[6] He writes, in a metaphor evoking fugitives from slavery, that he "can tell, even in the shadows, halfway across the field, whether it is a white man or Black man running."[7] Whereas the music valued by whites reflects "the softness and so-called 'well being' of the white man's environment," Black music creates "a place where Black People live . . . a place, in the spiritual precincts of its emotional telling, where Black People move in almost absolute openness and strength."[8] Given Black music's fundamental bond with Black lives, whites can only "steal" the music, cheapening it with their "constant minstrel need, the derogation of the real."[9] It is white performers and promoters who profit from the innovations of Black musicians. Baraka defines "integration" as "the harnessing of Black energy for dollars by white folks, in this case in the music bizness," and he argues that Brown "will never reap the *material* benefits that several bunches of white folks will, from his own efforts."[10] For Baraka, white appropriators demean Black music even as they steal and sell it.

White *New York Times* critic Albert Goldman, in contrast, emphasizes the psychological transformation undergone by white youth who imitate Black musicians. Goldman notes a change that distinguishes 1950s rock and roll from 1960s rock: "the kids who were once content merely to listen and dance to the sounds of Ray Charles and Little Richard have moved on to adopt a whole new identity of black gesture and language—of black shouts and black lips, black steps and black hips." But why, and with what authority? "Let's put it bluntly," Goldman demands as he stereotypes both sides of the equation, "how can a pampered, milk-faced, middle-class kid who has never had a hole in his shoe sing the blues that belong to some beat-up old black who lived his life in poverty and misery?" Goldman turns to Janis Joplin, "this generation's favorite culture creole," to ask "why do you work in vocal black face?"[11] Joplin's answer—"being black for a while will make me a better white"—proves revelatory for Goldman: "she had articulated this generation's great secret. They are *not* trying to pass. They are trying to save their souls. Adopting as a tentative identity the firmly set, powerfully expressive mask of the black man, the confused, conflicted and frequently self-doubting and self-loathing offspring of Mr. and Mrs. America are released into an emotional and spiritual freedom denied them by their own inherited culture." Having undergone "the adventure of transvestism . . . some of our leading culture chameleons" (he mentions Steve Winwood and Paul Butterfield) "are casting their black skins," developing musical styles of their own "that owed nothing, save intensity, to black tradition."[12] For Goldman, imitating blackness forms a necessary developmental stage for white rock musicians, who then must abandon their Black inspiration to assume their true selves. The "Woodstock Nation," Goldman argues, "no longer carries its soul in its genes."[13] As historian Jack Hamilton points out, this was a common argument among 1960s rock critics, who proposed that "black music provided the imaginative basis of rock's rebellion, but belonged to an earlier generation: it is not of a piece with rock, but rather something that preceded and enabled it."[14]

Meanwhile, white rock musicians asked their own questions. White hype man J. C. Crawford's call to "testify," delivered in an attempt at the fervid style of a Black preacher or perhaps a Black Panther, was aimed at a largely white audience in Detroit who had gathered to hear the MC5, a white quintet who justified their adaptations of James Brown and Sun Ra by claiming an affinity with the Black Power movement. The MC5, thanks to their manager, poet and critic John Sinclair, were aware of Baraka's arguments, but they believed that their political and musical dedication made them an exception to the rule against white appropriation. Jefferson Airplane, one of the most popular "acid rock" groups of the late 1960s, had turned by 1969 from introspective psychedelia to a militant political stance. Their song "We Can Be Together" directly quotes a notorious line—"Up against the wall, motherfucker!"—from a poem by Baraka, although their demand to tear that wall down is capped by a plaintive, decorous request: won't you try?

This book is about white rock musicians and activists who tried to tear down walls separating musical genres and racial identities during the late 1960s. Their attempts were often naïve, misguided, or arrogant, but they could also reflect genuine engagement with African American music and culture and sincere investment in anti-racist politics. With their music and their politics, the subjects of this book raised a fundamental question, later posed succinctly by jazz scholar Ingrid Monson: "Just what would an ethical white relationship to African American music look like?; furthermore, is there such a thing?"[15]

Rock, Race, and Revolution

This book considers this question by recounting five dramatic incidents that took place between August 1968 and August 1969. In each instance, white people involved in the rock scene made artistic and moral decisions inspired by their understanding of contemporary African American music and politics. While their decisions sometimes resulted in a new musical phrase, a new stage routine, or a change to a lyric sheet, at other times they led to fistfights and arrests. Each story sheds light on a significant but overlooked facet of 1960s rock—white musicians and audiences casting themselves as political revolutionaries by enacting a romanticized vision of African American identity.

The year 1968, when uprisings from New York to Mexico City to Paris signaled an international moment of youth protest, marked a watershed in the racial politics of the New Left.[16] Historians of the 1960s often draw a line between "cultural radicals," who sought individual liberation through changes in consciousness and lifestyle, and "political radicals," whose activism stressed more pragmatic and organized means of protesting such concrete political issues as racial discrimination and the war in Vietnam.[17] Rock critic Robert Christgau complains that in fuzzy, nostalgic accounts of the 1960s, "politicos and heads are conflated into a 'counterculture' that was never as homogeneous as that potentially useful term implied—that from my vantage looked bifurcated."[18] These categories were never hard and fast; Christgau goes on to explain, for example, that he and partner Ellen Willis bridged the divide in their lives and work and demonstrated "how roomy and heterogeneous a concept 'counterculture' could be."[19] A fundamental tension, however, persisted between the two camps, with political radicals belittling hippies as self-indulgent and apathetic while hippies dismissed political protesters as intolerably preachy, earnest, and dogmatic.[20] During and after 1968, however, these lines increasingly blurred in what historian Terry H. Anderson terms the "second wave" of the sixties.[21] As political radicals explored the new freedoms opened by the so-called "cultural revolution" of the hippies, cultural radicals shocked by the virulence of official crackdowns on their communities began to take a more hardheaded approach to political issues. Perhaps the most famous US group to fuse cultural and political radicalism were the Yippies, self-proclaimed "political hippies" who employed surreal humor and outrageous stunts to further what they called the "youth revolution."[22]

Synthesizing cultural and political radicalism required both sides to reconcile differing ideas about African American identity. White political radicals in the United States, despite their disparate agendas and viewpoints, derived much of their language, tactics, and values from the African American civil rights movement. By 1968, US radical groups included exclusively or predominantly Black organizations such as the Student Nonviolent Coordinating Committee (or SNCC) and the Black Panther Party, but white radicals outside such groups continued to draw on the rhetoric of Black leaders and to grant them special moral authority. Hippies like those in San Francisco's Haight-Ashbury or Manhattan's Lower East Side, in contrast, were largely white middle-class dropouts who lived in a "segregated Bohemia" and fetishized the cultures of India and of Native Americans rather than that of African Americans.[23] The fusion of cultural and political radicalism, then, did not mean simply that bohemians found themselves reassessing the value of political engagement; it also meant that they were revisiting the notion of African Americans as hip, idealized role models.

Many white radicals valorized the courage and sincerity of Black Power leaders and sought to appropriate their style and their rhetoric, which according to one observer posed a "moral demand" to white Americans by "calling America to its moral self."[24] As historian Doug Rossinow demonstrates, "black power and the burgeoning freak counterculture combined to help convince white leftists that the entire culture they had inherited was rotten but that they could make it anew."[25] Widely publicized figures such as Abbie Hoffman and Jerry Rubin of the Yippies embraced a stereotypical vision of macho, transgressive Black masculinity, going so far as to claim that they had effectively become Black by living in accordance with this stereotype.[26] As Nadya Zimmerman points out, often such identification said more about the private desires of white radicals than about interracial politics. For the counterculture, she writes, "'the political consciousness of black people' in the black power movement illustrated a way to live, rather than being heard as a call to fight alongside people who had been discriminated against for hundreds of years."[27] White activists with sincere intentions faced uncertainty about their role in the Black freedom struggle. As Christgau writes, "for years white anti-racists could arrive at no way to respond reasonably to the reasonable demand that black people run their own movement."[28]

This demand arose from a Black Power movement that resisted both liberal assimilationist politics and the counterculture and often sought distance from collaboration with whites. As historian William L. Van Deburg explains, many Black radicals felt that "unlike the poor blacks whose culture they attempted to imitate, all the hippies had to do to reap the advantages of their class was to clean up, clear out their drug-fogged brains, and rejoin the ranks of the economically secure. Surely, said a growing number of black activists, no lasting coalition could be made with such people."[29] While the Black Panthers' emphasis on class struggle rather than Black nationalism led them to form alliances with white activists of the New Left, their "faith in white radicals and Marxism" was "a belief shared by no other major Black Power organization."[30] Even the Black Panthers were deeply torn over white involvement in their activities, with the party's Honorary Prime Minister Stokely Carmichael warning the Panthers against becoming "the black shock troops of the white New Left and the 'counterculture'" and calling hippies "cowards," even as Minister of Information Eldridge Cleaver negotiated an alliance between the Panthers and the white activists of the Peace and Freedom Party, who nominated him for the US presidential race in 1968.[31] In his influential 1967 book *The Crisis of the Negro Intellectual*, critic Harold Cruse accused white radicals of appropriating Black politics as well as Black culture: "without an ideology relevant to America, white leftwingers are forced to attempt to take over the control of any incipient Negro trend that appears revolutionary."[32]

Despite such pointed criticism, white activists continued to get involved in Black Power causes, and some of the most visible were artists. Amy Abugo Ongiri notes that "white actors, artists, and intellectuals, such as Jean Seberg, Marlon Brando, Bert Schneider, Agnes Varda, Jean-Paul Sartre, and Romain Gary, and political activists such as Ulrike Meinhof of Germany's Red Army Faction, Abbie Hoffman and Jerry Rubin of the Yippies, and Bernardine Dohrn of the Weather Underground, all proclaimed an affinity for and affili- ation with the Black Panther Party, which was seen as providing important models not only for political and social change but also for a deeply personal transformation."[33] Ongiri argues against Tom Wolfe's famous dismissal of such affinity as merely "radical chic," a term that "flies in the face of the actual depth of the affiliations in question and the depth of the repression that faced those who engaged in them."[34] "To reduce the commitment of politically radi- cal but privileged whites such as Seberg to 'radical chic,'" Ongiri asserts, "is to paint a cynical and extremely reductive picture of the possibility and the cost of cross-racial identification in the 1960s and 1970s."[35] Singer-songwriter Elaine Brown, whose 1969 album *Seize the Time* promoted Black Panther ide- ology and who chaired the party from 1974 to 1977, believes similarly that "radical chic" was "a superficial stereotype," and that while some white sup- porters merely "imagined themselves vicariously linked to some dramatic revolutionary act . . . all of them, the strongest and the most frivolous, were helping us survive another day."[36]

The subjects of this book sought to employ Black music in the service of "revolutionary" aims that included spiritual metamorphosis, political protest, free publicity, and sometimes all of them at once. The notion of the "rock revolution" of the 1960s has become a commonplace, serving as shorthand for a conventional vision of the era's music and politics.[37] As historian Peter Doggett argues, during the late 1960s "'revolution' entered the rock lexicon— rarely defined or explained, but a catch-all refrain that symbolised a genera- tion's quest to overturn the old order and replace it with a new climate of liberation, that would free body, mind, and soul."[38] The racial implications of this purported revolution, however, are often overlooked. Historian How- ard Brick argues that the counterculture was constructed on a "mass-culture base . . . built around a market-mediated form of popular expression (rock music) inflected with the rebellious sentiments of the working class and oppressed peoples, particularly African Americans."[39] Rock, a form dominated by white musicians and audiences but pervasively influenced by African American music and style, conveyed deeply felt but inconsistent notions of Black identity in which African Americans were simultaneously subjected to insensitive stereotypes and upheld as examples of moral authority and revolutionary authenticity.

White rock musicians' desire to identify with Black radicalism and their anxiety over their own authenticity manifested themselves in both musical style and the value and significance placed on rock. Hamilton argues that "casting off the shackles of one's whiteness through musical performance was central to musical and personal authenticity" for white rock musicians during the 1960s.[40] But engagement with Black Power politics added new complexities to this quest for liberation. If white musicians could play Black music, did this earn them an authentic relationship to Black political struggle? Or was such struggle a prerequisite for performing authentic Black music? Or was acknowledging that they could *never* play Black music authentically the real struggle faced by white musicians? As jazz-turned-rock critic Ralph J. Gleason asked in a 1968 essay, "Can the White Man Sing the Blues?"[41]

Usurpers and Utopians

A reader well versed in popular music studies and concerned about racial issues might reasonably ask, why another book about white rock musicians? They have hardly been neglected in the literature on 1960s popular music, and they are often valorized in ways that implicitly or explicitly diminish Black performers. As John J. Sheinbaum points out, "the conventional narrative reasserts largely segregated spheres of activity in the mid-1960s at the same time that it disproportionately values those spheres."[42] Historical accounts that uphold white performers such as Bob Dylan and the Beatles as artistic "geniuses" often condescendingly depict Black musicians such as Aretha Franklin or Motown's stars as "'craftspeople' eager to make themselves acceptable to a general (read: white) audience."[43] An honest appraisal of the astonishing creativity and artistry of African American popular musicians of the 1960s such as Franklin, James Brown, and the Temptations belies the implication that white rock musicians were somehow more significant. To highlight Black musicians' imitators might confirm Nelson George's charge that "to applaud black excellence and white mediocrity with the same vigor is to view them as equals, in which case the black artist in America always loses."[44] Moreover, white musicians certainly were not necessary as musical propagandists for Black Power, a role ably served by such Black innovators as Curtis Mayfield (the Impressions' "We're a Winner"), Elaine Brown and Horace Tapscott (*Seize the Time*), or members of the Black Panther Party's own band, the Lumpen.[45]

One might respond that it is precisely white musicians' centrality to conventional conceptions of "rock" that demands that scholars rethink them as racial subjects in a contested musical and cultural environment rather than assume them to comprise an unmarked, normative category. This has long been a primary aim of whiteness studies, a field that seeks to defamiliarize whiteness and reveal its contingency and constructedness. I consider this an important project. At the same time, however, I am cognizant of some persuasive critiques of whiteness studies. One criticism is that whiteness studies, usually unintentionally, tends to reinforce racial categories rather than challenge them. As E. Patrick Johnson puts it, "a focus on whiteness may paradoxically reify the hierarchical racial binary between 'black' and 'white' that currently exists."[46] Another concern is that conducting scholarship on whiteness may give white scholars the smug but false sense that they have transcended its privileges. As jazz scholar Hilary Moore asks, "does complicating whiteness glorify and romanticize a racial identity inextricably linked with hegemony and privilege? Is it a 'get out of jail free card,' an opting out of the inescapable responsibility and guilt for past and present privilege and oppression?"[47]

I have tried here to find a way of addressing white musicians that avoids these hazards. This book is not as much about making whiteness visible as about rendering *blackness* newly *audible* in a music often understood as self-evidently white. As Jack Hamilton demonstrates, by the end of the 1960s "rock and roll music—a genre rooted in African American traditions, and many of whose earliest stars were black—came to be understood as the natural province of whites."[48] By the 1970s, the music later canonized as "classic rock," despite its significant debts to blues, soul, and jazz, was performed almost exclusively by white musicians who often failed to acknowledge those debts. The attention paid to Black performers such as Jimi Hendrix, Arthur Lee, and Sly Stone highlighted their token status rather than their centrality to the genre.[49] The radical rock of 1968–1969, unusually, continued to acknowledge Black influence, musical and political, at a moment when that influence was disappearing from rock's public image. The stories that I tell here thus reveal that rock has to be considered in light of a complex interracial culture. Such an approach seeks to counter the clichéd vision of 1960s rock as the soundtrack for a predominantly white counterculture. Hearing white rock musicians through a racial lens that makes their whiteness apparent does not inevitably perpetuate racial essentialism; rather, it can reveal the interconnectedness of racially diverse musicians and audiences in the creation of rock as it foregrounds the centrality of blackness.

I also have tried to remain aware of my own position as a white academic engaging a tradition in which I am a performer as well as a scholar. I have been a guitarist since middle school, when my interest in improvisation and my love of such blues-influenced classic rock bands as Led Zeppelin and Cream soon led me to begin playing, studying, and listening to blues and jazz. At my predominantly white, suburban Pittsburgh high school (class of 1992), I listened to *The Best of Muddy Waters* or John Coltrane's *Meditations* on my Walkman between classes. Black music, for me, wasn't about contemporary politics, about which I knew little—rather, it represented a kind of esoteric power that I could access through amassing used LPs, learning to play their lead guitar lines, and reading whatever romantic stories I could find about the musicians' lives. (That I sought to enhance my teenage masculinity by imitating Black men did not strike me as especially odd, as plenty of my white classmates fetishized Michael Jordan or Chuck D.) Throughout high school and college I played in post-punk and hard rock bands that covered songs by Black artists such as Jimi Hendrix and Smokey Robinson, as well as jazz groups in which I did my best to mimic Wes Montgomery or Grant Green. Although I remember once playing at a campus benefit for unhoused Philadelphians, the contexts in which I performed were almost never explicitly political. Nonetheless, I felt a sense of shared energy and warmth while playing at sweaty house parties and crowded bars that could be described as utopian.

This book, then, represents in part an attempt to answer questions I've been considering throughout my life in music. One of these has to do with my relationship to Black music. In the years since college, I have developed a more nuanced understanding of music's racial politics. Although I genuinely considered Black musicians heroic figures, and my love and respect for their music was sincere, my adolescent self didn't understand much about America's fraught history of racism and resistance. Now I understand that my performing and listening inevitably involved, and continues to involve, elements of misrepresentation and appropriation, in new variations on what Eric Lott terms "love and theft" in his influential study.[50] The white musicians whom I profile in this book attempted to grapple with similar concerns in complex ways that can be instructive even when they were not successful.

Another important issue running through this book is music's potential to bring about moments of utopia. This idea has been explored in detail by Josh Kun, who describes "audiotopias" as those "pieces of music" that reveal "music's utopian potential, its ability to show us how to move toward something better and transform the world we find ourselves in."[51] Audiotopias, in

Kun's telling, "encapsulate and articulate the meeting of different cultural and linguistic spaces," spaces "both sonic and social," sometimes subjective and sometimes literal and physical.[52] My early experiences revealed both music's power to unlock my individual imagination and the feeling of togetherness and mutual support that music can create between people. Many of the young people I discuss in this book had a palpable sense that music could change the world, and the conflict they felt between their utopian visions of society and their more realistic sense of music's limits continues to mirror my own.

But enough about me.[53] I hope that this book will be of use to white musicians wrestling with the ethics of involvement with Black music, as well as for politically engaged readers interested in white musicians' attempts to contribute to Black liberation movements during the 1960s. Readers of color, and African American readers in particular, likely will not be surprised to hear that there is a long history of white musicians performing and profiting from Black music. In this book, I relate episodes from this history not to uphold a triumphalist narrative of white victories over racism, but rather from a critical perspective that emphasizes these musicians' frequent missteps and insensitivities, often a result of their naïve unawareness of their own privilege. At the same time, I seek to highlight those moments when white musicians considered Black music and politics seriously and thoughtfully, in order to assess the political and musical strategies that made such moments possible.

Authenticity and Appropriation

An examination of white rock musicians also can shed new light on bigger questions about the connections between racial identity and popular music. To what extent is music-making fundamentally bound up with socially prescribed racial identities, and to what extent does it represent instead moments of hybridity, flux, and contingency? When musicians and listeners believe that they hear race in music, are they attending to something immanent and essential, or are they limited by cultural filters that prevent them from hearing sameness across racial lines?

Perhaps the most rigorous and thoughtful statement of the latter position is Ronald Radano's 2003 book *Lying Up a Nation: Race and Black Music*. Radano argues that the notion that an "immutable black essence" informs Black music relies on "strategies of containment" that ultimately reinforce belief in an unbridgeable racial difference rather than acknowledge "the interracial background from which ideologies of black music developed in the first place."[54] "The invention of 'Negro music,'" Radano writes, "may best be understood as a deferral of a potentially transgressive cultural achievement"—a tradition of interracial music-making repressed by official ideologies of race.[55] If white Americans "seek to claim" Black music for themselves, it is "precisely because these expressions grew from the same circumstances of national culture."[56] In a later essay, Radano points to the ironic process by which African American music became both a marker of racial difference and a symbol of shared national identity: "black music, as the ultimate expression of what is different between black and white, became the unifying folk music of the United States."[57] "Our investment in the truth of black difference," Radano argues, keeps us tied to arguments about authenticity rather than allowing us to perceive a musical culture "inherently built on racial contradiction."[58] For Radano, racialized conceptions of music, even when they serve as a source of Black pride and self-assertion, ultimately maintain a fiction of racial difference that prevents the recognition of our common humanity. Jack Hamilton brings a similar stance to rock scholarship by rejecting "ideas of cultural ownership, essentialist originalism, and racial hermeticism: a belief that there is a clear and definable boundary between 'black music' and 'white music' in America that resists porosity."[59]

Other scholars propose diverging arguments about the value and necessity of retaining some notion of racial authenticity. Critic and historian Guthrie P. Ramsey Jr. argues that while "ethnic identities like African Americanness are, indeed, 'socially constructed,'" they remain "powerful realities."[60] Ramsey contends that "all this talk about fluidity, indeed the idea of ethnicity as a process and not a static existence, does not prevent our understanding how people experience group identity from a reified, though contested, 'center.'"[61] Ingrid Monson, while she demonstrates "recursive cultural exchange" between Black and non-Black musicians, points out that such exchange has always been complicated by racial injustice.[62] Monson argues that African American musicians have never "been paid in proportion to their aesthetic contribution" and that "the discourse of racial authenticity . . . historically has been one of the few discursive weapons available to African Americans to protest the inequalities of the economic outcome, as well as to advocate for self-determination."[63] African American critics who point to white "'dilution,' 'imitation,' or 'stealing'" of Black music often seek justifiably "to emphasize the unequal economic playing field on which this took place."[64] White liberals' claims about "colorblindness" and music's universality serve "to censor African-American claims that they have a special relationship to the music by virtue of having endured the social experience of racism."[65] If scholars are to "critique claims of black authenticity," Monson contends, they must also address "the longstanding discourse of white resentment and the history of the racially stratified economic structure in music."[66]

It is important to note that these arguments overlap more than brief summaries might suggest. Radano, for example, acknowledges the significance of African retentions in African American music even as he rejects essentialist interpretations of them, and he also emphasizes the context of racial inequality in which conceptions of Black music developed, with particular attention to the horrors of slavery.[67] Monson, in turn, allows that "it is quite possible . . . for whites, Asians, Latinos, and members of any other constituency to have *real* relationships to the repertory [of African American music] and their own extensions of them without having to assert that those relationships are exactly the *same* as those of African Americans."[68] In this formulation, authenticity hinges on the possibility of multiple valid positions toward Black music rather than on a fixed racial identity. Critic Greg Tate, who accuses white appropriators of Black culture of taking on "everything but the burden" of blackness, nonetheless admires white musicians such as Bob Dylan or Frank Zappa who "found ways to express the complexity of American whiteness inside Black musical forms."[69]

This book builds on the work of these and other scholars to seek a middle ground between condemnation and celebration of white performance of Black music, a version of what Paul Gilroy terms "anti-antiessentialism" in a foundational essay.[70] Or one might consider my position in terms proposed by performance studies scholar D. Soyini Madison, who writes about a critical impasse between "cynics," who believe that any attempt to perform as or for "an Other is ultimately an act of crass appropriation, self-indulgence, and distortion," and "zealots," who believe that they "speak *for* the Other better than the Other can speak for herself, and they *know* what it means *to be* the Other." Between these two poles of "uncomplicated suspicion" and "uncomplicated enthusiasm" lies a third option that Madison terms the "performance of possibilities," marked by "an ethics guided by caution and a strategy informed by cultural politics."[71]

Such an exploration of possibilities, informed by ethical and political considerations, is what I attempt in this book. Although I acknowledge that interracial exchanges have been essential to the history of music in the United States and UK, to think of them only in terms of "borrowing" or "tribute" would be to ignore the structural racism that has allowed white musicians and promoters to profit from idioms innovated by Black musicians. Without reifying racial categories as natural or essential, I acknowledge the value of a notion of racial authenticity for African Americans upholding the value of their cultural traditions in the face of racism. Furthermore, as a white scholar,

I refuse to justify appropriation with appeals to hipness or a disingenuous rhetoric of colorblindness.[72] I'm also well aware of white Americans' and Europeans' tendency to embrace Black cultural expressions while ignoring or denigrating the people who create them.[73] Yet white imitation of Black music has taken on many forms and meanings.[74] Might some of its iterations support progressive racial alliances, or at least resist the legacy of misrepresentation and stereotyping?

Pretense and Possibility

I propose that radical white musicians during the 1960s were invested less in direct imitation of African American music than in adapting and synthesizing it, seeking to rework its practices and principles into forms that were relevant, and perhaps radicalizing, for their predominantly white audiences. Genres from avant-garde jazz to blues to funk were employed in a variety of creative ways to evoke a sense of militant commitment or encourage creative freedom. It is commonplace to explain the surreal juxtapositions of 1960s rock as signifying psychedelic explorations of an interior landscape, but few critics have noted the extent to which such juxtapositions are rooted in an exploration of signifiers of blackness. Indeed, the very construction of "rock" as a genre distinct from "rock and roll" was marked by a racial paradox: the interracial foundations of the music were masked even as its interracial borrowings became more adventurous and white musicians' anxieties about racial authenticity became central to the music. I hope to demonstrate that the white musicians I profile, while they cannot be excused from charges of appropriation, reflected a self-consciousness about the politics and history of appropriation. Examining this self-consciousness can shed new light on 1960s rock and its relationship to racial politics. In particular, it reveals that white performance of Black music could represent a reflexive, ironic tactic as well as more irrational expressions of racially charged fantasy and desire.

It follows that I am not especially interested in making judgments about whether or not the white responses to Black music that I describe were "authentic." As E. Patrick Johnson argues, "the key . . . is to be cognizant of the arbitrariness of authenticity, the ways in which it carries with it the dangers of foreclosing the possibilities of cultural exchange and understanding."[75] If one defines authenticity as inherent to those performers and audiences who possess profound understanding and experience of the complexities of African American life, one can readily concede that Jefferson Airplane or the MC5 were not authentic, but this concession cannot fully explain the cultural significance of their music. Instead, I prefer to historicize my subjects' own ideas about authenticity to see what they reveal about interracial music-making and political commitment during the 1960s.

This strategy leads me to assess a largely binary, Black-and-white model of race in this book, not because I seek to uphold this division, but rather because so many of the people I profile were so deeply invested in it. As Hamilton writes, "racial-cum-musical discourse" on rock during the 1960s "was almost entirely conducted on these grounds, at least within the critical and commercial mainstream."[76] Although images and sounds ostensibly drawn from Native American or Asian cultures were common within late 1960s rock—take the Grateful Dead's image as "psychedelic Indians," or the vogue for the sitar after its embrace by the Beatles—these influences often served as a source of exoticism and a connection to an idealized mysticism rather than as inspiration for political engagement.[77] Native American musicians made important contributions to rock, but their identity either went unmarked, as with the Band's Robbie Robertson during the 1960s, or was treated as a novelty, as when Mothers of Invention drummer Jimmy Carl Black announced himself as "the Indian of the group."[78] Latinx groups such as ? and the Mysterians and Sam the Sham and the Pharaohs achieved national popularity during the mid-1960s with a garage-band sound influenced by Mexican music, but "as rock reached its psychedelic phase in the mid to late 1960s, it seemed to tune out the Latin influence," and most audiences missed the influence of mambo and *guarácha* rhythms on groups such as the Rolling Stones and the Rascals.[79] For the rock press and many musicians and listeners, rock was essentially a white music with Black forebears, with the more obviously eclectic approach of a group such as Jefferson Airplane constituting a set of intriguing exceptions rather than the rule.

Neither was a notion of racial fluidity a significant part of the discourse of 1960s rock. Monson, addressing avant-garde jazz in the same moment, points out that "in the late 1960s the celebration of 'doubleness' or 'inbetweenness' was hardly in vogue," as many Black musicians instead embraced a cultural nationalism rooted in racial identity.[80] White rock musicians' attempts to leap over or break down racial barriers nonetheless presumed those barriers to exist in some fundamental way, and many of those I profile can rightly be termed essentialists.

White musicians' and radicals' essentialism encompassed the imitation and valorization of racial stereotypes, particularly the notion of Black men as hypersexual studs who demonstrated their power in part through subjugation of women. Their statements of solidarity, expressed through the ostensibly ironic employment of racial slurs or borrowed wholesale from Black Power rhetoric, were intended to shock then and often are simply offensive today—take Jerry Rubin's claim that "the hippie-yippie-SDS movement is a 'white nigger' movement," or "hip" white musicians' ubiquitous use of the racial slur "spade" to refer to African Americans.[81] I will often be quite critical of the pretentions and presumptions of my white subjects, whose relationship to Black music involved misrepresentation and self-aggrandizement as well as respect and homage. Most importantly, I do not claim that the *confusion* often felt by whites as they attempted to negotiate their place in Black music and Black radical politics was somehow more significant or more painful than the *exclusion* experienced by African Americans within the music industry and within US society more broadly.[82]

While acknowledging the patronizing and self-serving aspects of white radicalism, however, I also want to pay attention to the multifaceted ways in which white radicals fought against racist orthodoxies. My subjects generally proceeded from the liberal assumption that racism is wrong, and they attempted earnestly to undermine it with their music and their political involvement. But they diverged from liberal consensus by refusing to pretend to a colorblind worldview, assuming instead a fundamental racial difference between white and Black people that they (paradoxically) had the power to transcend. This difference was not framed primarily in terms of biology, but rather in terms of cultural authenticity. Whites who showed enough political and cultural commitment could not become Black, perhaps, but they could embody the soulfulness and righteousness that they associated with blackness. Such a position was both rigidly essentialist and insisted on the possibility that white radicals could contribute to Black liberation by listening respectfully and working courageously across racial lines.

This belief demonstrated the hallmarks of what anthropologist John L. Jackson Jr. terms "racial sincerity." "Questions of sincerity," Jackson writes, "imply social interlocutors who presume one another's humanity, interiority, and subjectivity. It is a subject-subject interaction, not the subject-object model that authenticity presumes—and to which critiques of authenticity implicitly reduce every racial exchange." He adds that "where authenticity lauds content, sincerity privileges intent—an interiorized intent that decentralizes the racial seer (and the racial script), allowing for the possibility of performative ad-libbing and inevitable acceptance of trust amid uncertainty as the only solution to interpersonal ambiguity."[83] Although intent is notoriously difficult if not impossible to prove, the actions and statements of the white musicians I discuss seem to reflect a presumption of Black "humanity, interiority, and subjectivity" alongside the acceptance of ingrained stereotypes and misperceptions. Contrary to Monson's assertion that "white Americans since the 1960s seem to have been interested primarily in the *fun* parts of

African American culture," or Goldman's assumption that white musicians took on blackness only in order to outgrow it, the musicians I address were serious about their relationship to Black political struggles, if only in halting and imperfect ways.[84]

Black activists, intellectuals, and musicians during the 1960s often asserted that the intent and sincerity of white musicians mattered. The Black Panther Party admired the music of Bob Dylan, whose "Ballad of a Thin Man," according to Bobby Seale, was analyzed by Huey Newton as a "history of racism" and was played and discussed repeatedly by party members working on the *Black Panther* newspaper.[85] Critic Albert Murray, although he disparaged white "jazzologists" who claimed expertise in Black music, praised "serious white jazz musicians" for their "intellectual and artistic sincerity," claiming approvingly that such musicians "eagerly embrace certain Negroes not only as kindred spirits but also as ancestral figures indispensable to their sense of purpose and to their sense of romance, sophistication, and elegance as well."[86] Archie Shepp, one of the most emphatic advocates of Black Power in 1960s jazz, was known for taking strong stands against white appropriation, asserting that "jazz is the product of the whites—the ofays—too often my enemy. It is the progeny of the blacks—my kinsmen. By this I mean: you own the music, and we make it."[87] Encountering Canned Heat guitarist Henry Vestine at an Albert Ayler recording session in 1969, Shepp "glanced at Vestine's long hair and pale face. 'I'd have liked your playing a lot better,' he told Henry, 'if I hadn't seen what you looked like.'"[88] Yet in 1968, he told jazz critic Nat Hentoff:

> The underlying symbolism of jazz . . . has always been black, and so have been the great innovators. But jazz is accessible to all people, if they're honest enough to receive it. [White trombonist] Roswell Rudd in our band is an example of that. It's an honesty that's necessary not only in jazz, but with regard to the most crucial problem in America—the racial problem. Most whites have allowed the relationship between the races to deteriorate, but there are some who are honest about what has to be done and who do see the need for profound and meaningful change in this country to end racism.[89]

While decrying the white-dominated music business and racism in the United States more broadly, Shepp suggests that sincere, "honest" white musicians such as Rudd may contribute to the solution.

Some Black musicians, particularly those invested in cultural nationalism, rejected Shepp's position and chose to avoid collaboration with whites. Chicago's Association for the Advancement of Creative Musicians, for example, expelled white vibraphonist Emanuel Cranshaw in 1969 amid concerns about preserving "its bona fides as a truly 'black' organization," while in Los Angeles some members of the Underground Musicians Association "developed an exclusionary stance toward nonblacks."[90] At the same time, however, even those Black musicians most associated with Black pride and Black Power sometimes chose to work with white musicians. James Brown, whose "Say It Loud—I'm Black and Proud" became an anthem in 1968, toured Vietnam during the same year with white bassist Tim Drummond on the grounds that "soldiers seeing a White man and a Black man sharing the stage together was a good thing."[91] Although Brown was ambivalent about the Black Power movement, Black musicians more overtly supportive of it also collaborated with white performers.[92] The Black Panther Party's band, the Lumpen, included white musicians, and the band's members "recount with pride the fact that when Black Nationalists refused to accommodate their white bandmates, the group as a whole responded in defiance and demanded that their white revolutionary musicians be treated as equals."[93] These examples, which involve groups led by Black musicians, differ from situations in which white musicians chose to play Black music on their own. Nonetheless, they reveal that there was more to the racial dynamic of popular music during the late 1960s than a simple conflict between appropriation and resistance.

Was there, then, any value in white radicals' faltering attempts to employ Black music in the service of progressive racial politics? If one takes a conventional view of political influence, the musicians profiled in this book failed, either because their interest in radical politics proved fleeting or shallow or because they rejected pragmatic political action in favor of utopian adventure. But perhaps these musicians proposed instead a "prefigurative politics," which historian Carl Boggs defines as "the embodiment, within the ongoing political practice of a movement, of those forms of social relations, decision-making, culture, and human experience that are the ultimate goal."[94] In other words, to practice prefigurative politics is to experiment with forms of social life that do not yet exist in the wider world. Boggs argues that the New Left was notable in "its glorification of spontaneity and subjectivity, in its celebration of everyday life, and in its hostility to 'politics' and all forms of organization."[95] As Wini Breines points out, more pragmatic political organizers tend to criticize such efforts as "utopian, romantic or unrealistic, and often irresponsible."[96] Prefigurative politics, then, tends to be aspirational rather than strategic: as Doug Rossinow puts it, "political radicals planned simply to demonstrate the superiority of the egalitarian and authentic way of life to which they aspired, and they hoped that their cultural alternative would triumph as a result."[97]

Yet such utopian experiments aren't necessarily without merit, as commentators from the 1960s to the present have asserted. Breines, quoting French activist Daniel Cohn-Bendit, describes "experiments that broke with existing society but could not last, experiments which allowed a 'glimpse of possibility' which was 'enough to prove that something could exist.'"[98] Stuart Hall, writing in 1968 on "The Hippies: An American 'Moment,'" argued that "it may be that all this is a utopian dream. But it is of such dreams that the revolutionary project is made."[99] And E. Patrick Johnson argues that "some sites of cross-cultural appropriation provide fertile ground on which to formulate new epistemologies of self and Other."[100] In 1968, some white rock musicians believed that performing and adapting Black music could contribute to what in the Black Lives Matter era is sometimes called "white allyship." This book explores their efforts and asks what lessons can be learned from them.

Honkie Soul

The MC5 at the Democratic National Convention
Lincoln Park, Chicago, August 25, 1968

On Sunday, August 25, 1968, on the eve of the Democratic National Convention in Chicago's International Amphitheatre, the MC5, a rock quintet, performed for protesters in nearby Lincoln Park. Early announcements by the Yippies, the playful radicals who planned a "Festival of Life" to protest the convention, had promised performances by a wide array of musicians, including Country Joe and the Fish, the Fugs, and the Steve Miller Blues Band, with invitations outstanding to everyone from Bob Dylan to Jefferson Airplane to the Beatles.[1] Yippie provocateur Abbie Hoffman proclaimed that "while they [the Democratic delegates] go through sterile roll calls, we will dance in the streets to Country Joe and the Fish."[2] The MC5, already notorious in their native Michigan for their hard-driving music and revolutionary politics, responded enthusiastically to the Yippies' invitation. In April, Yippie Walli Leff wrote to the band's manager, John Sinclair, to report that "we're looking forward to hearing all your Detroit heavy music and are working on getting sound equipment for the Park in Chicago to accommodate everyone who will be playing."[3] Shortly thereafter Sinclair defended the planned festival in a May letter to Jann Wenner, publisher of the recently founded *Rolling Stone*: "Hope your feuds with Jerry Rubin don't make you distort the real scene with the Yippies any more. All our bands are planning to make it to Chicago because we've been that way all along—ain't nobody leading us astray."[4] On August 7, the Ann Arbor *Sun*, a newsletter produced by Trans-Love Energies, the commune in which Sinclair and the MC5 lived, reported that the Yippies had "scheduled rock and roll concerts for each evening and afternoon of the Festival" and that Ann Arbor bands including the MC5, the Up, and the Psychedelic Stooges (as they were then known) also planned to perform.[5]

As it turned out, the MC5 was the only out-of-town rock band who played in Chicago.[6] In his column in Detroit's underground paper *Fifth Estate*, Sinclair boasted that "the Fearless 5 was the only group in the whole fucking country to show up and play for their brothers and sisters in the Youth International Party." (Sinclair acknowledged that Ed Sanders and Tuli Kupferberg of the Fugs, while not performing with their band, were involved in the protests, and that Country Joe McDonald had left town only after some South Carolina delegates beat him up in a hotel elevator.)[7] Years later, MC5 drummer Dennis Thompson still felt betrayed: "Chicago was supposed to be the show of solidarity, goddamn it. This is the alternative culture? Come on. Where were all the other bands?"[8] Guitarist Wayne Kramer remembered more sympathetically that "there were supposed to be bands from all over the country playing, West Coast hippie bands too, but they had second thoughts about it and, with hindsight, they were right."[9] Many musicians, recognizing the threat of violence if they came to Chicago, maintained their distance. San Francisco's Jefferson Airplane, for example, declined Hoffman's invitation to perform in Chicago. As guitarist and singer Paul Kantner later explained: "I appreciate the fact that some people did bother to go there and get their heads kicked in on our behalf, but I couldn't see any reason for us to go and get beaten up."[10] The MC5, as rock musicians committed to their Yippie "brothers and sisters," were an anomaly. Although folk stalwarts Phil Ochs and Peter, Paul, and Mary led protesters in song throughout the events in Chicago, rock musicians did not play a major role.[11]

Lincoln Park, then, hosted not a rock festival but rather a hasty set by a lone, obscure band. The MC5 had to perform at ground level because Chicago police refused to allow the Yippies to bring a flatbed truck into the park for use as a stage, and the band's Marshall amps (draped with US flags) were powered through a single extension cord that Ed Sanders, reeling from the effects of hashish-infused honey, managed to plug into a refreshment stand's outlet.[12] In his 1970 book *Shards of God*, a surreal fictionalization of events in Chicago, Sanders depicted the MC5's "ultra high energy set" as an erotic, life-affirming respite from the tensions of the protest: "on all sides of the stage the prone porn-mammals began to search out and touch one another upon the skin when the godful MC5 began their concert. They sang songs of strong communist realms of banned bras, artisan peace, hemp smoke, communal food, free electricity, and bunch punching. We were happy. Thoughts of mammal-peace filled our minds for a while, replacing the corrosive fear of police tails, Daley, satanism, brutality, clubs, and bullets."[13]

But the MC5 themselves were terrified. Kramer, in his 2002 essay "Riots I Have Known and Loved," insists that "the footage we've all seen a thousand times on TV, of demonstrators and police fighting in the streets, doesn't do justice to the tangible fear. It was an unsettling in the stomach; a gnawing, creepy feeling, like an inescapable cloak of dread. We felt it coming and there was absolutely nothing we could do about it." As government agents in the crowd of several thousand shot surveillance film of the band, "we played our set, and we could feel the tension building. There were no smiling faces in the crowd." Once the music ended, "we knew from experience to get our amps and drums packed double-quick for our escape and, sure as shit, the first phalanx of motorcycle cops muscled through the crowd as soon as we stopped playing."[14] For lead singer Rob Tyner, between the helicopters flying overhead, "people who looked like Lee Harvey Oswald walking around with funny-looking packages," and the paranoia induced by hash brownies, "it was scary, man."[15] Sinclair remembers that as police closed in and Abbie Hoffman "grabbed the microphone, and started rapping about 'the pigs' and 'the siege of Chicago,'" the band made a hasty exit to their van and drove straight home to Ann Arbor.[16]

Norman Mailer offered a more distanced account in his book *Miami and the Siege of Chicago*:

> A young white singer with a cherubic face, perhaps eighteen, maybe twenty-eight, his hair in one huge puff ball teased out six to nine inches from his head, was taking off on an interplanetary, then galactic, flight of song, halfway between the space music of Sun Ra and "The Flight of the Bumblebee," the singer's head shaking at the climb like the blur of a buzzing fly, his sound an electric caterwauling of power come out of the wall (or the line in the grass, or the wet plates in the batteries) and the singer not bending it, but whirling it, burning it, flashing it down some arc of consciousness, the sound screaming up to a climax of vibrations like one rocket blasting out of itself, the force of the noise a vertigo in the cauldrons of inner space—it was the roar of the beast in all nihilism, electric bass and drum driving behind out of their own non-stop to the end of mind.

Mailer, although he found the MC5's sound "harsh on his ear, ear of a generation which had danced to 'Star Dust,'" recognized its value to the "Hippies and adolescents in the house . . . a generation which lived in . . . the sound of mountains crashing in this holocaust of the decibels."[17] But not everyone appreciated the MC5's sonic onslaught. Mailer noted "the sight of Negroes calmly digging Honkie soul, sullen Negroes showing not impressed, but digging, cool on their fringe (reports to the South Side might later be made)."[18]

If one takes Mailer's word that the MC5's Black listeners were "sullen" and unimpressed (he doesn't seem to have asked them), it is not difficult to propose reasons for their skepticism. Some might have been put off by the

Yippies' presumption in equating the struggles of white radicals to those of African Americans generally, in what historian Marty Jezer terms "an image of hippie-black solidarity."[19] Yippie and satirical journalist Paul Krassner, for example, described the Yippies as "a community of voluntary niggers" in the *Ramparts Wall Poster*, a broadside distributed in Chicago during the convention.[20] While Hoffman had spent years working as a supporter of civil rights groups such as Friends of SNCC and the Poor People's Corporation, he had recently begun to compare the white counterculture to the people whom he now called "soul brothers" but also, in a willful affront to liberal piety, "spades" and "niggers."[21] Hoffman borrowed his rhetoric about "pigs" and "honkies" from the Black Panther Party, as did the Yippies when they satirically nominated a real pig ("Pigasus") as the Democratic presidential candidate.[22] Hoffman had failed to impress the Blackstone Rangers, Chicago's most prominent African American "street gang," who, despite a recent turn toward political engagement, refused to join forces with the Yippies during the convention.[23] The MC5's music and appearance also might have provoked some challenging questions. Why did this white band's sound evoke the avant-garde jazz of musicians such as Sun Ra, which some Black Power theorists had begun to promote as the soundtrack to Black revolution? Why did the singer style his hair into something resembling an Afro?[24] By what right did the MC5 play "Honkie soul"?

In this chapter, I argue that the MC5 did not simply mimic Black music but rather sought to transform it into a new musical idiom suitable for white musicians and radicals like themselves. Rather than attempt literal imitations of the music of James Brown or Pharoah Sanders, the MC5 self-consciously adapted the form and style of their African American influences into a new context. This approach also informed their political stance, which was itself an adaptation, sometimes reverential and sometimes whimsical, of Black Power ideology. The MC5 believed that their commitment to African American music inspired and justified their political activism, but this belief was always threatened by their tenuous position as white performers of that music.

White Panthers, Black Music

The political engagement the MC5 displayed in Chicago has made them familiar not only to rock fans but also to historians of 1960s radicalism. The band is well known today for its affiliation with the White Panther Party, a radical group founded in Ann Arbor in November 1968 from the circle surrounding poet, jazz critic, and arts promoter John Sinclair.[25] The White Panthers, whose name signaled their sympathy with the Black Panther Party, claimed to represent a "long-haired dope-smoking rock & roll street-fucking culture" and argued that "rock and roll is a weapon of cultural revolution." The party's ten-point program, which blended revolutionary sincerity with sly put-ons in the manner of the Yippies, called for "the end of money," the freedom of all soldiers and prisoners, free food, clothing, housing, drugs, and medical care for everyone, and "free time & space for all humans."[26] The MC5, who lived with Sinclair and over twenty others in Detroit/Ann Arbor's Trans-Love Energies commune, became the party's official band.[27] Their first album, *Kick Out the Jams*, released on Elektra Records in February 1969, featured incendiary liner notes in which Sinclair claimed that "the MC5 is totally committed to the revolution" and an exciting interplay of distorted guitars that many critics and musicians have credited with inspiring punk and heavy metal.[28] In 1969, Sinclair was sentenced to nine-and-a-half to ten years in prison for possession of two marijuana joints, a blatantly political persecution that sparked an international activist campaign leading to his release in 1971. Although the White Panther Party emphasized fiery rhetoric more than militant action, by 1970 their notoriety led the FBI to label them "potentially the largest and most dangerous of revolutionary organizations in the United States" and to make them the target of COINTELPRO surveillance.[29] Meanwhile, the MC5 broke with Sinclair and the White Panthers and released two more albums to declining sales before they disbanded in 1972.

Even sympathetic chroniclers tend to dismiss the White Panther Party as a prime example of 1960s "fantasy politics," stoned naïfs whose excesses were matched only by those of the authorities who oppressed them. Popular music scholar Neil Nehring describes the "common view" of the MC5 as that of "a respectable rock band with a laughable pretension to being revolutionary."[30] Historian Jeff A. Hale calls the White Panthers "a group of counterculture 'freeks,' who, in search of radical certification, created a largely fictional White Panther Myth—only to end up being portrayed by the Nixon administration as the epitome of a domestic national security threat and embroiled in a landmark constitutional case" (1972's *Keith* case, in which the Supreme Court ruled unanimously against the Nixon administration's warrantless wiretapping of the White Panthers).[31] Hale argues that this "myth" centered on a tenuous, self-proclaimed affiliation with Black radicalism: "the selection of the name White Panthers, which demonstrated a close identification with the Black Panthers, might appear as something of a contradiction, considering [Trans-Love Energies's] mostly white membership and sparse record of attention to black causes in Detroit." While the members of the party admired the Black Panthers' commitment to self-defense and their "national model of political organization," they also hoped to bolster their cultural cachet by association: "the title 'White Panthers' gave the group instant radical credentials and, they hoped, credibility as a 'vanguard' white revolutionary organization."[32]

In his important study of the MC5, Steve Waksman emphasizes the racially charged notions of masculinity that underlay White Panther ideology, explaining that the band's (and by extension the White Panthers') politics were "built upon a pronounced fetishization of phallic potency that centered around an idealized notion of black masculinity common among white male radicals of the 1960s."[33] This fetishization informed the MC5's appearance as well as their music. Kramer remembers that "Rob Tyner remarked that the Black Panthers looked pretty cool in their black leather jackets and berets, and we started incorporating their look into our style."[34] Waksman contends: "that this return to the body was to be led by 'pure' black men and that one of its goals was to reconstruct white men as sexually charged 'rock 'n' roll guerrillas' does not speak well for the Five's revolutionary vision."[35] As Waksman demonstrates, the White Panthers' radical visions of the future were rooted in a long tradition of stereotypes about blackness and masculinity.

At the same time, their serious engagement with Black music and musicians distinguished the White Panthers from what Jack Hamilton describes as "a long line of white rock and roll fans who have violently mined the music for racialized fantasies of hypermasculinity while strategically ignoring any real connection to black people."[36] Wayne Kramer, in contrast, asserts that he "viewed our role as cultural messengers and allies to the black liberation struggle."[37] Many of the "'pure' black men" admired by the White Panthers were musicians, and the group's professed commitment to Black liberation was inspired as much by Black music as by politics as conventionally defined.[38] Before he began working with the MC5, Sinclair had contributed to Detroit's bohemian scene as the co-founder of the Detroit Artists' Workshop, which sponsored concerts by Black avant-garde musicians, and as a poet and critic whose chapbooks paid tribute to such musicians as Ornette Coleman, Archie Shepp, Sun Ra, and John Coltrane and whose magazine *Change* covered avant-garde jazz.[39] The MC5, who began as an R&B-influenced garage band in the style of the Yardbirds or the Who, became avant-garde jazz acolytes under Sinclair's guidance.[40] Waksman writes that "what Sinclair explained to the band seems to have had much to do with the beauty and value of free jazz, itself a restless noisy outgrowth of African-American culture, which Sinclair perceived to parallel the Five's own brand of noise."[41] Black Arts Movement scholar James Smethurst cites the MC5 as rock musicians who drew from free jazz "the model of an avant-garde art that is both 'cutting edge' thematically and formally and yet rooted in popular culture, which itself is a sort of popular culture."[42] Their interest in the jazz avant-garde placed the MC5 in what Ingrid Monson identifies as a larger stream of white listeners "imagining a new idea of radical whiteness that rejected the racial status quo and found common cause with the revolutionary aspirations of their radical African American counterparts."[43] In 1969, the Detroit Police Department's personal file on Sinclair listed his alias as "Coltrane," a telling detail that suggests the close relationship between his radicalism and his love for jazz.[44]

The MC5's conversion to Sinclair's musical ideals played out in the pages of the underground press. In October 1966, Sinclair wrote in *Fifth Estate*: "That's the funny thing about all the 'psychedelic' music that people are screaming about—the 'acid-rock' bands I mean—because if these folks were ever exposed to a John Coltrane or Cecil Taylor performance they'd lose their minds! If they have any. And they do."[45] In the next issue, Tyner responded that "I was turned on to Coltrane long before I got into the rock thing," but he argued that "there is no comparison between jazz and rock. They are two different streams of music entirely, each with its own rules and goals."[46] Sinclair reconciled with Tyner in the following issue, writing that "if you'll take Robin Tyner's remarks [about rock] . . . as a guide to what the JAZZ I'm talking about is doing, then everything's all right too. Screaming & sweating, real human energy. That's where it's at."[47] By May 1967, Tyner had reversed his opinion, emphasizing (in an interview conducted by Sinclair) that although "seemingly there's no connection between rock & roll music and 'avant-garde' jazz—they seem to be totally unconnected—but they aren't."[48] In 1968, Sinclair seconded this idea, writing that by "rock and roll . . . we mean John Coltrane and Pharoah Sanders and Archie Shepp and Albert Ayler and Sun Ra and all those people as much as the Beatles and Jimi and the MC5 and Canned Heat and the Cream and the Grateful Dead and Big Brother & the Holding Company."[49] The MC5 cemented their association to free jazz by playing gigs with such luminaries as Joseph Jarman and Sun Ra.[50] More significantly, they attempted to make manifest the equation between rock and avant-garde jazz in their own music.

Beyond Minstrels and Hipsters

Extant firsthand accounts, as well as silent surveillance footage shot by the Department of the Army Special Photographic Office, fail to reveal what songs the MC5 played in Chicago.[51] Evidence from throughout 1968, however, confirms Waksman's observation that the band's live show emphasized cover versions "distributed among different styles of African-American music," particularly of songs performed by African American men.[52] A printed program for the MC5's May 10–11, 1968, shows at Detroit's Grande Ballroom reveals that half of the set list had been recorded originally by Black musicians, including Pharoah Sanders ("Upper and Lower Egypt," with new lyrics by John Sinclair), John Coltrane ("Tunji"), Albert King ("Born Under a Bad Sign"), Ray Charles ("I Believe to My Soul"), Screamin' Jay Hawkins ("I Put a Spell on You"), and Larry Williams ("Slow Down"). The program also included the blues standard "Stormy Monday," associated with T-Bone Walker and Bobby Blue Bland among many others.[53] A bootleg recording of a June 27 show at the Sturgis Armory in southwest Michigan includes the Sanders and King covers as well as Little Richard's "Tutti Frutti" and a James Brown medley encompassing "Cold Sweat," "I Can't Stand Myself," and "There Was a Time."[54] The Grande Ballroom concerts recorded on October 30 and 31 for the *Kick Out the Jams* album featured the Charles and Hawkins covers as well as Ted Taylor's "(Love Is Like a) Ramblin' Rose" and John Lee Hooker's "The Motor City Is Burning."[55] The MC5's repertoire thus drew on multiple genres of music often seen as distinct: funk, avant-garde jazz, rock and roll, and blues. Waksman argues that "what linked these disparate styles for the Five was their high energy, and a sensibility that represented to the band a subversion of the 'white honkie culture' and an affirmation of a new aesthetic and political order founded upon the celebration of bodily pleasure."[56]

The energy they perceived in Black music informed not only the MC5's repertoire, but also their stage presence. Critics consistently noted the seeming contradiction between the MC5's whiteness and their devotion to Black performance practices. Introducing the band to Australian readers in the *Sydney Morning Herald*, Lillian Roxon described them as "five young white boys from a lower-middle-class background who play that fierce and very energetic hard rock we have come to associate with black performers like Little Richard and Chuck Berry. That is, there's a lot of the screaming and sweating and leaping around that set the style for the whole rock revolution of the middle fifties."[57] *Village Voice* critic Richard Goldstein argued that "the MC5 come on live. They move with the kind of stylized energy long gone from pop, but not forgotten. Up on stage, they do the Chuck Berry cakewalk, the Little Richard split, the James Brown kneedrop, the Jackie Wilson leap."[58] Goldstein added, however, "ironically, it is the white boy rock 'n' roller jive that stays with you after the tonal assault dies down." [59] Bob Rudnick and Dennis Frawley, friends of the band, asked bluntly in a 1969 column "are Niggers and the MC-5 the only ones who entertain? Great stage act. Inspiration. James Brown, Mr. Dynamite."[60] Their comments reveal both that these white writers felt entitled to use a "hip" racial slur and that the MC5 were enacting a version of Black performance on stage. In his autobiography, bassist Michael Davis remembers that "Wayne wanted to be black more than he wanted to be white, and he worked hard at learning how to imitate the stage moves he saw the black performers doing."[61]

Clearly, the MC5 were engaged in a practice fundamental to American popular music—white imitation of Black music. More specifically, the MC5 represented white, male, working-class, heterosexist imitation of music associated with Black *men*—a more narrowly defined phenomenon widely noted since the nineteenth century. Most scholarly analysis of this tradition derives at some level from two basic archetypes: the minstrel and the hipster. Although I will suggest that these models are not fully adequate to explain the MC5, it will be useful to sketch them briefly first.

Minstrelsy dates to the early nineteenth century, when working-class men in northern US cities began performing in blackface in energetic shows featuring outlandish and often grotesque "black" protagonists. Early scholarly studies of minstrelsy emphasized the genre's undeniable racism and the legacy of offensive stereotypes that it created. Since the 1990s, scholars have tended to stress the subversive, subcultural aspects of minstrelsy, revealing its antielitism and its central role in crafting a white working-class identity. The most influential text of this era is Eric Lott's *Love and Theft* (1993), which draws on Marxist and Freudian theories to reveal minstrelsy's economic and psychological underpinnings. Without denying the demeaning and disturbing aspects of minstrelsy, Lott points to its ambiguities and instabilities, which involved "cross-racial identification" as well as revulsion toward African Americans.[62] Minstrelsy represented a paradox, Lott writes, "in which transgression and containment coexisted, in which improbably threatening or startlingly sympathetic racial meanings were simultaneously produced and dissolved."[63] Minstrelsy projected desire for the "repressed pleasure" of an imagined preindustrial, prerational past onto the bodies of Black men, who were at once the objects of masculine identification, sexual desire, fear, and disgust.[64]

The hipster, in contrast, exemplifies urban modernity.[65] The term first appeared in the 1940s to refer to a flashy subcultural figure associated with a distinct style of dress, an elliptical jive vocabulary, and an interest in drugs and modern jazz. While the hipster style began in African American and Latinx communities, it was quickly adopted by young white bohemians, who received their most influential assessment in Norman Mailer's 1957 essay "The White Negro." Mailer describes the hipster as "a philosophical psychopath" whose only moral law "is to do what one feels whenever and wherever it is possible."[66] For Mailer, the hipster is a kind of "barbarian" who represents "consciousness subjugated to instinct."[67] Mailer's vision of the hipster as the embodiment of primitive masculinity has since been widely criticized. Ingrid Monson, for example, argues that "the problem with white hipness" is that "well-meaning white Americans have confused the most transgressive aspects of African American culture with its true character."[68] Phil Ford puts the problem this way: "the literature of the White Negro sets up an unspoken and treacherous syllogism: if blacks are hip and hipness is criminal, then blacks must be criminal."[69] In other words, white hipsters enact a stereotype of Black men as sexually voracious and socially deviant that comes to represent blackness as a whole.

Cultural criticism centered on minstrels and hipsters demands attention to the legacy of mockery and primitivism that underlies white involvement with Black music. Viewed together, the two figures also reveal the complexity of this tradition. On the surface, minstrels and hipsters seem very different. The minstrel is a manic, uncontrolled buffoon, while the hipster always maintains his cool. The minstrel's claim to blackness relies on images of slavery and servitude, while the hipster's authenticity derives from close attention to the ebb and flow of modern life. While both are obsessively verbal, the minstrel's flamboyant malapropisms and enthusiastic banter contrast with the sly, knowing jive preferred by the hipster.

As portrayed by many scholars, however, minstrels and hipsters have something in common: both are irrational figures whose deeply embedded but largely unconscious racial obsessions are best examined through a psychoanalytical lens. Lott argues that "we might almost call [minstrelsy] a precognitive form."[70] Historian David Roediger describes minstrelsy in explicitly Freudian terms as a manifestation of "psychosexual anxiety" and "polymorphous perversity."[71] Mailer similarly identifies the hipster as a product of "infantile fantasy" who transcends "the sophisticated inhibitions of civilization."[72] Even Monson, who is critical of Lott's Freudian model, describes hipsters as "well-meaning white Americans" who "politically oppose racial discrimination" yet "perpetuate unwittingly primitivist assumptions," not fully aware of the implications of their own actions and beliefs.[73]

Much of the most compelling scholarship on white men who perform Black music thus has sought to uncover the tangled webs of fear and desire lurking under the surface. Here, however, I want to argue that this approach has its limits and can distort critical interpretation. Note that while historians sometimes point out the role of minstrels and hipsters in urban unrest, from the Astor Place Riot of 1849 to the Zoot Suit Riots of 1943, the presumed irrationality of both groups often leads scholars to depict them as fundamentally apolitical.[74] W. T. Lhamon, for example, writes that blackface "worked generally to confound political action," while Lott suggests that antebellum minstrelsy lacked what he calls "coherent, intentional politics."[75] Michael Rogin asserts plainly that "blackface did not engender a single interracial political working-class alliance."[76] Mailer argues that, while hipsters may have political potential, it remains inchoate and could go in any direction: "the hipster is equally a candidate for the most reactionary and the most radical of movements."[77] More recently, John Leland claims that "though it likes a revolutionary pose, hip is ill equipped to organize for a cause. No one will ever reform campaign finance laws under hip's banner, nor save the environment."[78] Hipsters and minstrels seem to transcend both collective action and individual agency, representing instead an inevitable, almost metaphysical impulse fundamental to white American identity.[79]

But what about those moments when white performance of blackness also constitutes a deliberate tactic employed by actors aware of its history and significance? Phil Ford points out that 1960s hipsters, including John Sinclair, often became political activists, if only in the utopian belief that "hip consciousness becomes revolutionary action in itself."[80] Of minstrelsy, Roediger writes that "the irrational, bacchanalian act of blacking up was . . . also an enterprise and even a scam."[81] In her foundational 1931 study of minstrelsy, Constance Rourke proposed that "with all their rude poetry it was about a mind that these myths centered, a conscious, indeed an acutely self-conscious, mind."[82] How might it change the conventional narrative about white performance of Black music to consider this enterprising, calculating, "self-conscious mind"?

My point here is not that white performers' capacity for rationality has been overlooked—on the contrary, white rock musicians are regularly lionized as serious, thoughtful artists, often in contrast (implicit or explicit) to Black musicians.[83] Nor do I deny that aspects of the minstrel and hipster models apply to the MC5, as perceptive critics noted even during the band's prime. Abe Peck, editor of the underground *Chicago Seed*, remembered that some skeptics saw the MC5 as "poseurs in symbolic blackface."[84] In 1969, critic Miller Francis Jr. castigated the band, arguing that "at its best the MC5 is an emasculated version of what The Who did years ago; at its worst it is a pasty-face derivative of black music (as if we needed yet another minstrel group!). The MC5, who I understand were a white rhythm & blues group before they were 'revolutionized' by John Sinclair, have simply wheeled their grimy Detroit vehicle up to a Black Power station and said, 'Fill 'er up.'"[85] Critic John Lombardi, in Philadelphia's *Distant Drummer*, attacked the MC5 as hipsters rather than as minstrels, reporting that J. C. Crawford, a white friend of the band who introduced them on stage in a style inspired by both James Brown and Eldridge Cleaver, "spoke in a grossly exaggerated hip spade manner, and soon succeeded in annoying those in the audience who don't believe anymore that 'all spades are cool.' He also bugged the real spades in the crowd with his second-hand impressions of how to talk like you're really from the South

Side."[86] More recently, Waksman, while he takes a more sympathetic view than did Francis or Lombardi, cites both Lott and Mailer in critiquing the macho posturing typical of the band's songs and stage performances.[87]

In many respects, however, the MC5 do not seem like minstrels. They took themselves too seriously, for one thing, and they imitated and openly credited specific Black musicians rather than a more generic stereotype. At the same time, their overt emotionalism and frenetic stage show seem to distinguish them from hipsters. To get at the significance of the MC5's approach to African American music requires us to historicize them rather than treat them merely as yet another interchangeable example of appropriative tradition.

A historically informed approach notes the reflexivity of racial representation in 1960s rock. By the 1960s, many whites with an interest in Black culture were themselves aware of minstrelsy's degrading legacy, so their performances sometimes aspired to ironic critiques of minstrelsy that sought to distance themselves from this tradition even as they reenacted aspects of it. In his work on the San Francisco counterculture of the 1960s, Sumanth Gopinath identifies what he calls a "minstrel avant-garde" including such significant figures as composer Steve Reich, cartoonist Robert Crumb, and the San Francisco Mime Troupe.[88] Such artists invoked outdated and offensive minstrel clichés as a way of attacking both racism itself and sanctimonious white liberals who claimed to transcend racism. "The irony," Gopinath argues, "was that this avant-garde . . . was recuperated into the system it so despised, resulting in minstrelsy's reappearance in the public eye with an ironic, postmodern flair that simultaneously mainstreamed the critical power of minstrelsy and returned classic minstrel stereotypes in new forms to mass audiences for consumption."[89] In other words, the radical minstrelsy of the 1960s winkingly mocked racism, but it also reinvigorated one of racism's most significant cultural manifestations. While the hipster was a more recent phenomenon, rock musicians, often influenced by the Beat writers and modern jazz, were similarly aware of the figure and its cultural ramifications. "The White Negro" may help critics explain the MC5, but it should be noted that members of the band may have been reading Mailer themselves.[90]

Soul by Proxy

It is possible to be precise about the intellectual influences surrounding the MC5, because the White Panther Party produced their own reading list, which they printed in the Ann Arbor *Sun* in July 1969. The list includes political tracts by Che, Mao, and Lenin alongside works by modernist literary icons such as Ezra Pound and William S. Burroughs.[91] Books by African American writers include Amiri Baraka's *Black Music* (published in 1967, before Baraka had changed his name from LeRoi Jones) and two works by Black Panther Minister of Information Eldridge Cleaver: *Soul on Ice* (1968) and *Eldridge Cleaver: Post-Prison Writings and Speeches* (1969).[92]

What do these texts say about white interest in Black music? Both Baraka's *Black Music* and Cleaver's *Soul on Ice* address the issue, and a selective reading of both might have encouraged Sinclair and the MC5. Cleaver praises white radicals' involvement with Black politics. He asserts: "that growing numbers of white youth are repudiating their heritage of blood and taking people of color as their heroes and models is a tribute not only to their insight but to the resilience of the human spirit."[93] Cleaver's vision of Black music centers on the supposedly essential rhythmic properties that Ronald Radano identifies as the trope of "hot rhythm."[94] Cleaver writes of white youth that "all they know is that it feels good to swing to way-out body-rhythms instead of dragassing across the dance floor like zombies to the dead beat of mind-smothered Mickey Mouse music."[95] Elsewhere, Cleaver credits the Beatles for making the physicality of Black music available to whites, describing the group as "soul by proxy, middlemen between the Mind and the Body."[96] Cleaver's notion that by "personifying the Body" Black people are "thereby in closer communion with their biological roots than other Americans" seems to reinforce primitivist stereotypes of African Americans as nonintellectual and irrational. Yet Cleaver upholds this stereotype in order to argue that in a technocratic society Black Americans "provide the saving link, the bridge between man's biology and man's machines."[97] Baraka's collection includes the 1963 essay "Jazz and the White Critic," which states that "the white musician's commitment to jazz . . . proposed that the sub-cultural attitudes that produced the music . . . could be *learned* and need not be passed on as a secret blood rite."[98] In the 1965 essay "Apple Cores #2," Baraka grudgingly credits British Invasion bands such as the Rolling Stones with having "actually made a contemporary form," unlike white American folk singers who make literal attempts to imitate old blues performers.[99] Cleaver and Baraka suggest in these passages that white musicians can genuinely access the physical and philosophical underpinnings of Black music, even if they can never imitate that music precisely.

A thorough assessment of these texts, however, reveals that Baraka and Cleaver often took more skeptical and critical positions. Cleaver argues that "a well-known example of the white necessity to deny due credit to blacks is in the realm of music. White musicians were famous for going to Harlem and other Negro cultural centers literally to steal the black man's music, carrying it back across the color line into the Great White World and passing off the watered-down loot as their own original creations."[100] Although Cleaver appears to exempt young bohemians such as the MC5 from this charge, it nevertheless registers as a warning against appropriation. Baraka is harsher in the famous 1966 essay "The Changing Same (R&B and New Black Music)," which concludes *Black Music*. He writes that for white Americans, "beginning with their own vacuous 'understanding' of what Black music is, or how it acts upon you, they believe, from the Beatles on down, that it is about white life."[101] While this suggests that the problem with white appropriation is cultural misunderstanding, Baraka also shares Cleaver's anger toward whites who profit financially from Black music. He describes the music of the Beatles and Rolling Stones as "a minstrelsy that 'hippens'" and points out that these white musicians have become wealthy stars while their Black models have not.[102] Although the MC5, still a struggling local band in 1968, might not have felt that this charge applied to them, it would have been harder to ignore Baraka's dismissal of underground, experimental bands such as the Fugs and the Mothers of Invention as "white kids playing around."[103] If at times Baraka and Cleaver offer some hope that white musicians can achieve an authentic relationship to Black music, they just as often suggest that such a relationship inevitably amounts to misrepresentation or theft.

Sinclair's writings and the MC5's performances often responded directly to Cleaver or Baraka. As early as 1966, Sinclair quoted from Baraka's poem "Leadbelly Gives an Autograph" in an admiring review of the MC5's performances at the Grande Ballroom.[104] The White Panthers' founding document, the White Panther Statement (printed on a duplicator owned by the MC5, according to a 1969 FBI memorandum), cites Cleaver's maxim that "you're either part of the solution or part of the problem," and Sinclair appointed himself the party's "Minister of Information" in imitation of Cleaver's title.[105] Cleaver's slogan appears again in J. C. Crawford's speech introducing the MC5 at the beginning of the *Kick Out the Jams* album, while Sinclair's liner notes for the album quote Baraka's saying "feeling predicts intelligence."[106] More generally, Sinclair adopted an aphoristic writing style clearly influenced by Baraka and an emphasis on the liberation of the body through Black music that recalled Cleaver.[107] Sinclair also mimicked the sexism and macho hubris sometimes characteristic of these writers.[108] All of these traits came together in the White Panther Statement, which proclaims:

> The actions of the Black Panthers in America have inspired us and given us strength, as has the music of black America, and we are moving to reflect that strength in our daily activity just as our music contains and extends the power and feeling of the black magic music that originally informed our bodies and told us that we could be free.
>
> I might mention Brother James Brown in this connection, as well as John

Coltrane and Archie Shepp. Sun-Ra. LeRoi Jones. Malcolm X. Huey P. Newton, Bobby Seale, Eldridge Cleaver, these are magic names to us. These are
men in America. And we're as crazy as they are, and as pure. We're bad.[109]

In promoting Black music as a path to embodied freedom, Sinclair drops the
names of avant-garde jazz musicians and radical political leaders in the same
breath, and concludes with a plea for recognition of a masculine authority
and authenticity inspired by and equal to that of these Black role models.

The presumption and pretension of Sinclair's comments is obvious, and
this is the sort of prose most commonly cited by scholars critiquing the MC5's
relationship to Black music.[110] An alternate reading of Sinclair's work, however,
reveals that he was sometimes more thoughtful about the issues of authenticity and appropriation that his rhetoric raised. The White Panther Statement
asserts that the party's music "contains and extends the power and feeling"
of Black music, an idea that Sinclair elaborated elsewhere. Promoting a John
Coltrane tribute concert in September 1967, for example, Sinclair argued that
"the MC-5 and the UP have translated Coltrane's huge energy force into the
electronic rock medium and are putting it to work in a popular context."[111] In
January 1968, Sinclair wrote that while the MC5's "total sound" drew on the
work of Coltrane, Pharoah Sanders, "and other non-electric innovators . . .
those elements have evolved in a form which is strictly precise and singularly
unique to the MC5 itself. That is to say, the band does not 'copy' anyone or
anything but they HAVE listened and learned."[112] In Sinclair's 1972 book *Guitar Army*, he expanded on this premise, writing that "we learned . . . by digging on black people's music and *assimilating* it into our own embryonic culture, letting it *interact* with the other terms of our lives and *mixing* it with the
elements of other people's cultures we picked up during our journey through
the darkness of the first half of the 60's, until we had a rainbow culture of our
very own which *reflected* all its sources but also *transcended* them to become
something absolutely unique in the history of civilization" (emphasis mine).
In the same essay, Sinclair says of Bob Dylan and the British Invasion: "it
was black rebellion which was most prominently evident in that music, having been *translated* into terms which related directly to our own situation as
the outcasts of Euro-Amerikan society" (emphasis mine again).[113] In these
passages, Sinclair emphasizes rock's *distance* from African American models,
and suggests that white performances of Black music represent a process of
transformation and translation.[114]

The MC5 propagated similar views even after their split from Sinclair
and a related turn from a style that drew on avant-garde jazz to one more
rooted in R&B and early rock and roll. During a 1969 interview preceding the

release of their second album, *Back in the USA*, journalist Sue Cassidy Clark asked the band if their music was influenced by soul.[115] Rob Tyner and Wayne Kramer responded:

TYNER: The reason that I mentioned the little properties that soul music has is because those properties that soul music has can be related to any other form of music, period. It's like listening to Black jazz. Black jazz and soul music and those forms of music that are played with a technical togetherness, man, and a rhythmical human quality—plus all the human vibration—that's the kind of music we want to play.

KRAMER: It isn't so much like we want to play soul music—

TYNER: But those principles can be used in any form of music, because that's just playing music right.

KRAMER: It isn't like we want to, you know, go up and get a horn section and be a soul band, 'cause that's—

TYNER: Not that we ain't gonna use horns.

KRAMER: Right, right. But there's all these properties of soul music and of the whole soul music scene.[116]

Here, Tyner and Kramer assert the right to employ and adapt the "principles" and "properties" of soul without explicitly claiming the privilege of playing soul per se. In similar terms, Kramer rejected Clark's suggestion that the band's recent music revived early rock and roll:

Well, see, in the first place, we're not really talking about going back to no old-fashioned sound. The thing you want to get out of that old material is the energy. The resensifier. The reality. Stuff that's talking about day-to-day, real-to-life experiences. Super real-to-life. In the lyric, and the reality of the energy in the music, the body-movingness of old rock and roll and of soul music, and on another level, you know, like new Black jazz. . . . Like, we do "Back in the USA" and "Tutti Frutti" on the record, but . . . we're not trying to copy Little Richard or Chuck Berry or nothing like that, 'cause that's just ridiculous, you know. That's just—that's nowhere. What we want to get is the life and the energy out of that music and apply it in a contemporary context, apply it to things that'll help these, you know, our people today.[117]

For Kramer, rock and roll, like jazz or soul, inspired imaginative invention and revision rather than demanding reverent repetition.

I May Be a White Boy, but I Can Be Bad Too

To consider more precisely the MC5's approach to adapting Black music, let's return to one of the cover versions that the band featured in their live shows. "Upper Egypt," as the MC5 called it, was their take on tenor saxophonist Pharoah Sanders's "Upper and Lower Egypt," from his 1966 album *Tauhid*.[118] Along with Sun Ra, Coltrane, and Archie Shepp, Sanders was one of the jazz avant-gardists most frequently cited as an influence by Sinclair and the MC5.[119] In interviews, Tyner described Sanders and Sun Ra as "musical prophets" while Kramer encouraged readers to "listen to Sun Ra . . . to Pharaoh [sic] Sanders . . . to John Coltrane. It'll save your ass."[120] Although the MC5's "Upper Egypt" never appeared on one of their albums, it formed a regular part of their show during 1968 and perhaps 1969. The May 10–11, 1968, concert program cited above explained that "Upper Egypt" is "inspired by the planet shaking '*Tauhid*' album by Pharoah Saunders [sic] . . . Lyrics by Detroit's noted Poet/Artisan/Lecturer/Dope & Sex fiend, John Sinclair, 'The Pharoah of the (now defunct) Hippies.'"[121] In the May 10, 1968, issue of New York's *East Village Other*, Bob Rudnick and Dennis Frawley singled out "Upper and Lower Egypt" as an example of the MC5's "fusion of rock and avant-garde jazz."[122] In 1969 *Creem*, *Fifth Estate*, and the White Panthers themselves each predicted (falsely, as it turned out) that the song would appear on the MC5's upcoming Atlantic album *Back in the USA*.[123] (My analysis below is based on the Sturgis Armory recording cited above.)[124]

Sanders's album *Tauhid* is significant as the recording debut of guitarist Sonny Sharrock, soon to become an important figure in the jazz avant-garde. Sinclair was an early admirer of Sharrock. In a 1969 review, he wrote that Sharrock "has created one working solution to the problem of plain old line runs on guitar, licks and shit—Sonny Sharrock plays flashes of amplified sound, weird spaced-out hums and sound drifts, spreading his sound out as far as he can get it until it takes in the whole spectrum of sound." Sinclair goes on to compare Sharrock's approach to that taken by the MC5's guitarists: "the other solution is to overpower the simple guitar and make the amplifiers sing the song, e.g. brother Fred Smith, brother Wayne Kramer, where the power of the machinery is written into the songs just as the notes and words are written in, or happen. So the sound itself, the totality, becomes the thing, the thing that moves you and makes you scream. Makes me scream, anyway. Just like Archie Shepp does, just like Pharoah."[125] Sinclair suggests here that although the MC5 don't sound like Sharrock, their extreme amplification shares the same aim as Sharrock's "sound drifts": movement beyond the limitations of conventional guitar gestures to create a visceral response in the audience.

Steve Waksman reads the MC5's sonic intensity as an updated variant of minstrelsy, arguing that "it was primarily by strapping on electric guitars, and in their use of technology more generally, that groups like the Five most clearly reproduced the logic of blackface."[126] For Waksman, the MC5's performances pitted the artifice of technology against the supposed naturalness of Black manhood. I contend that one can also hear the MC5's guitar sound as a calculated attempt to bring the energy of avant-garde jazz into a distinct but equally subversive musical form.

Sanders's recording of "Upper and Lower Egypt" comprises three sections. The first is a dense collective improvisation built around an E♭-minor pentatonic scale. The second features an unmetered improvisation by a spare ensemble of percussion, bowed upright bass, and piccolo. The third begins with bassist Henry Grimes playing an ostinato on two pitches: A♭ and B♭. Next, the rest of the rhythm section enters, with the guitar and piano playing a repeated cycle of four major chords—C D F G—over the bass pattern. Grimes then lowers his ostinato by a half step, creating the sense of a pedal point on A. After three minutes of this groove, Sanders enters on tenor saxophone with a fervid statement of the composed melody, followed by an improvised solo in his typically dissonant, intense style. After Sanders repeatedly sings a vocal version of the melody, the track fades out.

The MC5's "Upper Egypt" is far from a literal interpretation. Most obviously, it has words, written by Sinclair and sung by Tyner, that exhort the listener to "wake up" and "get out into the sun." Another significant difference is structural. The MC5 eliminate the first two sections altogether and pare away virtually every element of the third except for one: the bass ostinato. Even this ostinato serves a new function: rather than serving as a pedal point under shifting chords, the bass's insistently repeated A becomes the root of a single chord—Am7, or possibly A7♯9—that the MC5's guitarists hammer out in unison with the bass.[127] Between sung verses, the band plays an ascending three-bar riff that has no precedent in Sanders's original. Dennis Thompson plays busy, loud, shifting drum patterns rather than the gentle groove maintained by drummer Roger Blank on Sanders's recording. While Sanders's saxophone melody nestles neatly into the original harmonies, Tyner sings Sinclair's text in bluesy fragments. Although Sanders's "Upper and Lower Egypt" served as inspiration, what the MC5 play bears little obvious relationship to it.

One might condescend to the MC5 and say that they simply didn't know the right chords, and Wayne Kramer notes self-deprecatingly that "our harmonic sense was not that refined at that point."[128] Yet shifting major chords over a pedal point were a common sound in rock by 1968 thanks to the Who's Pete Townshend, and the MC5 themselves employed this technique in some of their original songs, such as "Come Together," which borrows its central guitar riff from the Who's "I Can See for Miles." I propose instead that the MC5 were in effect translating the fervor of Sanders's performance into their own language, creating what they called a "high-energy music" that reflected their ideas about ecstatic Black performance but added something new. Kramer remembers that "we could play the basic riff [sings the bass line], and we were so enamored of the music that we just wanted to be involved in it, we wanted to participate in it, even though we weren't trained jazz musicians, we were rock and roll players. So we did the best we could in reinterpret[ing] — deconstructing jazz tunes so that we could perform them."[129] By drawing on source material that was unfamiliar to many in their audience, but incorporating familiar elements of rock—harmonic simplicity, loud amplification, and hortatory lyrics—the MC5 created an adventurous hybrid that challenged their listeners.

Kramer remembers that the band saw it as their vocation "to upgrade our audience's listening taste. That was part of the mission . . . consciously to expose them to new kinds of music." As an example, he cites "the first time we brought Sun Ra and the Arkestra to the Grande Ballroom."

> Sun Ra had a policy of playing his most out, experimental, high-energy stuff right in the beginning to clear the room of any nonbelievers. But when they hit the stage at the Grande, the crowd was used to the MC5 doing it—we're their band, we're white guys, and we do all that weird music towards the end of our set. You know, we play real guitar rock all night, and then at the end shit gets weird . . . Now, Sun Ra starts where we end up, and for a couple of minutes there, I felt like, you know, this is touch and go . . . These greasers could react badly to this. You know, here's all these Black people up on stage dancing around, skronking on saxophones, not playing a two-and-four backbeat, and people were going "what the hell is this? What's going on here?" And it was really kind of . . . hmmm, this could get ugly. And after about five minutes of the Arkestra just *blasting*, everybody started cheering. Because they were able to make the connection between what Sun Ra and the Myth-Science Arkestra were playing and what their favorite rock and roll band, the MC5, played.[130]

In this moment, the example set by the MC5's "weird music" provided a gateway into avant-garde aesthetics and encouraged white listeners to keep open minds about an unfamiliar group of African American performers.

Although blues was more familiar to rock audiences in the late 1960s, the MC5 often made a point of adapting rather than imitating it.[131] The Grande

Ballroom program cited above boasted (in reference to "Stormy Monday")
that "the MC5 always include one stone blues in their live show because they
like it that way."[132] The band was particularly inspired by fellow Detroiter John
Lee Hooker. Tyner told Sue Cassidy Clark that Hooker "is the living embodiment of everything you're talking about, man. In the flesh—he stands there
just naked as shit right before you, man, it's just *unbearable*. You're blown
back by the sheer charge of the gentleman." He went on, perhaps thinking of
currently popular groups such as Led Zeppelin and Ten Years After: "I like
blues played by people who got the blues, you know what I mean? I mean,
nobody can tell me that some skinny English guy has got the blues, man! You
can't tell me that!"[133] The MC5's publicity touted their authentic relationship
to the blues tradition. In July 1969, for example, *Creem* ran a photo, taken at
the Saugatuck Pop Festival, of Wayne Kramer with his arm around Hooker,
reporting that "Hooker complimented the 5 on [their cover of his song]
'Motor City Is Burning' and suggested they take-on 'Boom-Boom.' Wayne
thought it was a far-out idea."[134]

Many white men in rock during the 1960s claimed a personal connection
to blues musicians and the masculine swagger they supposedly embodied,
but what made the MC5's take on blues unusual was the connection they
drew between the music and radical politics.[135] Popular music scholar Ulrich
Adelt demonstrates that during the 1960s many "white audiences of the blues
were beginning to demand an older and safer conceptualization of blackness
at the exact moment when calls for black power were becoming imminent."[136]
Blues played a very different role, however, in White Panther ideology, which
often echoed Amiri Baraka's influential book *Blues People* in claiming an essential connection between musical expression and political values. Just as
Baraka argued that "each phase of the Negro's music issued directly from the
dictates of his social and psychological environment," Sinclair claimed that
"we ourselves are developing a culture that has as its most exciting aspect . . .
its commonness with the blues culture, black culture, in that our music at
its best is a direct expression of the people who make the music, first, and
of the whole people out of which the musicians emerge."[137] In a special edition of the *Ann Arbor Argus* produced for the 1969 Ann Arbor Blues Festival,
Sinclair argued that "the blues has developed into a bridge between the black
people who have inspired our culture, and the freeky white mother country maniac people who have developed out of that inspiration through tons
of marijuana and LSD and into our current madness."[138] Sinclair added that
"though the particular quantity or quality of our oppression differs from that
of the blues people, the oppression is constant and will work to bring our
culture closer to theirs—it will unite us in our common struggle against the

common oppressor."[139] Here, Sinclair claims the spirit of the blues for white radical youth while acknowledging (if only vaguely) that differing kinds of oppression might result in different relationships to the music.

Two adaptations of Hooker's songs demonstrate how the MC5 tied blues to their political concerns. "Motor City Is Burning" (from the *Kick Out the Jams* album) is a relatively faithful take on Hooker's original, which addresses the Detroit uprising of July 1967, sparked by a police raid on a Black after-hours club.[140] Both Hooker and the MC5 were in Detroit at the time. While Hooker did not take part in demonstrations, he insisted (in Charles Shaar Murray's transcription) that "I know what they were fightin' for . . . Maybe they didn't have to do that, but they hoped to bring out the anger, straighten out a lot of the segregation."[141] Hooker describes a chaotic scene: "I could just look at the fire from my porch or my window, outside in my yard . . . I could see places goin' up in *flame*, hear guns shootin', robbin' stores, run-nin' the business people out of they stores. There was a lot of lootin' goin' on, y'know . . . the po-*lice* was even lootin'."[142] The White Panthers were energized by the unrest. The Trans-Love Energies commune displayed banners reading "Peace on Earth" and "Burn Baby Burn!" next to the Black Panther symbol, while police raided the MC5's apartment building and arrested Kramer and others "after finding a bag of reefer seeds."[143] In *Fifth Estate*, John Sinclair's im-mediate response was to celebrate the looting as "Robin Hood Day in merry olde Detroit, the first annual city-wide all-free fire sale" when "the people without got their hands on the goodies," and years later he still remembered this moment as "an exhilarating experience."[144]

The MC5's cover of "Motor City Is Burning" thus reflects a different posi-tion on the event than does Hooker's original. The most significant change the MC5 made to Hooker's song involves the words. Contrary to Stuart Cos-grove's claim that Hooker's "strident and uncompromising tone appealed to MC5," who were "fortified by the romantic message," Hooker's song sounds neither strident nor romantic about the uprising.[145] Instead, as Justin Schell has noted, Hooker's narrator "spins a tale of resignation and near-hopeless bewilderment."[146] Endangered by firebombs, he claims that "I don't know what the trouble is—I can't stay around to find it out" and vows to escape with his family. Rob Tyner, in contrast, portrays a young revolutionary excited and invigorated by the rebellion.[147] Where Hooker sings "there ain't a thing in the world that I can do," Tyner sings "there ain't a thing in the world they can do," mocking those authorities who hope to stop the protest. Similarly, Hooker's line "I don't know what it's all about" becomes Tyner's "it made the beat cops all jump and shout" and "it made the pigs in the street freak out," suggest-ing that the police, not the hip narrator, were caught unaware. The "snipers" who prevented fire trucks from doing their work are celebrated specifically as "Black Panther snipers" in the MC5 version. Hooker's "I don't know what the trouble is" becomes Tyner's "your mama and papa don't know what the trouble is," imputing ignorance to square parents rather than to the presumably youthful listener.[148] Tyner sings Hooker's lines about getting out of town with his family, but he follows it by boasting that "before I go . . . I just might strike a match for freedom myself" and pleading that "I may be a white boy, but I can be bad too . . . yes, it's true now."[149] The pared-down music reflects this aggressive attitude. The MC5 simplify the bass line and slow the tempo of Hooker's original. Heavy, distorted guitars, highlighted during two choruses in which Kramer and Smith improvise simultaneously, create a thick, menacing sound.[150] Nonetheless, the MC5's "Motor City Is Burning" remains recognizably a slow twelve-bar blues.

A more radical revision strategy informs the MC5's reworking of Hooker's "I'm Bad Like Jesse James": "I'm Mad Like Eldridge Cleaver," recorded live at the Grande Ballroom on October 27, 1968, at a benefit for left-wing Michigan state senator Roger Craig.[151] Hooker's song centers on a slow, one-chord vamp, over which he delivers a monologue as a man vowing violent revenge against a former friend who claims to be having an affair with his wife. The entire performance is so exaggeratedly threatening and sinister that it seems intended as dark humor. The MC5's performance, which Sinclair later described as "eighteen minutes and fifty-two seconds of improvised madness," uses Hooker's song as a springboard for something both more earnest and more experimental.[152] Introducing the song, Kramer prepares the Grande audience for its formlessness while highlighting the influence of Hooker and Cleaver:

> It's a little thing that we're gonna just put together now. We've been wanting to work it out, but traveling around and . . . being lazy and all, we never had a chance to get in the practice room . . . It's this little political song. At least it's gonna start like that. It's hard to tell what happens when you get carrying on, and gettin' wild and deep into it, goin' crazy. For those of you that dig John Lee Hooker . . . we're gonna start off something like that and take it into a little more contemporary lyric . . . "I'm mad like Eldridge Cleaver's mad!"

Tyner begins an angry monologue—"I'm mad out in the street! I'm frothing at the mouth pissed!"—over a percussive, atonal backdrop of fingers tapped on choked guitar strings. Guest musician John Sinclair enters on tenor saxophone, trading squawking sounds with the guitars. Gradually the band begins playing a slower version of the groove from the Hooker recording. Tyner recites the first two lines of Hooker's song, but then turns to a comparatively abstract (and perhaps improvised) text about a world of machines and assembly lines that can be overcome only by "anger" and "down in the street howling rage." His vocal culminates with the claim that "a white boy like me can get mad / Can get bad / like Eldridge Cleaver, mama, yeah, yeah." As the collective improvisation of guitars and saxophone builds intensity in the background, Tyner insists that "I'll run the gutters red / Before I let 'em stay ahead" and boasts that he's mad like Muhammad Ali, LeRoi Jones, and Jerry Rubin. After some collective improvising around Hooker's riff, the band spends the remaining ten minutes of the performance shifting through a range of grooves and styles, including an exploration of the familiar "Bo Diddley" rhythm; a rave-up centered on a tonic pedal point in the bass, in the style of the Yardbirds or "Psychotic Reaction" by the Count Five; a passage in which Sinclair's squealing sax trades short, dissonant melodies first with Tyner's scat singing and then with the guitars; a dense, dissonant group improvisation featuring Tyner on flute; a four-on-the-floor groove, built on a 7$\sharp$9 chord, that recalls Jimi Hendrix; and finally, a coda that gradually accelerates as it ascends in pitch toward a climax. The performance concludes without ever returning to the original riff—as feedback rings out from the guitar amps, Tyner sings "Don't you know I'm mad again—always been." In this performance, blues and avant-garde free improvisation are juxtaposed and reinterpreted to support a statement of solidarity and identity with a famous Black radical.[153]

The MC5's relationship to blues thus encompassed not only the inevitable influence that any rock band owed the tradition, but also deliberate reconceptions openly concerned with questions of authenticity and difference. In 1970, Sonny Sharrock dismissed most rock guitarists, explaining that "there are certain places on the guitar where you can play blues runs and licks, and all you have to do is go buy a Mickey Baker blues-volume-one-book and figure out where on the neck they are and then you just get them faster and faster."[154] This charge does not apply neatly to "I'm Mad Like Eldridge Cleaver," and the MC5 thus might have seen themselves as transcending simple imitation. At the same time, Tyner's protest that even a "white boy" can "get mad" and "get bad" reveals an anxiety about his place in both blues or avant-garde jazz and the Black liberation movement, an anxiety that required special pleading beyond the dedication apparent in his band's music.

What the MC5 challenged their audience to hear is a self-conscious variation of Black music mobilized to serve a particular political agenda in a specific historical moment. To consider the MC5 as willful agents rather than unwitting links in a chain of tradition does not deny the value of a psychoanalytic approach to their lives and performances, nor does it exonerate them from charges of cultural insensitivity and appropriation. Rather, it reveals how minstrels, hipsters, and other white performers of Black music constantly comment on their own tradition, which in the process accrues layers of what Ingrid Monson terms "intermusicality."[155]

The Only Thing We Play Is Music

But how did contemporary audiences hear the MC5? As we have seen, some commentators felt that the band's performances veered too close to direct appropriation or hipster name-dropping. In the *Los Angeles Free Press*, critic Robert Gold dismissed the band as "a bunch of pretentious assholes who give Sun Ra a bad name by merely mentioning him."[156] Others, however, made comments suggesting that they heard the group as synthesizers and adapters of Black music. Richard Goldstein wrote that while the MC5 "are fiercely proud of the elements of angry black jazz they retain in their music," they also make "allusions" to R&B and "choose their reference points with a poet's sense of style."[157] In the *Village Voice*, Sandy Pearlman argued that "the 5's into amazing syntheses. They've made a Cosmic Show of all such hack ready-mades. Too much like Sun Ra is most accurate. And that's a winner."[158] A reporter for the University of Iowa's *Daily Iowan* explained that "the MC5, in a peculiar way, is into the same things in the rock format that Sun Ra is into in jazz—there is also an awful lot of Coltrane, Coleman and Shepp in both the phrasing of the guitars and the ensemble sound of the band. Without, apparently, making much of a conscious effort in that direction, the MC5 is well on the way to producing a rock-jazz synthesis based primarily on the common denominator which the two forms have always shared—complete spontaneity."[159]

Some observers linked the MC5's musical style to social and political issues. London's *OZ* cast Detroit industry as a metaphor for their approach, writing that "they thrust raw chunks of Hendrix, the Who, Screaming Jay Hawkins into their sound, melting and binding them with Detroit's incessant pulses of metal, engines and fire."[160] Art Johnston, in *Fifth Estate*, claimed that "the MC5, virtually alone among contemporary rock musicians, are trying to encounter the black man's music of the present: the anguish and violence of burning ghettos; not the nostalgic up-tempo electrified R&B that Muddy Waters and Bo Diddley were playing at rent parties in the thirties [*sic*]. The Five are trying to fuse this experience with the purest of their own culture (itself a derivative of black music), the hard rock exemplified in their road show opener, Carl Perkins' 'Tutti-Frutti.'" The result, Johnston argues, is music that both "the blacks" and "the really wigged out revolutionaries" can "dig."[161]

Yippie Jerry Rubin suggested more provocatively that the approval of Black radicals was beside the point, writing that:

> Revolutionary whites relate to black soul politics the way white musicians relate to black soul musicians . . .
>
> Whites, without a culture of their own, took the soul and guts of black feeling and adapted it to their own reality.
>
> The White Panthers was born and their origins were jazz and rhythm and blues and rock and the Black Panthers. They did not ask the Black Panthers for permission. They just did it.
>
> *It is one of the beautiful, soulful ironies of history that the children of the oppressor achieve their freedom through learning from the oppressed.*
>
> And so these freaks became White Panthers the way Janis Joplin became a blues singer.[162]

Yet Black radicals were often less than enthusiastic about the White Panthers and the MC5's adaptations of "the soul and guts of black feeling." Wayne Kramer remembered a cordial relationship with the Black Panthers' Ann Arbor chapter that revolved around drinking, smoking pot, and firearm practice in the woods, but he admitted that "the official party line from the Black Panther party in Oakland was that we were 'psychedelic clowns.' They said we were idiots and to keep the fuck away from us."[163] Some of the band's critics were closer to home. William Spencer Leach of the Black Panther Party's Detroit branch published a scathing piece in *Fifth Estate* in January 1969 accusing the White Panther Party of "mak[ing] a joke out of the revolution" and becoming "our (the movement's) biggest headache." In a clear swipe at Sinclair's vision of cultural politics, he added that "music ain't revolution. Black folks have been singing, dancing, and blowing instruments, and we still ain't free."[164] Around 1970, Bobby Seale made a similar argument, explaining to an interviewer that "the White Panthers created themselves and they had some kind of psychedelic program, and we ran them out of our office—we didn't have time for it . . . psychedelic programs ain't going to solve these problems of Black people." This reads as a criticism of Sinclair's hedonism and perhaps the "psychedelic" rock of the MC5. Seale added that once Sinclair "put some politics into it. . . . it came down righteously . . . the cats turned out to be some beautiful cats," but the compliment nonetheless implied that psychedelia and politics should not mix.[165] One of Sinclair's harshest critics, novelist Ishmael Reed, wrote:

> John Sinclair of the MC . . . whatever the fuck his group is called can come on with a neo-aljolson shout all corny and off the wall like . . . "brothers and sisters get out d jams" but for sure there is no tribute to blackness or negritude

on that album—no tribute to the experience that only affords him the limousine service to Max's Kansas City where they tell black people at the door "I'M
SORRY BUT WE IS ONLY SERVING DINNER" . . . John Sinclair you hard
working, dedicated would-be nigger and naturally born werewolf think abt
this shit when you are making coins from our music. We got some dolls for
you. Dolls with pins in them.[166]

For Reed, Sinclair was a cultural imperialist in the guise of a political ally.

Sinclair defended the White Panthers by citing the Black Panther Party's
encouragement of white radicals such as Jerry Rubin, but he also stood up for
the role of rock in the revolution, asserting that "we are not playing. The only
thing we play is music. The rest of this shit we are dead serious about—but
that don't mean you can't have a good time while you're doing it." In a spirit
of reconciliation, he told Leach that "we'll be happy to play benefits to raise
money for the Black Panthers if that would fit in with your plans."[167] Leni
Sinclair, then married to John, recalls that the two parties occasionally got
together for "political education classes" and protest rallies and that "over the
years we started a working relationship with them" in which White Panther
Pun Plamondon served as distribution manager for the *Black Panther* newspaper in southeastern Michigan.[168] Perhaps as a result, Plamondon, whom
historian Jeff A. Hale describes as "the most influential Black Panther advocate within the collective," seems to have grown skeptical of Sinclair's narrow
focus on the cultural development of white youth. In a meeting of the party's
Central Committee recorded in Ann Arbor in June 1969, Plamondon insisted
that "we have to be able to relate to the Vietnamese—if they read our stuff and
we say 'music is the revolution,' you ain't gonna be able to *tell* no Vietnamese
that! We ain't gonna tell no Black Panther that!"[169]

If, in the final analysis, the MC5 had only a tenuous relationship to the
Black Panther Party, their unpredictable variants on jazz and blues demonstrated one mode in which aspiring white allies sought to relate to Black
culture—reworking it rather than seeking to imitate it outright. Scott Saul
writes that "in the late 1960s, Sinclair's greatest debt to the jazz world may
have been how he applied jazz's insistence on self-improvisation to the life
of the activist, reinventing himself like his heroes Malcolm and Coltrane, re-
acting to every twist of the radical screw and every slap of the backlash."[170]
Similarly, the MC5's self-inventions revealed their sincere love for African
American music, even as they reflected the band's immersion in primitivist
stereotypes of Black masculinity. But the MC5's "Detroit heavy music" was
not the only kind of response that white rock musicians made to Black Power.
We turn now to San Francisco's Jefferson Airplane, whose engagement with
blackness was less ideological but just as theatrical.

Blue Eyes and a Black Face

Jefferson Airplane and the Rock Revolution
The Smothers Brothers Comedy Hour
(CBS-TV), November 10, 1968

On November 10, 1968, five days after Richard Nixon's victory in the hotly contested US presidential election, the CBS television network broadcast the latest episode of *The Smothers Brothers Comedy Hour*, a variety show well known for controversial political satire. The episode, which had been taped in late October, featured Jefferson Airplane, one of the best-known bands to arise from San Francisco's much-publicized rock scene. The band performed "Crown of Creation," the title track from their recently released fourth album. Aficionados of acid rock might have been impressed by the song's unusual formal structure, its brief foray into a 5/4 meter, or its obscure, apocalyptic text. No viewer, however, could have missed the most unsettling aspect of the performance—white singer Grace Slick appeared covered in dark brown makeup, and gave the Black Power salute at the song's end.[1] In January 1969, a staged photograph of Slick with brown face and raised fist, perhaps taken backstage, appeared on the front cover of *TeenSet* magazine with the provocative cover line "Grace Slick and Jimi Hendrix on Being Black."[2]

Because Slick's appearance evokes, first and foremost, the ugly specter of blackface minstrelsy, the first reaction of many observers both in 1968 and today might be offense. Slick likely intended to scandalize "square" viewers, as in her appearance in an Adolf Hitler costume (alongside actor Rip Torn dressed as Richard Nixon) for a 1969 show at New York's Fillmore East.[3] Some commentators on the *Smothers Brothers* performance emphasize its sheer shock value rather than its relationship to racial representation. Slick's biographer Barbara Rowes, for example, downplays the significance of the incident by implying that Slick's alcohol problems had exacerbated her "sarcastic exhibitionism."[4] According to this reading, Slick's performance was not intentionally racist, but only another absurdist provocation typical of the freewheeling sixties. Historian Peter Doggett similarly minimizes the performance's racial implications, arguing that "though [Slick's] appearance has passed into rock myth as 'blackface,' it actually resembled a street urchin who had recently rolled through mud."[5]

Slick's own explanations of her blackface performance, however, reflect engagement with the controversial legacy of minstrelsy as well as a desire to distance herself from it. A press release, issued on November 12 by Jefferson Airplane's PR firm Rogers, Cowan & Brenner and widely quoted in the underground and rock press, reported on the incident:

> Grace Slick, one of the group's vocalists, appeared on the television show, singing two songs, in black face [*sic*]. At the close of one of the songs, she also raised a black-gloved hand in the Negro militant's close-fisted salute seen a month earlier at the Olympics.
>
> Miss Slick included in her list of reasons for wearing black makeup: "Listen to the words in 'Crown of Creation' and think about a Negro singing them; it makes sense. Also, women wear makeup all the time, so why not black? Next time I might wear green. Besides, I think it very weird to have blue eyes and a black face. And . . . there weren't any Negroes on the show and I thought the quota needed adjustment."[6]

Although this jumble of justifications acknowledges the racial charge of Slick's gesture, it spans the gamut from radical ("Crown of Creation" as a militant anthem for a Black singer) to (mock-) liberal (blackface as affirmative action) to aesthetic (black as just one of many colors worn by women; the "weird" juxtaposition of black skin and blue eyes), suggesting that Slick was unwilling to pin down its significance. The rock magazine *Fusion* quoted Slick explaining that "black is beautiful. Also, I've heard that black shows up on television better than white. To me, black is just a color. I could just as easily have worn green makeup."[7] In *Jazz and Pop* in January 1969, Slick asserted that "we wear make-up, no reason not to wear all different colors," and when an interviewer asked "was there any black and white theme there? Or hadn't you even thought of that?" she added that "if you get a whole mess of stuff out of it, that's the purpose of it. We just mess around and see what people do."[8] In more recent accounts, Slick explicitly distinguishes her gesture from minstrelsy while implicitly acknowledging its influence, speculating: "I think if I'd done a regular Al Jolson with the lips that might've made people even more furious," or "I wasn't interested in some funny Al Jolson look, though. I wanted to get it as real as possible."[9]

Of course, a gesture as provocative as Slick's blackface performance was bound to accrue meaning regardless of her intention. While the MC5 drew strategically on Black music and rhetoric, Slick's action may have reflected not a concrete political stance but rather a more experimental desire to "mess around" with some potent cultural signifiers to "see what people do." If by 1968 minstrelsy per se was no longer a living tradition, it remained a source of both racist imagery and ironic commentary. Rather than uncritically invoke the minstrel tradition, Slick acted from a privileged position to make a self-consciously obscure artistic statement, a "mimicry of racial mimicry" that perhaps deconstructed minstrelsy but perhaps simply perpetuated it.[10]

In this chapter, I propose that Slick's blackface stunt embodied ongoing changes in the relationship between bohemian hedonism and political radicalism, changes that centered on a new appreciation of Black militant style and rhetoric. At the same time, Slick's appearance invoked a long, troubling tradition of white women "blacking up" as a way of rejecting social and sexual conventions. At a fundamental level, Slick's gesture was presumptuous, a cheap, disrespectful way of claiming credit for edgy radical sympathies without making a genuine commitment to Black causes. At the same time, Jefferson Airplane's music often reflected a comparatively sensitive understanding of the nuances of African American musical traditions and the band's ambiguous connection to them. Grace Slick and Jefferson Airplane thus represented a key dynamic in 1968 rock: flamboyant political posturing wedded to innovative and complex musical forms and practices.

Up Against the Wall

To understand Slick's statement, one might look first to her Black Power salute, which seems intended to defamiliarize blackface by linking it to an assertive Black political movement. More specifically, her salute evokes an iconic event of 1968, when African American Olympic track stars Tommie Smith and John Carlos achieved international attention by raising black-gloved fists as they received their medals. This incident took place on October 16, 1968, only days before the Jefferson Airplane performance was taped. Comments by journalist Ralph J. Gleason as well as Rogers, Cowan & Brenner's press release make it clear that contemporary audiences would have understood Slick's gesture as a reference to the Olympic protests.[11]

Understanding Slick's blackface performance in a more precise, local context, however, requires an examination of the fusion of cultural and political radicalism underway in 1968 and epitomized in the Bay Area by the distinctions between Haight-Ashbury and Berkeley. Jefferson Airplane, founded in San Francisco in 1965, became an integral part of the burgeoning hippie movement in Haight-Ashbury, helping publicize that scene far beyond the

Bay Area with their 1967 hit singles "Somebody to Love" and the psychedelic anthem "White Rabbit." Jefferson Airplane's guitarist, singer, and songwriter Paul Kantner recalled that "there was a difference between Berkeley
and us. . . . We didn't give a shit about politics. . . . So people in Berkeley were
disdainful of us in San Francisco. We would support them, but we didn't want
to live the way they did."[12] Jefferson Airplane's initial apathy toward political
issues supports Kantner's claim. During 1967, the band told an interviewer
that "politics and music are the two dirtiest businesses in America today,"
and their most visible connection to radical politics was the criticism they
received for recording radio commercials for Levi Strauss while its workers
were on strike.[13] Students for a Democratic Society (SDS) passed a resolution
condemning the band, and a pre-Yippie Abbie Hoffman complained:

> I realize that they are just doing their "thing" but while the Jefferson Airplane
> grooves with its thing over 100 workers in the Levis-Strauss [sic] plant on the
> Tennessee-Georgia border are doing their thing which consists of being on
> strike to protest deplorable working conditions that characterize most South-
> ern textile factories. Perhaps many in the hippie community find the accep-
> tance of this contradiction mind-expanding; personally all I get is a headache.[14]

At a press conference early in 1968, the band claimed to be apolitical and
requested "don't ask us anything about politics," and in the spring they even
appeared on a radio show promoting the US Army, hardly a conventionally
radical gesture.[15] As we have seen, they refused Hoffman's invitation to perform in Chicago during the Democratic National Convention in August. In a
December interview with the *Chicago Kaleidoscope*, they defended this decision in various ways, with drummer Spencer Dryden asking "who wants to
be a martyr, man" while Slick argued that "there are some people who are
more effective at doing what was done in Chicago and who want to do it"
and Kantner surreally suggested that "I'd love to fill Mayor Daley's house with
cement."[16]

In September 1968, however, the band released a surprisingly militant
statement: *Crown of Creation*, an album whose cover featured a double-
exposed image of the Airplane superimposed on a photograph of the atomic
bomb blast at Hiroshima.[17] Kantner recalled in 1996 that "*Crown of Creation*
[was] just a beginning political reaction to the forces around us as the Haight-
Ashbury got darker and the jackboots and the anti-dope and the crushing
forces came in to squelch Communism and God knows what else is going on
here."[18] The title track featured atypically aggressive, hostile lyrics compiled
almost verbatim by Kantner from John Wyndham's 1955 science fiction novel
The Chrysalids, in which the words are spoken by postapocalyptic mutants

who wage a war of rebellion against an oppressive race of genetically "pure" humans.[19] Critic Craig Morrison argues that "the enforced conformity of the survivors [in the novel] and the persecution of those with the deformity of being able to communicate through mental telepathy paralleled the 'us and them' thinking that pitted the freaks (hippies) against the straights (ordinary citizens)."[20] Kantner recalled with amusement that he sent this song to Hubert Humphrey, the Democratic presidential nominee, when his staff asked the Airplane for a "hip" "campaign anthem" (it was promptly and predictably rejected).[21] The final song on *Crown of Creation*, "The House at Pooneil Corners," alluded cryptically to the devastation following a nuclear holocaust. Both songs featured unsettling melodies emphasizing the flatted second scale degree, a musical trademark of the band since their 1967 "White Rabbit," which evoked an exoticized conception of Spanish music.[22] Both also highlighted dissonant vocal harmonies and strained singing timbres, jarring tempo changes, and thick instrumental textures marked by distortion and feedback. These had also been prominent aspects of the Airplane's previous album, *After Bathing at Baxter's* (1967).[23] While the band's musical style resembled that of their earlier recordings, the apocalyptic thrust of some of *Crown of Creation*'s lyrics seemed to link that style to muted political protest as well as psychedelic inner exploration. In October 1968, the band taped their Smothers Brothers appearance, and in November they were filmed playing an illegal show on a Manhattan rooftop for Jean-Luc Godard's film *One A.M. (One American Movie)*, which also featured an interview with Eldridge Cleaver and a street performance by Amiri Baraka.[24] While they did not advance a specific political platform, Jefferson Airplane nonetheless played a highly visible role in the trend toward radical rhetoric in rock during 1968.

Jefferson Airplane's next album, 1969's *Volunteers*, made their revolutionary stance explicit.[25] Kantner remembered in 1996 that, with *Volunteers*, he wanted to assert that "in a sort of utopian way . . . yes, even though we are sharded amongst ourselves, we can all be together in fighting this common enemy, or this common force, that is not doing things in our best interest."[26] Its cover depicted the band, wearing grotesque masks, superimposed on an image of the American flag, while an insert in the form of a mock underground newspaper (the "Paz Progress") satirized the moon landing, the Peace Corps, and marijuana laws and included such surreal, irreverent headlines as "How to Tell Your Self from Richard Milhaus [*sic*] Nixon" and "Feed and Water Your Flag," as well as an "Editorial: By Tommy Smothers" with most of its words redacted. The album's first track, "We Can Be Together," presents a romantic, stirring proclamation of solidarity with and among the young "outlaws" of the counterculture. The song, credited to Kantner, takes almost every phrase of its verses from a manifesto published in the *Berkeley Barb* in October 1968 by the radical "affinity group" Up Against the Wall/Motherfucker (UAW/MF or the Motherfuckers for short).[27] The song's most controversial line, "Up against the wall, motherfucker," resulted in a censorship battle with RCA.[28] (Although the line remained on the record, the lyrics printed on the insert read "Up against the wall fred.") The album's last song, "Volunteers," featured the refrain "Got a revolution / Got to revolution" and promoted a youth rebellion, proclaiming that "one generation got old / One generation got soul." In these songs, the band adopted comparatively accessible formal structures and chord changes—both are based around the standard I-♭VII progression ubiquitous in 1960s rock.[29] The songs thus seem designed to attract listeners to their message rather than to evoke social turmoil through dissonance or formal complexity.

The Airplane's notorious use of the phrase "up against the wall, motherfucker" deserves special attention because of its direct link to both radical movements and racial representation. "Motherfucker" had been a word emblematic of African American speech since at least the 1940s. Kurt Vonnegut Jr., remembering World War II in his 1969 novel *Slaughterhouse-Five*, recalled that the word "was still a novelty in the speech of white people in 1944."[30] Mezz Mezzrow's 1946 glossary of Harlem jive presents it in bowdlerized form as "motherferyer," defined as an "incestuous obscenity."[31] The San Francisco Mime Troupe used "motherfucker" several times in their controversial 1965 play *A Minstrel Show, or Civil Rights in a Cracker Barrel,* some of whose cast was prosecuted (unsuccessfully) on obscenity charges after a 1966 performance in Denver.[32]

By 1968, "motherfucker" had become associated more precisely with the rhetoric of Black radicalism.[33] The full phrase sung by the Airplane became prominent in radical parlance after the publication of "Black People!," a poem by Amiri Baraka (then LeRoi Jones) that appeared in the December 1967 issue of *Evergreen Review*. In it, Baraka exhorts Black readers to attack white-owned businesses: "All the stores will open if you say the magic words. The magic words are: Up against the wall mother fucker this is a stick up!"[34] "Black People!" attracted wider attention when, at Baraka's trial for illegal weapon possession in January 1968, the judge read it aloud in court (substituting "mother blank" for the offending words) and cited the poem's content as reason for imposing a maximum sentence of two-and-a-half to three years (later overturned on appeal).[35] On April 22, 1968, shortly before a student occupation of campus buildings shut down Columbia University for a week, Columbia's SDS chairman (and future founder of the radical Weatherman organization) Mark Rudd wrote an open letter to university president Grayson

Kirk, describing the protests as a "war of liberation" and adding "I'll use the words of LeRoi Jones, whom I'm sure you don't like a whole lot: 'Up against the wall, mother fucker, this is a stick-up.'"[36] Protester Dotson Rader recalled that, shortly before they were finally routed by police on April 30, Columbia's student strikers chanted "UP AGAINST THE WALL MOTHERFUCKERS" as a "defiant slogan."[37] The UAW/MF group, also involved in the Columbia actions, took their name from Baraka's poem.[38] When Jefferson Airplane sang "Up against the wall, motherfucker" in "We Can Be Together," they were actually quoting the byline at the end of the UAW/MF manifesto.[39] In turn, the Yippies produced a 1970 pamphlet that quoted "We Can Be Together" in its entirety, ending with "UP AGAINST THE WALL MOTHERFUCKER / TEAR DOWN THE WALLS / TEAR DOWN THE WALLS."[40] Jefferson Airplane's song had become a link in a chain of radical texts.

Besides the Airplane's, the best-known utterance of "motherfucker" in 1960s rock appears in the introduction to the title track of the MC5's *Kick Out the Jams*, recorded live at Detroit's Grande Ballroom in October 1968, during which Rob Tyner yells "Kick out the jams, motherfucker!"[41] The White Panthers reveled in the word in their 1968 publications. John Sinclair, for example, ended a *Fifth Estate* column with "Up against the ceiling, motherfucker!" while his brother Dave concluded his poem "Pontiac's Speech to the White Man" with "in my dreams I hear / the triumph of my forest speech / in another time, and it says, it / screams with a vengeance / UP AGAINST THE WALL MOTHERFUCKERS!"[42] As Steve Waksman points out, Tyner's "cry in its fullness was a paean to impoliteness," and screaming it in unison created a "collective euphoria" that unified audiences at the band's performances.[43] Controversy over the line led some stores, such as Detroit's Hudson's chain, to refuse to sell the album, to which the MC5 responded with a full-page advertisement in the *Ann Arbor Argus* reading "KICK OUT THE JAMS, MOTHERFUCKER! And kick in the door if the store won't sell you the album FUCK HUDSON'S!"[44] The advertisement, which featured the Elektra logo without the company's permission, led the MC5 to lose their recording contract, but it also helped establish their radical credibility.[45] The Groove Shoppe, a Detroit record store, ran a supportive advertisement reading "The Groove Shoppe Sells Plastic Motherfuckers . . . 'We refuse to censor the MC5 album.'"[46]

While such rhetoric was at some level a means of generating publicity through scandal, it had the power to rile up commentators holding a variety of political positions. By 1969, Abbie Hoffman had come around to "rock folks," claiming that "you cats got some good shit goin, like . . . Gracie Slick saying 'motherfucker' on the Dick Cavett Show. . . . If you get into digging the music it's all 'tear down the walls, motherfucker' and 'kick out the jams, motherfucker' . . . That's good enough politics for me."[47] From the other side of the political spectrum, right-wing anti-Communist columnist Susan L. M. Huck sardonically cited "the Airplane's repeated use of the compound revolutionary noun, 'mother******,'" and argued sarcastically that "teaching Grace Slick, or Paul Kantner, or others of the Jefferson Airplane not to hurl obscene insults at anyone within earshot would, at best, be a repressive thing to do."[48] More moderate observers strove to make sense of the recent popularity of "motherfucker," a task made challenging by newspapers' refusal to print the word under discussion. Cultural critic Benjamin DeMott cited Columbia students' adoption of Baraka's "Up against the wall, mother—" as an example of the rhetorical "overkill" that he believed was taking over the United States.[49] A letter to the editor of the New York Times argued that before Baraka popularized it, "this 'literary' phrase was once a standard command used by our police as a prelude to frisking suspects," while reporter Nan Robertson noted that "some believe that the reverse side of the coin is what the police say in Harlem when they frisk suspects, front to the wall."[50] Allan Silver, a Columbia sociologist, argued that "the use of obscene language might be a manifestation of a deep-seated wish of white radicals to identify with the rhetoric and argot of the poor. 'Obscenity is very much a feature of proletarian life, of black city life. They chose this style instead of the genteel university style they are revolting against,' he said."[51] Such commentary reveals that a broad public associated "motherfucker" with both urban African American speech and student radicalism, and that moreover the word signified the connection between the two.[52]

Slick's blackface gesture, like the ubiquitous "motherfucker," reflected racial concerns already prevalent among the counterculture. Musicologist Nadya Zimmerman argues that in San Francisco "racialized elements were thrown in the pluralistic mix of signifiers that underscored the counterculture's cultural landscape, allowing the counterculture to deal *implicitly* and indirectly with racial politics without being pinned to a particular cause or *explicit* racial agenda."[53] More specifically, "the counterculture conceived of itself as a risk-taking outlaw culture, and it shaped that self-image by trading upon symbols of racially charged 'outlaw' cultures in the Bay Area—namely, the Black Panthers and the Hell's Angels."[54] The counterculture, however, was more interested in the style of Black radicalism than in its substance, "appropriat[ing] the antiofficial, outlaw sensibility of the [Black] Panthers . . . while remaining one step removed from participatory racial politics."[55] African Americans served as romantic symbols of authentic experience and identity, rather than pragmatic political strategists to be emulated.

Jefferson Airplane's limited engagement with racial politics exemplifies the sense of idealistic detachment that Zimmerman describes. Beyond surface gestures such as Slick's Black Power salute and a sign outside their shared San Francisco mansion reading "Eldridge Cleaver Welcome Here," the band made little overt comment on the racial turmoil of the late 1960s.[56] At times, their rhetoric seemed to mock traditional ideas about Black identity, but it is often hard to tell whether they were making fun of stereotypes or simply perpetuating them through what Sumanth Gopinath terms "radical minstrelsy."[57] "Jefferson Airplane," for example, was an abbreviation of "Blind Thomas Jefferson Airplane," a fictitious country blues persona invented for guitarist Jorma Kaukonen by his friend Steve Talbot.[58] The band's frequent, casual references in interviews to African Americans as "spades" may have been intended to evince a hip, ironic sense of superiority to racism, or perhaps the presumption of solidarity between white members of the counterculture and oppressed African Americans expressed in Abbie Hoffman's slogan for the radical Diggers group, "Diggersareniggers," or Jerry Farber's 1967 essay "The Student as Nigger."[59] Even at the time, the Airplane's comments on race impressed some observers as merely offensive rather than subversive. Susan L. M. Huck, for example, noted with biting sarcasm that "Grace always calls Negroes 'spades.' If she says it, it *must* be all right."[60] More recently, Zimmerman, criticizing the pervasiveness of such language among whites of the counterculture, argues that "the transformation of a racist slur ('spade') into a term of praise is, at the very least, a deeply patronizing gesture when coming from a white audience."[61] Others criticized the band's racial rhetoric for its lack of substance. Rock critic Michael Lydon singled out the group's Cleaver sign as an example of their "mushy politics—sort of a turned-on liberalism that thinks the Panthers are 'groovy' but doesn't like to come to terms with the nasty American reality," a stance that Lydon dismissed as "the politics of the much-touted 'rock revolution.'"[62] Lydon effectively critiques Jefferson Airplane's relationship to Black politics. But why did Slick choose blackface as a means of addressing that relationship?

White Women in Blackface

Although I have argued above against employing minstrelsy as a one-size-fits-all explanation of white performances of Black music, Slick was clearly referencing the minstrel tradition. The MC5 sought to adapt African American music into a form relevant for white radicals. Slick, in contrast, was playing not on Black music but on *blackface*, a form bound up with racist stereotypes, for a self-consciously hip rock audience who fancied themselves sophisticated enough to have moved beyond those stereotypes. Her perfor-

mance commented less on blackness as such than on the complex history of
white (mis)representations of blackness. But was this transgressive gesture a
moment of anti-racist critique? Or was it merely empty provocation? And by
what right did Slick make it?

Slick's performance places her in the persistent but often overlooked tradition of women in blackface. The substantial body of scholarship on minstrelsy has emphasized male spectators and performers, who, as Eric Lott puts
it, sought to access "black culture in the guise of an attractive masculinity."[63]
Lori Harrison-Kahan writes that "in fictional representations and historical
accounts" of the early twentieth century, "women performers appear to experience a deeper resistance to assuming blackface. This resistance stems in part
from a social protest against the inherent racism of minstrel practices, but
much more so from the ways that darkening their appearance would place
them at odds with white feminine ideals."[64] Those women, such as Sophie
Tucker, who performed in blackface during the vaudeville era often resisted
"uniform beauty standards" by flaunting what audiences regarded as "virile
voices and big ugly bodies."[65] Some white women in blackface portrayed the
desexualized "mammy" stereotype.[66] This convention fails, however, to account for Slick, a "public sex symbol" known for what her biographer calls
her "cool, dark beauty and haunted aspect."[67] Slick recalls that "in those days
I made a habit of putting on makeup, shaving my armpits and legs, and wearing dresses or skirts," although she adds that "the language that came out of
my low-end voice was a counterpoint to the refined image I might otherwise
be projecting."[68]

Slick's suggestion that her conventionally "refined" appearance contrasted
with the obscenity of her words and the sometimes harsh grain of her voice
recalls M. Alison Kibler's argument that blackface signified "unruly womanhood."[69] Daphne A. Brooks writes that the blackface performances of
nineteenth-century actor Adah Isaacs Menken "transgressed white patriar-
chal circumscription from within its very borders rather than simplistically
succumbing to its seductive burnt-cork rhythms."[70] Blackface often licensed
white women to engage in otherwise forbidden performances of sexuality. A
closer analogy to Slick's performance is the light brown "café au lait" makeup
worn by Ziegfeld Follies "girls," which allowed these white performers to
"safely act out the (bad) sexuality Ziegfeld Girls supposedly did not have."[71]
Zimmerman argues that "Slick . . . became for the counterculture the antithesis of middle-class repressed female sexuality. And as one of few female
rock musicians, she could encourage female sexual assertion, both through
her music and via her position as a role model."[72] Other blackface perform-

ers, such as May Irwin, took on "the persona of a combative black man," a persona that in Irwin's performances reinforced the primitivist stereotypes of "coon songs" but in Slick's mimicked the dignified self-assertion of the Olympic protesters.[73]

But if blackface represented "unruly womanhood," what did that mean in the specific context of 1960s radicalism? One might contrast Slick with Grace Halsell, who during 1968 undertook a more extended experiment with blackface. Halsell, a white journalist inspired by John Howard Griffin's *Black Like Me*, underwent skin-darkening treatments and then attempted to live as a Black woman first in Harlem and then in Mississippi. *Soul Sister*, her bestselling 1969 account of her experiences, is an earnest but awkward mixture of liberal piety and self-absorption. Halsell's aim was to report authentically on racial injustice by becoming its victim: "now I know what it cost me, psychologically, to bear, for one minute in time, what every black American bears all his life: discrimination, segregation, injustice. I truly journeyed into areas of *apartheid*."[74] Her account, however, also reflects her desire for belonging within a stereotyped vision of a Black folk community: "I need this experience. I have been on the outside looking in. I have smelled the colored people's collard greens and their living-up-close-together smells. I am now going to knock on their doors and say, black people let me in there with you!"[75] Halsell's experiment, while predicated on color-consciousness, ironically allows her to claim that she has achieved colorblindness. She writes that, only days into her new life as an ersatz African American, "I become aware that I have begun to see beyond the blackness of Harlem. A black among blacks, I have forgotten to 'see' black so much as people, individuals: fat, short, clean, dirty, pretty, ugly."[76] Literary critic Baz Dreisinger writes that "*Soul Sister* not only maintains sharp distinctions between black and white but also preserves the essential whiteness of its protagonist, who hopes to become a more enlightened, more nearly perfect white person by taking that whiteness off—at least for a little while."[77] Halsell's story appears to have inspired "I Am Curious (Black)!," a 1970 issue of DC Comics' *Superman's Girl Friend Lois Lane* in which intrepid reporter Lane undergoes a temporary racial transformation (thanks to Superman's Kryptonian "Plastimold Machine") so that she can report on "the *inside story* of what it means to be *black*!" In the end, the issue's liberal lesson is learned by a Black militant who stops hating "whitey" after Lane, who has saved his life with a blood transfusion, reverts to whiteness and reveals her true identity.[78] Neither Halsell nor Lois Lane overtly resemble Slick. Slick hardly seems to have been promoting colorblindness—in fact, the brazen artifice of her costume forced viewers to think about skin color. But the visibility of that artifice may also support the fundamental premise of Halsell's work, belief in an essential, binary division between Black and white that can be bridged only in an all-or-nothing way.

A more telling comparison links Slick with Bernardine Dohrn, a highly visible member of SDS at the moment of Slick's performance and by the end of 1969 one of the founders of the radical Weatherman group. Slick and Dohrn each came from an upper-middle-class family. Dohrn, raised in affluent Whitefish Bay, Wisconsin, was a graduate of the University of Chicago Law School, while Slick, by her own account, grew up "right in the middle of the WASP caricature of family life" in Palo Alto, California, and attended Finch College, a New York "finishing school for girls from wealthy or prominent families."[79] Student radicals of the 1960s often rebelled against such class identities. Historian Jeremy Varon points out that "the status of the Weathermen as largely middle-class whites was essential to their politics of transgression."[80] Women radicals, moreover, could flout both gender and class norms by rejecting conventions of genteel feminine behavior. *New York Times* columnist John Leo highlighted "the obscenity issuing from the lips of apparently demure girls at political demonstrations," noting that "the official slogan of the Columbia rebels—of which 'Up against the wall, mother' is a polite contraction—is used almost as frequently by Barnard women as by Columbia men." Psychologist Philip Zimbardo informed Leo that "lower-class women don't curse, at least before men," and that "he believed that the women at Columbia were consciously exploiting class differences to enrage policemen who were viewed as oppressors."[81] Although Slick, unlike Dohrn, was not committed to street protest, both employed obscenity to shock and provoke their audiences, and both recognized the power of playing their class privilege against their unruly behavior. This explains Slick's sardonic proposal after her Smothers Brothers performance that "perhaps a bored socialite can do the same thing and go shopping in blackface and maybe pick up some bargains."[82]

Both Slick and Dohrn also combined a glamorous image with a reputation for resolve and self-assurance. Larry Grathwohl, an FBI informer who infiltrated the Weathermen, remembered Dohrn leeringly as a "high priestess," "sexually appealing in long dark boots, a short miniskirt, and a see-through blouse with no bra," while adding that she "radiated confidence and displayed a poise that can be acquired only from countless public appearances."[83] Weatherwoman Susan Stern remembered how Dohrn "spoke and moved; such control, such self-assurance, such elegance."[84] After 1969's Days of Rage protest in Chicago, "other than the limp, there was no discernible reminder that [Dohrn] had just been through a violent battle with Chicago's finest. She looked like a fashion model. Short black leather jacket, nice slacks, neat purple blouse—everything just so."[85] Slick had literally worked as a fashion model for San Francisco's I. Magnin department store before beginning her musical career, and later *American Bandstand's* Dick Clark (ostensibly) complimented her as "extraordinarily beautiful, very mannequinlike."[86] At the same time, Slick projected an authority that belied Clark's implication of passivity. Rock critic Gillian G. Gaar argues that "Slick's sarcastic, sometimes menacing demeanor . . . made her one of the strongest female rock personalities of the time."[87] In 1970, Tom Hayden, decrying the sexism of the New Left, wrote that "Bernadine [sic] Dohrn and Bernadette Devlin are seen as revolutionary sex objects, Janis Joplin and Grace Slick as musical ones, Joan Baez and Judy Collins as 'beautiful and pure.'"[88] Slick and Dohrn thus occupied a similar place in the radical imagination as both sexually desirable and admirably revolutionary.

Although Dohrn was not known to wear blackface, she demonstrated her identification with the Black Panthers and related groups through language that recalled that of the White Panthers, speaking of "organizing against the pigs" and describing white radicals as "honkies" obliged to prove themselves through "armed struggle."[89] Varon argues that "Weatherman's talk . . . of frightening 'Honky America' appears a rather transparent and forced mimicry of a black radical idiom."[90] At their most outrageous, the Weathermen celebrated the Charles Manson murders and "debated the ethics of killing white babies, so as not to bring more 'oppressors' into the world and denounced American women bearing white children as 'pig mothers.'"[91] In less theatrical moments, however, Dohrn sincerely engaged the question "what is the political relationship between the black liberation movement and the white radical movement, and how do we forge that relationship?"[92] At the SDS national convention in 1969, Dohrn led the Revolutionary Youth Movement in expelling the Old-Left Progressive Labor Party from SDS in favor of a platform of "anti-racist solidarity." Historian Dan Berger notes that "beyond the messy process of faction fights was the reality that a sizable sector of white American radicals had broken with white supremacy and deliberately, consciously, and proudly allied themselves with people of color and national liberation struggles."[93] Dohrn explained that "building a white Left movement from the ground up means we need the Panthers and black radicals there—at the ground level."[94]

Yet the Black Panthers themselves were divided about affiliating with Dohrn and Weatherman. After the "Days of Rage" in October 1969, when the Weathermen smashed windows and fought with police in Chicago, Fred Hampton, chair of the Black Panther Party's Illinois chapter, "denounced" the group for their undisciplined actions, asserting that "we do not support people who are anarchistic, opportunistic, adventuristic, and Custeristic."[95] Elaine Brown reports that when "Dohrn and other Weather leadership demanded a meeting with him," Hampton "kicked Dohrn and the others out of the Chicago office."[96] In his 1993 autobiography, former Black Panther Party Chief of Staff David Hilliard recalls that the Weathermen were "extremely immature" and "often anti-Panther. They never wanted a black group that had a real following . . . They were completely into their own exclusivity and their own elitism."[97] At the same time, "the New York Black Panthers largely cheered Weather's militancy," and even Hampton "maintained a friendly relationship with Weatherman/SDS" before his murder by Chicago police on December 4, 1969.[98] But clearly it was difficult for even the most committed whites to negotiate their relationships with Black radicals. How, then, could Grace Slick claim a connection to the Black Power movement?

I Still Wouldn't Call It Blues

Such a connection is more likely to be found in Jefferson Airplane's performances and recordings than in their sporadic public comments about politics. To what extent did Slick's blackface performance, for example, signal her identification with African American politics and culture, or perhaps her desire to convince audiences of that identification? The history of white women performing in blackface includes those, such as Sophie Tucker, who strove to persuade audiences (if only temporarily) that they were, in fact, Black. Tucker "cultivat[ed] a specifically black sound through both aural and aesthetic avenues," and her early blackface performances climaxed when she removed her glove "to reveal a white hand and demonstrate that she was, in fact, a white female."[99] Even after she abandoned blackface, "Tucker's appeal increasingly resulted from her ability to provide a sensationally incongruous blend of white face and black sound."[100]

In 1960s rock, an updated version of this stance was made famous by Janis Joplin, whose biographers highlight her strong sense of affinity with African American music and culture and her dream of becoming what she called "the first black-white person."[101] Joplin's sister Laura remembers that "Janis needed acceptance from black society, from those whom her high school friends had defined as the heroes of the underbelly of America, the guideposts of her life."[102] This need made Joplin anxious about singing authentic blues— astounded in 1968 by the power of a B. B. King show, she lamented that her own band, Big Brother and the Holding Company, were "just a sloppy group of street freaks" by comparison—and led her to an obsession with the music and life of Bessie Smith.[103] As her alter ego "Pearl," "Joplin cultivated aspects of her own character that correlated with what she knew of Smith's: a taste for alcohol, a fondness for ornamenting herself with feathers and beads, bisexuality, and a reputation as a 'good-time girl' who talked frankly about her sexual needs."[104] Biographer Myra Friedman captures Joplin's obsession with Smith's mythos: "from Janis's own darkness of heart came the enchantment with Bessie's style—hard-drinking, hard-suffering, loser to men, and the victim of early death."[105] Robert Crumb's famous cover art for Big Brother's 1968 album *Cheap Thrills* satirizes Joplin's blues fixation by depicting her dragging through the desert a "Ball and Chain" with a thought balloon reading "Big Mama Thornton" (in the adjacent panel a wildly stereotypical Black mammy sings "Summertime" to a wailing white baby).[106]

Some critics took strong positions against Joplin's approach to Black music. In 1968, *New York Times* reviewer William Kloman dismissed *Cheap Thrills* as a "stereophonic minstrel show," and the following year writer Stanley Crouch, then a Black nationalist, attacked Joplin as an "imitation nigger" like the Beatles and the Rolling Stones.[107] More recently, Michael Awkward has argued instead that Joplin respectfully and thoughtfully adapted the "sonic conventions and cultural wisdom" of the blues "to her own social, cultural, and material circumstances."[108] But none of these critics contests that Joplin sought to embody Black music, just whether that embodiment was appropriate or successful. In April 1968, Joplin told the *Village Voice* that "make-up . . . is 'a lot of insignificant crap. Sometimes I wish I was black or of some exotic race, where, baby, it's your face alone that's working for you, no camouflage.'"[109]

Slick, in contrast, wore blackness overtly *as* camouflage in her blackface performance, as something that obviously could be put on or taken off at will, and despite her appreciation of African American musicians, she did not style herself a "black-white person" à la Joplin. In her 1998 autobiography, Slick argued that she was so distanced from blackness that even her blackened face was not legible as such:

> The trouble was that my features were angular and not right for the part, so apparently none of the viewers even noticed that I was in special makeup. Since nobody wrote in to the show and said, "What the hell was that?" they must have thought I had on some jet black tanning lotion or that the color on their TV sets had gone haywire. Maybe it was just getting harder to shock the couch potatoes.[110]

If Slick is correct that viewers failed to notice her masquerade, the reason might not have been her features or viewers' TV reception, but rather that no aspect of her public persona other than her temporarily darkened face seemed to evoke blackness.

Slick was, however, influenced by Black musicians, primarily those associated with the folk revival, such as Bay Area singer Stan Wilson, exiled South African Miriam Makeba, and especially guitarist and singer Odetta, who employed her rich contralto in a repertoire that included Child ballads, spirituals, and blues. Slick explains that "since I have a low-end voice, I could relate to Odetta's style better than, say, a Joan Baez or a Joni Mitchell reedy soprano."[111] Slick remembers that at a backstage meeting in Greenwich Village around 1957, Odetta "encouraged my moderate ability and gently warned me that being a musician was sort of a hit-and-miss occupation."[112] In her autobiography, Slick self-deprecatingly relates her first attempt to make it into the music business around 1959, when she responded to a classified ad reading "Singer wanted for new record label" without realizing that the label wanted a Black musician.

> Two men in a small recording studio with a closet-sized control room waved me over to a microphone to do the song I'd rehearsed. Unfortunately it was "Summertime." For an all-black record label? . . . Through the double-glass window of the control booth, I saw gentle smiles—not condescending—just two black men watching a little white dufus squirming under the weight of her own self-inflicted hubris.
>
> I didn't get a callback.[113]

While "Summertime" was a mainstay of Joplin's repertoire, Slick was too self-conscious about racial difference to feel comfortable performing a song so strongly associated with Black performers, at least in front of a Black audience.

The other members of Jefferson Airplane were inspired in their formative years by a variety of African American musical practices and genres. Drummer Spencer Dryden, who cited Elvin Jones, Art Blakey, and Philly Joe Jones as influences, began his career in jazz big bands and worked for two years with jazz saxophonist Charles Lloyd.[114] Lead guitarist Jorma Kaukonen was a blues fanatic who revered Black musicians from Muddy Waters to Reverend Gary Davis.[115] In 1967, he told *Hit Parader* magazine that "I got very, very interested in blues music when I was in my early teens. Jack Casady, our bass player, and I grew up together. He and I and his brother used to listen to 'The Best of Jimmy Reed,' 'The Best of Little Walter' and 'The Best of Muddy Waters.' Those were the first three albums I ever bought."[116] Casady also claimed the bass players featured on the Motown and Stax labels as important influences, and he had played briefly with rhythm and blues legends Little Anthony and the Imperials in the early 1960s.[117] In a 1967 interview, Casady asserted that "there are a lot of good jazz bass players. But there aren't too many really good white bass players in rock. But I've been running into more good ones lately. There have always been good Motown bass players."[118] Paul Kantner, perhaps the Airplane member least obviously influenced by Black music, explained that his song "The Ballad of You and Me and Pooneil" (from *After Bathing at Baxter's*) "has a little bit of 'Memphis' by Chuck Berry and a little bit of 'Spoonful' by Howlin' Wolf in the music."[119] Kantner added, however: "but I still wouldn't call it blues. To me blues are the classic things like Gary Davis."[120] Whereas the MC5 were adamant that they could play "stone blues," Kantner alluded to the music without claiming it as his own tradition. Critic James Lichtenberg suggested something similar in 1969 when he described Jefferson Airplane as "amazing the world with art-blues" rather than seeking to play blues in its "original" form.[121]

The term "art-blues," however, assumed an implicit racial hierarchy in which the "original" blues produced by Black musicians served as raw material to be refined into "art" by white musicians. Jefferson Airplane themselves rarely discussed their music in this way, and their public comments often reflected a relatively sophisticated understanding of the issues raised when white musicians drew on Black music. Nadya Zimmerman demonstrates that musicians such as Joplin and Jerry Garcia were either unaware of or unworried about the racial politics of appropriation and believed that genres such as the blues should be available to anyone who chose to perform them.[122] Jefferson Airplane, in contrast, were informed at least in part by the principle that Black musicians deserved autonomous control over their own music. Spencer Dryden, for example, remembered with equanimity the experience of being excluded from some African American jazz groups. Dryden commented that "it's coming *time*, man, for the American Negro to do his thing . . . And I still have a lot of good [Black] friends; it's just that they're in their section of what they're doing right now. They're sort of like doing their thing *together*."[123] Singer Marty Balin speculated that "a lot of Negro cats come up and say, 'Wow, man, I dig your voice. Too much!,'" perhaps because, unlike white blues revivalists like Paul Butterfield, he did *not* strive for "a communication with a Negro type of sound."[124] In October 1968, a reporter for the *Daily Californian* seconded this idea, arguing that "Marty Balin . . . is the most authentically independent white male vocalist in rock. Not only does he stubbornly refuse to mimic Negro blues stylists, but he sings beautifully."[125] Unlike many of their overtly political statements, the band's comments on their musical style sometimes displayed a nuanced sense of music's racial significance, rather than a pretense of performing Black music authentically or embodying it personally.

Both *Crown of Creation* and *Volunteers* demonstrate Jefferson Airplane's flexible, adaptive approach to African American models. *Crown of Creation* includes "In Time," a song whose verses begin with what sounds like the first eight bars of a twelve-bar blues before deviating away from the form. The oscillating minor-ninth progression underlying the verses of "Triad" (written by David Crosby) mimics the voicings played by pianist McCoy Tyner in John Coltrane's "My Favorite Things." "Star Track" fits the melody and chords of Reverend Gary Davis's "Death Don't Have No Mercy" with new lyrics by Kaukonen.[126] Kaukonen's guitar solo (on this and many other examples) reflects immersion in the electric blues, but his unconventional phrasing as well as aggressive use of wah-wah and distortion distance his guitar style from that of his influences. *Volunteers* features "Good Shepherd," Kaukonen's reworking of a nineteenth-century hymn recorded by blues and gospel guitarist Jimmie Strothers in 1936, and his "Turn My Life Down," inspired by Smokey Robinson's "The Tracks of My Tears."[127] "Wooden Ships," composed by Kantner, Crosby, and Stephen Stills (and recorded earlier in 1969 by Crosby, Stills, and Nash), tells the story of a wandering band of nuclear survivors over lulling minor-ninth chords that once again evoke the sound of modal jazz.

Beyond their incorporation of African American influences, Jefferson Airplane's style tended toward eclecticism, reflecting what Nadya Zimmerman terms a "pluralistic" "countercultural sensibility."[128] Jack Casady described the group as "a conglomeration of really radically different backgrounds."[129] Reminiscing in her autobiography, Slick envisioned the rock scene as a melting pot:

> I really believed the whole world would look like that in about sixteen years—the different skin colors weaving in and out of the tapestry, the unrestricted language and lack of cultural animosity, and the beautiful power of our main language: rock and roll. The blend of African American, Native American, Scottish folk, East Indian, Irish, Spanish, and even classical music all folded into German-Japanese electronic technology to produce art for everybody, our endless anthems celebrating the differences and similarities of the new global family.[130]

In the extensive series of interviews Ralph J. Gleason conducted with the band around 1967, they cite a broadly inclusive range of inspirations and interests. These include Dylan and the Beatles, but also the electronic music of Edgard Varèse and the choral harmonies of Bulgaria, as well as Asian influences including sitarist Ravi Shankar and veenaist S. Balachander, the Japanese koto and shakuhachi, and the traditional music of North Borneo.[131] Slick, employing her usual racial slur, explained that Spanish music, another influence, "is actually very universal . . . it's spade music and it's Eastern music, European, both North and South, and I can hear all the stuff that's gone on with all these different people, within that one music."[132]

This diverse range of influences is apparent throughout Jefferson Airplane's music, sometimes as a source of exotic color and sometimes in more formally significant ways. The bolero figure and Phrygian harmony of "White Rabbit" reflect what Zimmerman terms an "Orientalist" vision of flamenco filtered through Ravel's *Bolero* and Miles Davis's and Gil Evans's *Sketches of Spain*.[133] The dense, complex three-part vocal harmonies that characterize much of the band's work, including the conclusion of the song "Crown of Creation," might reflect the influence of Bulgarian choral music.[134] *Volunteers*, the band's most politically "revolutionary" album, is a freewheeling blend of genres. Jeff Tamarkin describes "The Farm," an affectionate country-music satire featuring pedal steel guitar by the Grateful Dead's Jerry Garcia, as a "commentary on the back-to-the-land movement finding favor with many hippies at the time."[135] Probably the album's most unusual track is "Meadowlands," a brief organ rendition, played by Slick, of a Soviet army song accompanied by the voice of a stereotypical Jewish shopkeeper advertising "Mendel's Department Store."[136] If the juxtaposition was intended to make a point about the Cold War or Russian Jewish identity, that point remains opaque.

Their devotion to eclecticism rather than to African American music in particular means that Jefferson Airplane's most militant music was not necessarily their "blackest." Consider the treatment of "motherfucker" in "We Can Be Together." Despite the controversy surrounding the line, its musical setting renders its meaning ambiguous. In one of the few contemporaneous reviews of *Volunteers* to devote close attention to the music as well as the political implications of the lyrics, Miller Francis Jr. of the *Los Angeles Free Press* noted:

> By now you've probably heard that the Airplane sings those famous lines, "Up against the wall, mother fuckers," and they do; but the way this statement is handled in the context of this song is very clever and imaginative indeed. It follows a brief pause in the song and appears after the lines, "Everything they say we are we are / And we are very / Proud of ourselves" so that these specific lines are emphasized, and sing like a piece of dialogue complete with quotation marks. The Airplane is obviously more into tearing down walls than putting people up against them, and the song ends with a positive statement of cosmic revolution.[137]

Francis suggests that the band's use of the revolutionary catchphrase is ironic, an evocation of radical sentiment rather than an endorsement of it. Indeed, the line in question is sung in soaring three-part harmony, crowned by Slick's warm alto, over a consonant I-V-IV progression that evokes a sense of security and coherence rather than revolutionary rage or violence.[138] The line that follows, "tear down the walls," is set similarly. While "tear down the walls" was another of the rallying cries of striking students at Columbia, Tamarkin reports that Kantner actually took the line from the 1964 album of the same name by folk singers Vince Martin and Fred Neil, the latter one of Kantner's most important early influences.[139] Unlike "We Can Be Together," Martin and Neil's song "Tear Down the Walls," with its references to church bells and freedom songs, is squarely in the tradition of earnest liberal protest associated with the 1960s folk revival. J. Lawrence of *Changes* magazine, who described "We Can Be Together" as "folk-rock; it sounds like 'This Land Is Your Land,'" added that "Kantner borrows 'Tear Down the Walls' from a Fred Neil 'folk' song of five years back and puts it in a more relevant musical and political environment."[140] The song's intended meaning is thus more ambivalent than the text alone might suggest. As Tamarkin asks, "was this a literal call for rampant and random violence in the streets, or a symbolic plea to eliminate all barriers?"[141]

What Kind of Revolution Is That?

Jefferson Airplane themselves often seemed uncertain of the answer to Tamarkin's question. Like their records, Jefferson Airplane's public statements demonstrated an uncertain view of revolution. Those comments that might have been interpreted as radical or revolutionary were generally spontaneous rants against local authority. Slick, for example, began a 1968 performance for "moneyed, well-dressed, smug, upper-classers" at New York's Whitney Museum by "riff[ing] on for about ten minutes on socialites and their strang [*sic*] habits and quaint attire" and referring to the "assembled rich" as "'filthy jewels" (or perhaps, more objectionably, "you Jewish broads with your jewels").[142] At a 1969 concert in Miami, when the band's power was turned off after a "designated curfew," Kantner "cursed out the police and pressed the crowd . . . into action. 'Wait till we burn down *your* society!' he shouted, as the audience of 10,000 cheered him on."[143] Such outbursts likely reflected genuine frustration with "the Establishment," but in hindsight they look like petulant explosions of annoyance and contempt rather than effective political gestures.

A revealing glimpse of the band's conflicted politics is provided by a conversation between Slick, Kantner, and Yippies Abbie and Anita Hoffman, published in the *East Village Other* in June 1970.[144] As the group banters, Slick and Kantner sometimes try to match the militant fervor of the Hoffmans.

Kantner, for example, claims that he has ordered an AR-18 assault rifle for self-defense, while Slick explains glibly that "I prefer not to kill people, but I'd like to destroy as much property as possible." (This line attracted the attention of the FBI, which quoted it in a 1970 memorandum on Slick.)[145] More often, however, they express a vision of cultural revolution that reveals their continued engagement with the dropout ideology associated with Haight-Ashbury. While Kantner praises the "good old revolutionary crazies" that attend the band's shows, he describes them as "just stoned, dancing and having a really good time" in contrast to "up against the wall" radicals such as the Weathermen. He also draws the familiar distinction between "Dionysion" [sic] San Francisco and "uptight" Berkeley, and argues that "instead of protesting about the war with 20 people I'd rather take those same 20 people out into the woods and get 'em high and swimming in a stream. And just doing that shows them a much better way to live and will convert them alot [sic] faster than yelling in their faces at a rally."[146] When questioned about their "model for revolution," Kantner and Slick retreat into utopian fantasy, with Slick asking "why kill something that's already dead?" and Kantner claiming that "the government's already been overthrown. It just has to realize it." Kantner is particularly critical of the Hoffmans' comparatively pragmatic approach to revolutionary politics. Pressed by Anita Hoffman on whether Mick Jagger's performances are "more dashing as gesture than meaningful politically," Kantner grumbles, "that's 'cause you put a pretty dull picture of what he should have been, on him." When Abbie Hoffman argues that young people should (probably metaphorically) "kill their parents and take over," Kantner demurs: "There's no need to kill 'em. That's sort of a harsh thing to subject the typical American teenager to. What do you mean by that?" While Anita Hoffman describes radical bombers (presumably those in groups such as Weatherman) as "heroes," Kantner asserts that "it's wrong to blow up property." Kantner claims rather defensively that "we think our politics speaks through our music," but he also protests that "We Can Be Together" is "not an anthem . . . It's fun to sing."

A survey of critical reporting on Jefferson Airplane reveals that their revolutionary rhetoric met with a range of receptions, even among presumably sympathetic members of the counterculture. Several reports in the alternative press expressed support for the band and their political statements. In San Francisco's *Rolling Stone*, white critic Ralph J. Gleason argued that Slick's blackface makeup and Black Power salute were positive signs of "a new way of life emerging in this society."[147] *Distant Drummer*, a Philadelphia underground paper, described *Volunteers* favorably as "a scathing scatological attack on standardized valve [sic] systems."[148] At a Fillmore East performance of

"We Can Be Together" in November 1969, *East Village Other* reporter James Lichtenberg found himself moved to "tears and sobs a total crack up, head and hart [*sic*] lifted out of the body, held, caressed and returned."[149] Miller Francis Jr. touted "We Can Be Together" as "the hippest thing I've ever heard in the way of 'political' rock," praising the way the song "combines militance in its verbal stance . . . with a lyrical kind of sentimentality in the way it is performed."[150] In 1970, Francis, inspired by an Atlanta concert at which Marty Balin stood up to police who "hassled kids" in the audience, quoted both "We Can Be Together" and "Crown of Creation" in a call for revolution: "If 'private property' is the target, as the Airplane puts it, and 'We' are its enemy, we'd better start getting together some mass, collective actions to Stop the Pig/Serve the People. *In loyalty to their kind, they cannot tolerate our minds / In loyalty to our kind, we cannot tolerate their obstruction.* Got a revolution to make!"[151]

Other countercultural observers were more skeptical, often invoking what historian Thomas Frank terms the "theory of co-optation," the argument that "emblems of dissent" are "quickly translated into harmless consumer commodities, emptied of content, and sold to their very originators as substitutes for the real thing."[152] *Georgia Straight*, a Vancouver paper, attacked *Volunteers* for its "inspecific politics and packaged, consumerized anti-Amerikanism."[153] Lester Bangs, writing in Detroit's *Creem*, called the Airplane "radical dilettante capitalist pigs."[154] Baltimore's *Harry* ran a review of an Airplane concert at which the police arrested rowdy members of the audience while others stood idly by, singing along to "Volunteers." Reporter Thomas V. D'Antoni asked pointedly, "What kind of revolution is that? No matter what kind of revolution you're into—political, cultural, spiritual or all three—what kind of shit is waving your fist as your friends are dragged off? And singing 'got to revolution' at the same time. Somebody please explain that to me."[155] In the leftist journal *Ramparts*, Ed Leimbacker accused the Airplane of hawking "harmless words and grand gestures rather than truly radical actions."[156] Even the conservative *Time* magazine took a similar view, citing Slick's blackface routine as an example of "revolutionary hype."[157] For these critics, the poetic revolution advocated by Jefferson Airplane amounted only to a self-satisfied narcissism, limited by what Michael Lydon described as the Airplane's belief "that the place for the revolution to begin and end is inside individual heads."[158]

White critic Lydon's skepticism toward the rhetoric of these white musicians' radicalism mirrored that of many politically engaged African Americans during the Black Power era. If Black radicals were ambivalent about the white counterculture generally, they appear to have been largely unconcerned with, or unaware of, Jefferson Airplane's occasional attempts at political engagement. A survey of the *Black Panther* newspaper, as well as the mainstream publications *Ebony* and *Jet*, reveals no mention of Slick's blackface appearance or Black Power salute during the weeks following the Smothers Brothers broadcast. For most African Americans engaged in political and social struggles, Jefferson Airplane were simply irrelevant.

It is easy to be cynical today about the rock revolution represented by Jefferson Airplane, especially given the vagueness and ineffectiveness of their political rhetoric. John Strausbaugh argues that "by 1969 the Jefferson Airplane were quite practiced in marketing revolutionary hipness to receptive youth."[159] Looking back, the band's members have sometimes concurred. Casady, for example, remembered that "naturally, nobody wanted people to die in a war, but I don't think there was tremendous deep thought about the situation. Paul waving his guitar over his head like Che Guevara, and pumping his guitar in the air in military fashion, was all okay theater at the time." Kaukonen agreed: "I always thought that Paul was very politically naive. And I always thought that I was very politically savvy because my dad was a government guy. After the fact, I suspect neither one of us really knew very much about what was going on. But it was better to have an opinion than to have none."[160] Kantner himself argued in 1996 that the Airplane didn't do "political things. We didn't encourage voting drives. We just continued the Timothy Leary of the drop in, tune out, drop out situation, which had worked quite effectively for us up until that point."[161] He went on to contrast Jefferson Airplane with the politically engaged folk musicians of the previous generation: "we didn't want to go out and be the Weavers—or I didn't—and be in labor unions, and support Communism, and do the Wobbly thing, and carry on singing Lead Belly songs for our life, but I think the spirit of addressing your community, the world that you live in through your own particular optic, is what I learned at the Weavers' knee."[162] Slick claimed in 1987 that "Volunteers" "doesn't make any sense, and it never did."[163]

Slick's blackface routine, in which she seems to play at revolution by imitating African American radicals, exemplifies the frequent emptiness and arrogance of rock's politics. If one views the Airplane as musicians as well as public figures, however, their relationship to African American culture and politics becomes more complex. If, as I have argued, one of the significant features of 1960s US radicalism was the tendency of white radicals to admire and seek to emulate African American role models, Jefferson Airplane were in the vanguard as artists, if not in politics as typically conceived. Jefferson Airplane's music often reflected a respectful and thoughtful effort, not simply to revive or mimic various aspects of Black music, but to creatively synthesize them into new forms of expression. If Jefferson Airplane tore down walls during the 1960s, they did so as much through continued exploration of African American musical tradition as through utopian visions of political and cultural revolution.

One Plus One

Jean-Luc Godard Meets the Rolling Stones
London Film Festival, November 29, 1968

On November 29, 1968, *One Plus One*, a film starring the Rolling Stones and directed by French New Wave pioneer Jean-Luc Godard, received a contentious premiere at London's National Film Theatre as part of the London Film Festival.[1] Godard, infuriated by producer Iain Quarrier's decision to revise the film's ending while also retitling it *Sympathy for the Devil*, spoke beforehand. In halting English, he asked the audience to vote on the proposition that they leave the theater, demand a refund at the box office, and then send the money to the defense fund for Black Panther Eldridge Cleaver, then in hiding to avoid trial for attempted murder charges. Most members of the audience either failed to understand Godard's request or rejected it. In the London underground paper *IT*, Joel Finler explained that

> Godard was understandably peeved at this, remarking that this was exactly what he had expected. Somebody in the audience yelled out that wasn't it possible to do both, see the film AND donate 10 shillings to Cleaver? And Godard replied that this was a typical "liberal" reaction, for it missed the main point, that this was meant to be a gesture with regard to the British cinema and the film festival and not just the Black Nationalists. Then others in the audience began to shout out some rather nasty remarks calling Godard a bastard and attacking him for not turning up to give a lecture at the NFT a month ago.[2]

Godard, in turn, denounced the audience as "fascists," punched Quarrier in the face, stormed offstage, and marched out into the night. Critic Martha Merrill reported that most of the audience remained in the theater to view a version of the film that included both Godard's and Quarrier's endings; or, according to Finler, they saw only Godard's, because despite the controversy the Quarrier version had yet to be completed. Meanwhile, Godard addressed (in Merrill's sardonic account) "a group of non-fascists assembled on the cold ground under Waterloo Bridge who are there to see a showing of his personal copy" of *One Plus One*.[3] Godard had offered this print of the film to the Open Festival, which was screening films for free in competition with the main festival.[4] "He stays only for a minute," Merrill reported, "and then glassy-eyed, begs off, saying that he has a plane to catch the next morning, and so departs for dinner with Bernardo Bertolucci and a few other luminaries."[5] Over the following weeks, the dispute between Godard and Quarrier became a minor scandal, covered by both the London *Times* and the *New York Times* and by Liberation News Service, which supplied stories to the underground press.[6] The *San Francisco Express Times* even published a mock-pretentious poem inspired by the incident (it concludes "Jean-Luc left in a rage / not before Producer / a-punched / in said / mouth").[7]

Despite Godard's initial passion for his film, *One Plus One* has been dismissed by most critics and scholars (and eventually by Godard himself) as a lesser film in the director's oeuvre, a transitional work bridging the stylish New Wave narratives that made him famous and his difficult Marxist treatises of the late 1960s and early 1970s.[8] Critics often see the film as sloppy, an unfinished synthesis that, despite the promise of its title, doesn't add up to much. Godard's biographer Colin MacCabe, for example, writes that "while the footage of the Stones is extraordinary, and while the film often intrigues, there is no doubt that the montage has too much work to do. Heterogeneous ideas are yoked together, but the links between Black Power and the Stones' music or Fascism and pornography are asserted rather than explored."[9]

Unlike many critics, I consider *One Plus One* a compelling film, but I am not going to argue for its excellence below. Nor do I intend to provide a complete analysis of its wide variety of images and implications. Rather, my interest in the film derives from Godard's perspective on the role of African American music and rhetoric in 1960s rock. In his allusive and willfully obscure way, Godard assumes a critical stance toward rock's racial tensions and political aspirations. While contemporaries such as John Sinclair proclaimed a direct correspondence between the energy and style of rock and political and cultural revolution, Godard's film pushes viewers to acknowledge the troubling possibility that both rock music and revolutionary politics are social and textual constructions, created through the circulation of borrowed texts rather than rooted in any essential reality. This profound skepticism toward any claim to objective representation is typical of Godard's films of this period. One of his most famous aphorisms, for example, appears in the 1969 film *Le Gai savoir*: "In each image one must know who speaks." As Kaja Silverman points out, Godard challenges here "the notion of a transcendental subject who thinks from a position outside language" or occupies an unmediated relationship to truth.[10]

In my close examination of *One Plus One* below, I will discuss Godard's often oblique illumination in the film of some ironic disjunctures between 1960s rock and revolutionary politics. *One Plus One* highlights the discrepancy between the Stones' music and its African American influences. At the same time, the film suggests provocatively that Black radicalism itself is also constructed through rhetoric and mediation. In short, *One Plus One* is a critical, multilayered essay on the elusiveness of an authentic political stance, and it casts a cynical eye on rock's revolutionary aspirations and interracial mimicry.

A Question of Black

As is typical for a Godard film, the form and content of *One Plus One* changed considerably over the course of production. The project began in 1967, when Eleni Collard, a "novice Greek producer," contacted Godard with an offer to produce a film on the subject of abortion.[11] As critic Richard Roud recounted, "then the abortion laws were changed, and the project took a new turn: Godard said he would make a film in England, providing the producers could get either the Beatles or the Rolling Stones."[12] Godard came to London to begin shooting on May 30, 1968. A report published during shooting explained that although the film "began about abortion," Godard's plan "changed to parallel themes of construction (the Stones making a song) and destruction (suicide of white girl, played by Anne Wiazemski, Godard's wife, when deserted by her black boy friend in favour of a Black Power guerilla band), and has since changed again."[13] A report in *L'Express* claimed that the story was to involve a love triangle involving a French girl, "un Texan réactionnaire," and a Black militant.[14] The film was beset by difficulties and delays. Roud reported that "during shooting, [Rolling Stones guitarist] Brian Jones was arrested, as earlier was Terence Stamp who was due to play the Quarrier role. The roof of the Stones' recording studio caught fire, and as a result Godard went back to France. He later returned, only to have the shooting of the Black Power sequences jinxed by rain. He left for Paris again, came back . . ."[15] Despite these misadventures, the film premiered only six months after filming began.

In the completed film, as critic Jan Dawson pointed out after the premiere, "for the first time, Godard has abandoned even the slenderest pretence to a narrative line."[16] *One Plus One* comprises ten sequences, each based on a single continuous shot approximately ten minutes long.[17] In five of these sequences, we see the Rolling Stones in London's Olympic Studios, where they are working on the arrangement and recording of "Sympathy for the Devil," the song that opens their 1968 album *Beggars Banquet*. The film's other sequences, which alternate with the Stones footage, include staged tableaux of Black militants in a junkyard reading Black Power texts and ritually murdering white women, hippies in a pornography shop listening to a recitation of Hitler's *Mein Kampf*, and a woman named Eve Democracy (played by Wiazemsky), seen first in a lush forest being interviewed by a television crew and later running alongside Black militants on a beach, where she is shot with a rifle, covered with obviously fake blood by Godard himself, and raised into the air on a camera crane. Each of these sequences is frequently interrupted, visually with brief shots of Wiazemsky spray-painting political slogans on walls and cars in London, and on the soundtrack by excerpts from an unidentified pornographic novel whose characters are contemporary political and religious leaders.[18]

The film's obsession with political rhetoric reflects the moment of its production: Godard reluctantly left France during the student protests and general strike of May 1968 to begin shooting the film in London, and "One Plus One" was one of the many radical slogans written on the walls of the Sorbonne during that month.[19] In all, the film suggests two separate films woven together: the first a documentary about the Rolling Stones as they painstakingly pursue the challenging project of assembling a satisfying work of music, and the second an odd, disjointed, overtly contrived collage of political symbolism and imagery. Godard told an interviewer that "the only theory about it was only to match two different kind[s] of discourse. Musical one, a political one, maybe a sentimental one—and the only theory was just to put it like that and to see what happens."[20] The result, as film scholar Des O'Rawe puts it, is "a cinematographic exercise in keeping contradictions in play, not resolving them."[21] It is notable that the altered ending that Godard found so objectionable at the London premiere featured the final recorded version of the song "Sympathy for the Devil," which is never completed in Godard's version of the film.[22] For Godard, 1 + 1 was never meant to equal 2, at least in this film.[23]

The fragmented, incoherent form of *One Plus One* itself is paralleled within the film by the Rolling Stones' arduous quest to find a "groove" for their song. This goal is acknowledged explicitly during the film by record producer Jimmy Miller, who teases the band by announcing that "if we can get a groove happening, we'll probably be all right" (51:00) after hours of rehearsal and experimentation have finally begun to yield a satisfactory rhythm track for "Sympathy for the Devil."[24] Although it is a phenomenon easier to recognize than to define, a groove can be characterized as a state of rhythmic cohesion in which each element contributes to a unified whole. Or, as ethnomusicologist Steven Feld puts it, a groove is "an intuitive sense of style as process, a perception of a cycle in motion, a form or organizing pattern being revealed, a recurrent clustering of elements through time."[25] Feld argues that "getting into the groove also describes a feelingful participation, a positive physical and emotional attachment. . . . A groove is a comfortable place to be."[26] "Groove" thus describes a level of togetherness and completeness that the Stones must struggle to reach. Significantly, this sense of "groove" has long been associated specifically with African American music and musicians—jazz performers have used the term since the 1930s.[27] A 1970 review of *One Plus One* celebrated the Stones' interracial influences, explaining that "near the center of the film, when the Stones have reached creative fusion, have given their music an embryonic form and Black soul, the camera enters the studio and spills out into light."[28]

Godard's view of the racial politics of rock is, however, more skeptical than this quotation suggests. Take, for example, the startling juxtaposition between the first and second sequences of the film. The first sequence, introduced (at 00:47) by a title card reading "THE STONES ROLLING" (with all of the letters in the word "one" highlighted as here), features the Rolling Stones in the studio, working persistently but languidly on their song. The camera meanders through the studio, cluttered with wires, microphones, amplifiers, and baffles, from musician to musician, often capturing them in moments of boredom and inactivity. At first, Mick Jagger, Keith Richards, and Brian Jones strum a preliminary version of "Sympathy for the Devil" on acoustic guitars as Charlie Watts noodles on his drums and bassist Bill Wyman sits idly. Next, the band tries out an electric version of "Sympathy," playing sporadically but spending much of the time talking with the producer about technical details such as headphone and amp volumes and with one another about the song's form. This sequence is twice interrupted briefly by shots of Wiazemsky painting graffiti while the pornographic political novel is read on the soundtrack. Moreover, a recitation from the novel is dubbed incongruously onto the studio footage for a minute or so, making it clear that we are watching an intentionally perplexing art film rather than an attempt at transparent documentary. Beyond these distractions, however, there is no narration or editing, and the film provides a rare opportunity to watch these famous musicians at work in a seemingly natural, unaffected moment.

Then, joltingly, Godard cuts to the next sequence. A new title screen (at 11:27) reads "OUTSIDE BLACK NOVEL" (with the letters in the word "love" highlighted as here), and the film's second section begins with a shot of a bearded Black man sitting in a wheelbarrow with the Thames flowing behind him and two wrecked cars by his side. (The sequence was filmed in London's industrial Battersea district.) The man reads aloud from a book about blues music. After about forty-five seconds of this static shot, a second Black man wearing sunglasses walks into the frame and hands a rifle to the first. The camera then follows the second man as he walks away, revealing that the sequence is set in a large auto junkyard. We see two more Black men, one reading from a printed text while another repeats his words into a tape recorder; layered on the soundtrack on top of their speech is another seemingly irrelevant passage from the political novel. From its beginning, it is clear that the second sequence is staged and stylized, in contrast with the naturalistic, documentary approach taken in most of the first.[29]

The transition between the two sections is jarring, to say the least. Yet there is a connection in each sequence's references to the blues.[30] At the end of the first sequence in the studio, guitarist Keith Richards noodles some generic blues licks during one of many listless moments. The unidentified text read at the beginning of the second sequence comes from *Blues People*, Amiri Baraka's foundational 1963 work on the history of African American music. The passage we hear is the opening of a chapter entitled "Classic Blues," which begins: "What has been called 'classic blues' was the result of more diverse sociological and musical influences than any other kind of American Negro music called blues."[31] Baraka goes on to argue that classic blues was created by Black musicians who incorporated ragtime and the music of popular theater and vaudeville into older forms of African American musical expression. For Baraka, blues is the epitome of authentic African American music, a "changing same" that maintains its essence while constantly adapting to stay one step ahead of a white mainstream that seeks to dilute and commercialize it. Later in the sequence (beginning at 17:45), the same reader recites a long passage from Baraka's "The Changing Same" in which Baraka complains that "not only the Beatles, but any group of Myddle-class white boys who need a haircut and male hormones can be a pop group" and goes on to reflect: "Stealing Music . . . stealing energy (lives): with their own concerns and lives finally, making it White Music."[32] The immediate juxtaposition of the Stones and Baraka, and the "Myddle-class white boys" passage in particular, thus implicate the Stones in a long tradition of white (and specifically British) appropriation of Black music. The marginalized radicals holed up in the junkyard, moreover, seem to represent an authentic Black underclass, in contrast to the Stones in their high-tech recording studio and mod London fashions. Critic Gary Elshaw argues that "the scene illustrates the marginalisation of blacks within white culture and their revolutionary stance against white imperialism," represented by the Stones' "co-opting" of Black music.[33] Interviewed shortly after the film's premiere, Godard encouraged such an interpretation, asserting that "Leroi Jones is quite correct. Whites stole black music and transformed it to suit their taste."[34]

The transition between the second and third sequences presents a variation on this theme. The second sequence ends with another static shot including two radicals. The first, leaning out of a wrecked car, reads aloud from a text by Stokely Carmichael, while the second, played by real-life Black militant Frankie Dymon Jr., sits in a wheelbarrow and faces the camera as he repeats Carmichael's words into a tape recorder. The reading concludes (at 22:17): "That is how dehumanized we are. We are so dehumanized that we can't say 'Yes, we hate you for what you've done to us.' Can't say it. Can't say it. It's not a question of right or left. It's a question of black!"[35] At this point, the film cuts abruptly to a title screen reading "SIGHT AND SOUND" (the name of the premier British film journal), with the letters SDS (presumably for Students for a Democratic Society) highlighted. The third sequence then begins with a close-up of Stones guitarist Brian Jones in the studio. Jones wears a bright white shirt, and the studio lights create shiny highlights in his blond hair. Godard's sudden exhibition of Jones's obvious whiteness, in light of the preceding quotation from Carmichael, appears intentionally sardonic. If, as cultural critic Richard Dyer argues, "whiteness as race resides in invisible properties and whiteness as power is maintained by being unseen," Godard seems to be challenging this power by presenting whiteness as a particular, contested identity rather than an assumed norm.[36] A similar juxtaposition occurs at the end of the film's seventh sequence. Jagger, recording the vocal track for "Sympathy for the Devil," ad-libs "Get down! Yeah!" (1:15:30).[37] The film cuts immediately to the title screen for the eighth sequence, which reads "iNSiDE BLACK SYNTAX." While such associations are subtle, their cumulative effect is to reinforce the notion of the Rolling Stones as inauthentic appropriators of Black culture.

No Place for a Street Fighting Man

The Rolling Stones, whose very name comes from a Muddy Waters song and who began their careers as avowed disciples of blues and R&B musicians such as Chuck Berry and Elmore James, provide an easy target for this kind of condemnation. As Jack Hamilton illustrates, "the Rolling Stones' relationship to black music, and race itself, is among the most complex and controversial of any white artists in the history of rock and roll. Over the long course of their stardom the band has weathered charges of minstrelsy from Black Arts Movement poets and white academics alike."[38] The Stones sometimes seemed happy to wallow in racist stereotypes: take, for example, the well-known "Brown Sugar," from 1969, with its "lascivious celebration of sexual clichés associated with slavery."[39] According to some sources, the band consistently underpaid Black performers who toured with them, including B. B. King and Ike and Tina Turner.[40] At the same time, however, the Stones "remained devoted to surrounding themselves with present-day black music and black musicians in ways that were becoming increasingly uncommon in late 1960s rock."[41] They often paid sincere tribute to their African American influences, praising Waters and Berry and insisting that Howlin' Wolf appear with them in 1965 on television's *Shindig*, where they literally sat at his feet as he performed.[42] Jagger, asked in 1969 whether the Stones' music "was nothing more than imitation black blues," replied "we're an imitation, certainly, but so is black blues—of *some*thing—but by being derivative, a new music results."[43] Here, Jagger attempts to distance himself from debates about authenticity by arguing that imitation and innovation are two sides of the same coin, and that derivative music, paradoxically, can also be significantly novel.

Beggars Banquet, the album that the Stones are seen recording in *One Plus One*, is often cited by critics as the band's triumphant return to a more direct blues-based style after the rambling psychedelia of their previous album, 1967's *Their Satanic Majesties Request*.[44] In 1969, producer Jimmy Miller asserted that "whereas [sic] *Banquet* is at is old Negro blues, hard driving dirty stuff."[45] The influence of the blues, from Richards's Berry-inspired guitar lines to Charlie Watts's solid backbeat, pervades the album, and "Parachute Woman" is a straightforward twelve-bar blues, with gritty production values that evoke the early Chess recordings that first inspired Jagger and Richards. The Stones also draw, however, on several other genres of Black music. "Sympathy for the Devil," the album's first song, begins with polyrhythmic drums and rattles playing in a groove augmented by a guest musician, Ghanaian conga player Kwasi Dzidzornu, known to the Stones as "Rocky Dijon."[46] (At the band's Hyde Park concert in 1969, they intensified the polyrhythm of "Sympathy" by featuring a large ensemble of African drummers.)[47] Jagger's grunting and shrieking, however, makes the opening of "Sympathy" sound less like a studious imitation of West African music than a stereotypical evocation of "hot," "jungle" rhythm, a cliché often associated with fear of the primitive and thus, perhaps, seemingly appropriate to the song's celebration of threatening, malevolent forces.[48] Scholar Sheila Whiteley reinforces this interpretation, arguing that the "extremely rhythmic" music "evok[es] an ecstatic tribal response with Jagger cast in the role of leader of the dance."[49] More critically, historian Peter Doggett asks of the Stones' collaboration with African drummers in Hyde Park: "Was it meant to signify the Stones' primeval roots, or their empathy with Africa, or was it simply an exhibition

of radical chic—a way of saying, look, we're down with the Negroes too?"[50]
Polyrhythmic percussion recurs in different contexts throughout *Beggars
Banquet*; for example, at the end of "Stray Cat Blues," where it undergirds
a distorted Chuck Berry shuffle pattern in the rhythm guitar, and throughout "Factory Girl," where congas and tabla provide rhythmic counterpoint to
a pastoral arrangement featuring mandolin and fiddle. Elsewhere, the band
draws on African American religious music. "Prodigal Son," the Stones' version of a religious song by Memphis guitarist Rev. Robert Wilkins, can be
heard as either an earnest tribute to Southern gospel or condescending mimicry highlighted by Jagger's intentionally slurred, sloppy diction.[51] "Salt of the
Earth," the final track on the album, ends with the rousing up-tempo singing
of Los Angeles's Watts Street Gospel Choir (Miller explained dismissively that
"we added some colored chicks").[52] Although the Stones' borrowings from
Black music in *Beggars Banquet* can be fairly criticized as condescending or
contrived, the diverse uses to which they are put support Jagger's claim that
the band wanted to synthesize a "new music" rather than simply emulate an
existing genre. A reviewer for the *Ann Arbor Argus* agreed, writing that on
Beggars Banquet "the Stones play the blues, and it's not a rehash of something
that's already been done; it's new and original and yet so bluesy you can taste
the wrinkles."[53]

Many Black critics took a more skeptical view. As we have seen, Amiri
Baraka and Eldridge Cleaver, whose words are prominently featured in *One
Plus One*, were at best ambivalent about white performance of Black music,
with Baraka a particularly acerbic commentator. In a 1965 essay, Baraka asked
rhetorically, "does anybody really think it's weird that all these English 'pop'
groups are making large doses of loot? It's pretty simple, actually. They take
the style (energy construct, general form, etc.) of black blues, country or city,
and combine it with the visual image of white American non-conformity, i.e.,
the beatnik, and score very heavily."[54] In 1966, he made specific reference to
the Stones, writing of white musicians: "They steals, minstrelizes (but here
a minstrelsy that 'hippens' with cats like Stones and Beatles saying, 'Yeh, I
got everything I know from Chuck Berry,' is a scream dropping the final . . .
'But I got all the dough . . .') . . . Actually, the more intelligent the white, the
more the realization he has to steal from niggers. They take from us all the
way up the line. Finally, what is the difference between Beatles, Stones, etc.,
and Minstrelsey [*sic*]. Minstrels never convinced anybody they were Black
either."[55] Cleaver, although he regarded white appreciation of Black music as
a step forward for whites, whom he believed "were discovering new aspects
of the Body, new possibilities of rhythm, new ways to move," could also con-
demn white musicians as appropriators, acerbically noting "the 'Yeah, Yeah,

Yeah!' which the Beatles high-jacked from Ray Charles" and describing Elvis Presley "ripping off fame and fortune as he scrunched his way . . . sowing seeds of a new rhythm and style in the white souls of the white youth of America."[56] The Stones and other white British rock musicians faced similar criticism closer to home. Obi Egbuna, founder of the British Black Panther Movement, wrote angrily that "songs that owe their origin to unknown Black back-street night clubs in the ghettoes of England have frequently appeared in the top ten under the names of soul-less White 'stars.'"[57]

Many white radicals, less concerned about racial appropriation, looked directly to the Stones for inspiration. During the band's 1969 US tour, an anonymous manifesto distributed at their Oakland, California, concerts welcomed the band to town and promised that "we will play your music in rock 'n' roll marching bands as we tear down the jails and free the prisoners, as we tear down the State schools and free the students, as we tear down the military bases and arm the poor, as we tattoo BURN BABY BURN! on the bellies of the wardens and generals and create a new society from the ashes of our fires."[58] Godard, although he similarly expressed support for "revolution," took an approach that was, predictably, more intellectual and critical. In a 1969 *Rolling Stone* interview, he complained that "the new music" of the Stones and other rock groups "could be the beginning of a revolution, but it isn't. It seems more like a palliating to life." According to Godard, the Stones erred by exploring only one of the three sources of "correct ideas" identified by Mao—"scientific experiment"—while neglecting the other two—"the struggle for production" and "the class struggle." Perhaps more to the point, Godard expressed disappointment that the Stones refused to make a statement in support of his preferred ending for *One Plus One*. Godard claimed that "it was very unfair for them to accept their being emphasized over all the others in the film . . . It's unfair not from a personal point of view, but from a political point of view, unfair to the Black people."[59]

Godard's disappointment was perhaps inevitable, because the Stones normally refused to make direct political statements and often expressed ambivalence or antipathy toward "the revolution." Interviewed in May 1968 by *IT*, Jagger bucked the counterculture's trend toward revolutionary utopianism, arguing instead that change in England was always moderate and gradual.[60] When asked by young reporters at a 1969 press conference in Oakland why the Stones had made no public statements about "U.S. youth movements, marches, and battles with the police," Richards flatly replied, "we take it for granted that people know that we're with you," and Jagger explained that "we admire your involvement, but we're primarily . . . musicians."[61] In 1969, Richards said of the band's American fans: "I don't think they understand what we're trying to do . . . or what Mick's talking about, like on 'Street Fighting Man.' We're not saying we want to be in the streets, but we're a rock and roll band, just the reverse. Those kids at the press conferences want us to do their thing, not ours. Politics is what we were trying to get away from in the first place."[62] During the same year, Jagger refused Abbie Hoffman's request for money for the Chicago Eight's defense fund, and stated flatly in an interview: "if you get involved with politics, you get fucked up."[63]

The band's comments on *One Plus One* in an *IT* interview conducted shortly after its release reflected their disengagement from politics as well as their distaste for what they saw as Godard's pretensions. Jagger downplayed the film's political significance, arguing that "I don't think Godard understands anything about black people, I'm only guessing really as I haven't seen the film but I've read things he's said to people about black power and what he said about us and black power and the film and everything. He's such a fucking twot, you see." Jagger and Richards's own observations on Black Power did not reveal much intellectual depth, however. Jagger described the Black Power movement as "very young and . . . very negative. I think they should just walk into South Africa and take over and forget about America. . . . Do they want to be part of American society or not?" Richards pontificated, "first of all they're trying to give the negros [sic] some pride in themselves. That's the first stage. That's why their [sic] coming on too strong with all this, 'Kill/Fight/Kill' scene." Jagger added puzzlingly that "the black people are bound to use more violence because they're the bourgeoisie. They are a different type of cultural strata."[64] Here, Jagger and Richards seem to drop leftist buzzwords rather than spell out a coherent political stance.

More recently, critics have argued that the Stones are much better understood as libertarian hedonists devoted only to personal freedom than as radicals of any intentional sort. Marcus Collins describes the "tensions between their essentially individualistic form of rebellion and the collective claims made by new social movements," and argues that Jagger's "dalliance with the anti-capitalist New Left in the late sixties and early seventies was a brief diversion from the normal business of pop."[65] Peter Doggett suggests that Jagger was drawn to protests by his own "atavistic relish of violent confrontation" rather than by political aims, and asserts that after the band's infamous 1969 Altamont concert, at which white Hells Angels serving as "security" murdered Black spectator Meredith Hunter as the band performed, "nobody would ever mistake the Rolling Stones for political radicals."[66] Sheila Whiteley argues that the New Left embraced the Stones largely because the band's narcissistic emphasis on sexual "satisfaction . . . mirrored the views of the underground element which most strongly identified sexual freedom and total freedom."[67] According to Tim Barnes, the Stones' primary contribution to the counterculture was as a generalized symbol of nonconformity, expressed through what he calls "Black American body language."[68] In this view, the Stones were not willfully radical, but rather attracted radical attention inadvertently through their appropriation of Black style.

The Stones' self-proclaimed apathy toward politics seems disingenuous, however, given their repeated flirtations with political rhetoric. "Sympathy for the Devil," for example, makes references to the Russian Revolution, Nazi Germany, and the Kennedy assassinations, with Jagger, as Lucifer, claiming responsibility for, or at least approval of, each. On the basis of the text alone, Jagger's urbane devil, inspired by the suave but sinister Woland of Mikhail Bulgakov's *The Master and Margarita*, seems like a jaded, deceitful villain, and the song is easy to interpret as a warning or a protest against evil.[69] Composer Ned Rorem, in a nasty 1969 review, understood this as the song's (failed) intention, claiming that "Mick Jagger's presumably-guilt-inspiring whine of 'Who killed the Kennedys?' is cheap Brecht."[70] Yet the music encourages a different reading: the infectious, up-tempo polyrhythm and Jagger's engaging performance encourage listeners to identify with the devil, making him a romantic antihero and implicitly endorsing the disorder, violence, and nihilism that he foments.

While the Oakland manifesto quoted above epitomizes the apocalyptic revolutionary rhetoric in vogue among some factions of the New Left in 1968, Jagger's portrayal of an aristocratic devil who exemplifies "wealth and taste" seems to clash with the antiestablishment ideology of such groups.[71] "Street Fighting Man," also on *Beggars Banquet,* similarly plays on radical rhetoric without explicitly endorsing it. The song was inspired by Jagger's brief, tentative participation in an anti–Vietnam War march in London on March 17, 1968, and perhaps by his reflections on the May 1968 events in France.[72] While "Street Fighting Man" was threatening enough to be banned from Chicago radio following the Democratic National Convention in 1968, its ambivalent text, which asks "what can a poor boy do?" and explains that "there's just no place for a street fighting man," actually seems to undermine radical idealism.[73] As John Platoff has shown, however, critics tended to ignore this ambivalence and interpret the song as a call for revolution, to the band's frustration.[74]

Other songs on *Beggars Banquet*, in contrast, draw on old-fashioned populist rhetoric about the dignity and value of common laborers, but it is often unclear whether these references are meant sincerely. "Factory Girl," which evokes a sense of folk authenticity with its largely pentatonic melody and gentle acoustic arrangement, may be intended to pay tribute to the title character, but lines describing her broken zipper, stained dress, and fat knees appear to poke fun, particularly when sung by the famously glamorous Jagger. The verses of "Salt of the Earth," sung by Keith Richards, celebrate the working masses in very conventional terms, but the song's bridge, sung by Jagger, contemplates his inability to relate to the "faceless crowd" that Richards glorifies. Although Jagger may have been grappling earnestly with his social responsibility, the song is hardly a ringing statement of solidarity with the working class. Peter Doggett argues that "isolated from the proletariat and activists alike, happy to lean on an imaginary source of evil as the explanation for political unrest, Jagger remained as uncommitted an artist as he had been a demonstrator" at the London protest.[75] In all, the Stones seem to have been attracted more to the sense of moral authority, and perhaps the publicity, associated with political commitment than to any specific political stance.

Inside Black Syntax

By thus juxtaposing the apparently cynical, self-centered Rolling Stones with fervent, militant Black radicals in *One Plus One*, Godard might seem to be dramatizing a conflict between inauthentic and authentic political commitment.[76] In the "iNSiDE BLACK SYNTAX" sequence, for example, the militants pass rifles from one to the next while loudly reciting Baraka's ubiquitous poem "Black People!" in what one reviewer termed an "up-against-the-wall-motherfucker fugue."[77] Critic Norman Silverstein points out "the parallel passage of cigarettes among the Rolling Stones and of rifles among black militants," which might imply a contrast between the Stones' hedonism and the militants' seriousness.[78] Another, more subtle connection between the Stones and radicalism is drawn when Frankie Dymon, reciting from Stokely Carmichael (21:11), asserts that "one of the ways of bringing our people home is by using patience, love, brotherhood, and unity. Not force—love, patience, brotherhood, and unity. And we try. And we try. And we try." While the latter repetition is drawn directly from Carmichael's text, it also recalls the repeated "And I try" so familiar from the Rolling Stones' "Satisfaction," revised with a collective "we" and a final warning: "if they become a threat, we off them."[79]

Godard's Black Power sequences reflect the increasing popularity and influence that the British Black Power Movement, "distinct from but in conversation with its American namesake," had begun to wield by 1968.[80] The Universal Coloured People's Association (UCPA), founded in June 1967, sought to approach "white racialism in Britain not in isolation but as a part of a worldwide phenomenon, and conceived combating racialism in international, rather than national, terms."[81] In July 1967, Stokely Carmichael's appearance at the Dialectics of Liberation conference in London further encouraged the nascent movement.[82] Journalist Dilip Hiro explained that "being a negro by race, a Trinidadian by birth, and an American by nationality, Stokely Carmichael was instantly able to establish a rapport with his Afro-Asian-Caribbean audiences. His speeches and activities in London had an immediate and electrifying effect, especially on the coloured British."[83] In April 1968, the UCPA's Obi Egbuna split with the group and founded the British Black Panther Movement.[84] These burgeoning Black Power groups contended with a growing backlash against non-white immigration epitomized by the Commonwealth Immigrants Act of March 1968 and by Conservative MP Enoch Powell, whose notorious "Rivers of Blood" speech, delivered in Birmingham on April 20, 1968, warned that "in this country in fifteen or twenty years' time the black man will have the whip hand over the white man."[85] On July 25, 1968, while *One Plus One* was in production, Egbuna and two others were arrested for written statements "threatening to kill police officers at Hyde Park, London," and then held without trial until December.[86] Godard himself explained in 1969 that the Black militants in the film "were rehearsing, trying to learn from their comrades in the U.S., who are engaged in a more dangerous fight than their own in England."[87] This suggests that Godard hoped to depict the militants as serious participants in a volatile international political movement.

It is important to note, then, that Godard's Black radicals are made to look even less genuine and sincere than the Stones in their studio. While the Stones are a real, recognizable rock band practicing their professional craft, the revolutionaries in the junkyard are obviously archetypes. They speak not in their own words, but only through quotations from such writers as Baraka and Cleaver, read directly from their books. These quotations are filtered through layers of alienating technology, dictated into microphones and tape recorders that create an artificial distance between the speakers and their speech. As Marina Roumenova Grozdanova points out, "the recitation represents a variation of the repetition of musical sound" highlighted during the Rolling Stones sequences, drawing a parallel between the band and the Black radicals.[88] Gary Elshaw points out that while "the figures in the junkyard in *One Plus One* may be part of a united guerrilla organisation . . . communication between the individuals seems to be impossible without the presence of the tape recorder to give speech a purpose."[89] In his 1969 review of the film, British critic Raymond Durgnat argued that "all the impedimenta of communication (from books through tape-recorders to a-camera-before-the-cameras)" signaled that "an iron (or safety) curtain of theory has dropped across the world's stage. Life is reduced to footnotes about the theory of life's possibility."[90] Godard's obsessive display of recording technology recalls better-known films of the period, such as Michelangelo Antonioni's *Blow-Up* (1966) and Francis Ford Coppola's *The Conversation* (1974), in which photography or audio recording lead their users into paranoia and confusion rather than an enhanced understanding of the world around them.

The readers in the junkyard often speak in flat, unemotional tones, suggesting a sense of detachment from the words that they recite. Moreover, the speakers' accents suggest that they are not American, unlike the authors of the texts. This may have been a matter of necessity rather than a conscious strategy: *Variety* reported that British Actors' Equity insisted that Godard use British rather than US actors.[91] The resulting cast included actors from the UK's postcolonial immigrant communities, such as Tommy Ansah (Ghanaian), Danny Daniels (Guyanese), Clifton Jones, Rudi Patterson, Linbert Spencer, and Roy Stewart (Jamaican), and Glenna Forster-Jones (Sierra Leonean).[92] Such casting led some British viewers to see the militants as inauthentic. Durgnat asserted that "Godard's Black Panther guerillas, real in the Congo, real in the USA, are purely hypothetical in London 1969. Their rootless pathos is the effect desired."[93] This view reflects the broader dismissal of the Black Power movement in England; as historian Anne-Marie Angelo demonstrates, British "figures in the media, politicians, and cultural leaders" typically "denied the existence of Black Power in the United Kingdom" and claimed that "Black Power was an inherently American phenomenon."[94]

Frankie Dymon Jr., the central figure in *One Plus One*'s Black Power sequences, further blurs the lines between ostensibly authentic radicalism and inauthentic performance because he was already involved with both political activism and the world of rock and popular entertainment. According to the underground newspaper *Other Scenes*, Dymon had been "a pop singer in the days of the Twist," and he appears as a drummer in the 1962 juvenile-delinquent musical *Some People*.[95] By 1967 he had become a familiar figure in the London counterculture, featured in November at the "Ying-Yang Uprising: A Three Day Conference at the Arts Laboratory," which also included well-known Black activist Michael X as well as Beat novelists William S. Burroughs and Alexander Trocchi, rock singer and writer Mick Farren, and journalist and promoter Barry Miles.[96] By 1968, Dymon, as "Frankie Y," had become part of the group surrounding Michael X, who were involved in both Black politics and the Swinging London counterculture.[97] A 1970 Foreign and Commonwealth Office report on the Black Power movement profiled "*Frankie Y (Frankie Dymon)*. A former lieutenant of Michael X and one of the few members of the Black Muslim Brotherhood of Britain, Dymon has a penchant for colourful talk about teaching his people karate, handling of explosives, and terrorist tactics in urban areas. He has said that caches of arms

to be used for Black Power purposes exist, but this seems doubtful. His out-
rageously violent speeches seem a mixture of exhibitionism and an attempt
to draw attention to the frustration of young intelligent coloured people."[98]

Although Dymon represented the world of popular entertainment and
media hype as well as sincere commitment to Black Power, Godard took his
politics seriously. When an interviewer asked "why you wanted a man [pre-
sumably Dymon] who is actually a black power militant," Godard explained
that "I prefer it but I was a bit afraid to because its [*sic*] more honest for me to
take actors because if black power people say 'you were not right saying that,'
because I'm not so good . . . Well then I can say, well maybe I'm right, maybe
I'm wrong but at least people know it is actors and will not take it as if it is a
real person."[99] During the production of *One Plus One*, Dymon claimed his
own pragmatic reasons for participating: "'In this film I am playing myself—
getting across a point of view—an attitude helping my people,' he adds wryly,
'And I'm getting bread for it!' He was reluctant to talk about Black Power: 'I'm
working for the man (Godard) and that is what I am concentrating on now.
If you want to know about the movement, I'll tell you but not here—it would
take too long."[100] Inspired by Godard, Dymon went on in 1969 to direct his
own film, *Death May Be Your Santa Claus*, which "explores a black man's fantasy relationship with a white girl" and recalls *One Plus One* with a "nonrealist
narrative" including footage of a Black militant reading aloud from a Fidel
Castro book and a political voiceover superimposed on its accompanying images.[101] At the same time, Dymon claimed that Black Power "was yesterday"
and now declared himself an "Afro-Saxon" determined to "offer to black people and white a new horizon, a bridge, something they can aim for without
the hang-up of color."[102] Far from the cartoon radical presented by Godard,
Dymon was an unpredictable cultural figure who staked out his own shifting
positions in response to both Black Power and cinema.

Perhaps most significantly, Godard's confrontational invocation of disturbing stereotypes makes it difficult to see the Black figures in the film as
anything but caricatured icons of radicalism. The most inflammatory example occurs during the film's second sequence, when three young white women
wearing white robes are led into the junkyard (14:30). In a long static shot,
a militant gropes one of the women as another militant reads a passage by
Eldridge Cleaver in which an elderly Black man details his obsessive veneration of white women.[103] The women in the film are then shot and killed off
screen. Here, according to James S. Williams, Godard "conjures up the colonial specter of the indigenous black male as a sexual rival stealing and raping
white women," a gesture that for Williams negates the "rare, exciting moments celebrating radical black expression in his work."[104] A contemporary

reviewer compared the scene to the formerly enslaved Gus's assault on the white innocent Flora in *The Birth of a Nation*.[105] Although critic James Roy MacBean argues that the "theatricality" of the film's Black militants should be seen as akin to a "primitive hunting or war dance" in which each militant "prepar[es] himself to do in reality what he does first in art," the primitivist language to which MacBean resorts underscores Godard's apparent point that the "reality" of Black radicalism is necessarily apprehended through a filter of stereotypes and rhetoric.[106]

The "myth of the hypermasculine black male" was a common trope of Black Power, whose leaders often "seemed to feel that these ostensibly regressive myths could be transformed into a viable political tactic," but this myth's treatment in *One Plus One* is so exaggerated and lurid that one may read Godard as satirizing, rather than endorsing, the misogyny of Cleaver's text and hackneyed notions of aggressive Black male sexuality.[107] Gary Elshaw, for example, interprets the scene as Godard's attempt to "provocatively illustrate a stereotypical, mediated perspective of black militancy."[108] But Godard's staging of Cleaver's words misrepresents their original context. In *Soul on Ice*, this passage is narrated not in Cleaver's voice but by a fictional character, an "old fat Lazarus" and "Uncle Tom" who rejects violent revolution. Lazarus spells out a vision of racial oppression in which the white "Omnipotent Administrator" seeks to reduce Black men to the status of the "Supermasculine Menial," ideas that mirror Cleaver's own, and his obsession with phallic masculinity also recalls Cleaver. But Lazarus's acquiescence to this system is met with contempt from a group of "young, strong, superlative Black Eunuchs" including the narrator. Although labeling these characters "eunuchs" suggests that they are emasculated, perhaps a humiliating flaw given Cleaver's "hypermasculine" persona, Lazarus and his obsession with white women do not represent a viable alternative: as the essay ends, "he turned and faded from our sight, from our lives."[109] Cleaver seems to present Lazarus's views in hopes of moving beyond them. By giving Lazarus's speech to a young Black militant, Godard proposes such rhetoric as a tenet of Black Power rather than the subject of critique within the movement.

One Plus One, then, is not simply an attack on white rock musicians for appropriating an authentic Black culture, but rather makes the more subtle suggestion that any political or cultural expression that looks transparently authentic is actually constructed rhetorically.[110] O'Rawe notes that "there are no heroes in *One Plus One*, no rousing call to arms or revolutionary manifesto, only *particular* contradictions, and even these contradictions are open to contradiction: white musicians capitalising on black culture, black activists fetishising militarism, a mass media mystifying democracy, freedom of expression censoring expressions of freedom, and so forth."[111] Film scholar Shaun Inouye argues that "the film's political didacticism, exhibited in fictional episodes that juxtapose the Stones footage, caricature[s] rather than endorse[s] the militant idealism of the period, aligning the futility of documented 'truth' with the stagnation evident in countercultural revolution."[112] Observers at the time of the film's release often took a similar view. In 1971, Roberta T. Ash argued that "Godard heralds the postindividualistic future" by depicting "a revolutionary dawn which proves to be yet another mass-media event."[113] A 1970 letter to the editor in *Great Speckled Bird* claimed that in the film "black militants engage in the same blind parroting of the revolutionary 'word,' the same cruelty as the white revolution. . . . The implication is that the ideas of the Black revolution are merely second-hand ideology."[114]

Godard's portrayal of Black radicals thus may seem to unfairly trivialize them, particularly if one contrasts *One Plus One* with contemporaneous films about Black Power that represented the movement and its leaders more clearly and sympathetically. Agnès Varda's *Black Panthers* (1968), which was screened immediately before Godard's controversial appearance at the London Film Festival, includes interviews with Huey Newton and Kathleen Cleaver as well as footage of a speech by Stokely Carmichael.[115] California Newsreel's *Black Panther* (1968), also known as *Off the Pig*, features Newton and Eldridge Cleaver along with images of police violence, urban decay, and a "Free Huey" rally at the Alameda County Courthouse. William Klein's *Eldridge Cleaver, Black Panther* (1970) is a detailed profile of Cleaver, then in exile in Algiers, as he participates in the Pan-African Cultural Festival of 1969. These films employ music largely in conventional ways, sometimes diegetically (Varda opens with an outdoor concert by a funk band, and both she and Newsreel feature the Panthers' call-and-response song "Off the Pig") and sometimes to provoke viewers' emotion (Newsreel superimposes the sound of a polyrhythmic percussion ensemble onto images of windows shot out by the police, while Klein scores a montage of racist violence with Elaine Brown's ballad "The End of Silence").[116] These films respect their subjects' claims to authenticity by presenting their voices in a direct and seemingly unmediated way.

As commentators have noted since the 1960s, however, Black Power leaders were calculating about both their rhetoric and their public image, which they manipulated strategically and self-consciously. Scholar of political rhetoric Charles J. Stewart argues that Stokely Carmichael's "militant black power rhetoric" "created a symbolic realignment within the movement by replacing words such as Negro, Negro people, ghetto, segregation, and integration with black, black masses, colony, colonialism and liberation that altered how audiences saw the ghettos of large American cities and American institutions and linked the civil rights movement with the African movements for independence from colonial powers."[117] Craig Peariso writes that the Black Panthers' "early efforts to gain national publicity seemed almost to invite cinematic comparisons," such that "the 'vanguard' of the struggle for black liberation . . . had begun to look very much like they had been lifted straight from a Saturday matinee."[118] Peariso argues that Cleaver, in particular, simultaneously celebrated and questioned stereotypes of Black militancy: "although some called in earnest upon an authentic blackness as the key to maintaining one's critical distance from the workings of American culture and society, Cleaver's 'super-masculine' posing pushed the viewer to recognize that distance was in itself nothing more than an illusion, that any purportedly 'authentic' blackness was inherently compromised, constrained by the very system it opposed."[119] *One Plus One* implies that Black Power rhetoric and the radical posturing and interracial borrowing of rock formed interrelated, if perhaps irreconcilable, parts of a complex political culture. If Godard seems to accuse the Rolling Stones of appropriation or inauthenticity, he also implicitly defends them by suggesting that nobody is unequivocally authentic.

Godard's critique was inevitably self-reflexive, because, as the director himself pointed out, his own authority to represent Black Power was dubious at best. He justified himself as using his relatively privileged position to get Black radical voices on screen. During production of *One Plus One*, he told an interviewer that "if Stokely Carmichael wants to make a movie about Malcolm X, he can't do it. And even if he finds the money, if Mao gives him the money, or Kosygin, but I don't think he would, then no theatres would show it."[120] After the film's premiere, Godard explained that "culture has to come from the bottom up rather than the top down. It must involve more those who are themselves involved in revolutionary action. Take myself, for example, I can't *talk* about blacks, but I can record their statements. Very few people do."[121] By 1970, however, Godard had decided that the controversy over the film's title and ending no longer mattered because he had realized that it was "a bourgeois picture" that "has nothing to do with the revolution."[122] In 1972, he elaborated that "I don't even know [the Black Panthers]; I didn't even know them before. Maybe I may still have sympathy for the black people because they are oppressed as I may have sympathy for women because they are oppressed by men, especially by me. There is nothing I can say specifically."[123]

Longing to Be Involved

Godard's convoluted layers of irony and uncertainty disappointed at least some of the original audience for *One Plus One*, which was shown at a single theater in Paris in 1969 and more widely distributed in the United States in 1970.[124] Many professional critics rejected the film, with leftists attacking it as racist, sexist, or "reactionary" and more conservative reviewers mocking its revolutionary pretensions.[125] Theatrical audiences were often less critical. Literary critic Leo Hamalian attended the film's showing at New York's Hunter College, where "the audience was made up of academic types and post-hippies, and the air was redolent with the fragrance of pot." Hamalian believed that "most people were taking the film at face value . . . 'Watch the intellectuals have an orgasm over this flick,' sneered one of my evening's companions. 'You saw the movie. What you saw is what it's about.'"[126] The *Daily Planet*, a Miami underground newspaper, reported that "everyone cheered and applauded" when the Rolling Stones appeared in the opening credits, and that "the audience called out in unison 'right on' during the film." Reviewer Bill Rasch wrote approvingly that the film's "answer to all those liberal arguments about 'What are you going to replace the system with, once it has been burned down'" is "to beat on a drum awhile and find out." Rasch concluded his review by reporting that "post-show festivities included the new shipment from Mexico and making the scene. No revolutionary activities or any genuine concern was reported in Miami."[127]

Reviews of this sort suggest that the film's most receptive audience comprised young members of the counterculture who had a utopian sense of rock's potential to change "the system" but little interest in political nuance. More politically engaged viewers were often frustrated or enraged by the film's seeming cynicism and obscurity. A review in the *Berkeley Tribe* fumed that instead of "positive ideas and directions," "we are confronted in theater after theater with Godard's message, fuck the Redbook, fuck black rhetoric, fuck hip culture, fuck leaders and fuck followers, fuck symbols, drone, drone. Well, fuck you, Jean-Luc, we don't need that anymore." The film was especially disappointing, reviewer Lee Davidson felt, because it failed to unite the radical community: "when I entered the theater for each of Godard's films [*One Plus One* and *La Chinoise*] the audience was vibrant, longing to be involved. But we were polluted with dry and depressing images, and we left the theater without looking at each other, without touching."[128] Godard's message of alienation may have been received loud and clear, but it was not what young revolutionaries were looking for.

Godard continued his attempt to represent the relationship between rock and Black Power in his next film, the unfinished *One A.M.* (*One American Movie*), which he began shooting in and around New York and Berkeley during the weeks before *One Plus One*'s London Film Festival premiere.[129] The Public Broadcasting Laboratory had contracted Godard to direct a film in the United States in collaboration with American documentary filmmakers Richard Leacock and D. A. Pennebaker, the latter then enjoying great acclaim for his recent concert documentary *Monterey Pop*. Richard Brody explains that "Godard's idea was to film people expressing views that interested him and then to refilm those discussions as fictionalized recitations and performances by actors."[130] Art historian David Fresko argues that "to draw the spectator's attention to the relationship between fiction and documentary by placing each in dynamic contact with the other would . . . make even more explicit what was already intuited in *One Plus One*, namely, that reality itself is always already mediated and mediation functions as a social relation in the production of subjectivity."[131] Keith Beattie writes that "Godard intended the process in which an actor 'fictionalized' the experiences of subjects by repeating their speech to be a performance that would draw attention to the artificial and constructed nature of representation as well as the ability of representation to reframe and rewrite 'real-life' experiences."[132] Godard, Leacock, and Pennebaker filmed interviews with Eldridge Cleaver, white radical Tom Hayden, and Wall Street lawyer Carol Bellamy, as well as Amiri Baraka leading a performance of music and poetry on the streets of Newark.[133] In separate sequences, the film's main actor, Rip Torn, recited excerpts from these speakers' statements in ironic contexts and while wearing deliberately offensive costumes. Torn, for example, enters a junior high school classroom of Black children (in Ocean Hill–Brownsville, Brooklyn, cite of a racially charged teachers' strike in 1968) wearing a Confederate military uniform and recites Bellamy's comments about the role of business in social progress in a mocking "feminine" voice (54:50).[134] In another sequence (3:30), Torn, in a Native American headdress and buckskin shirt, plays back Hayden's voice on a tape recorder, repeating each line with different inflections. Although Godard never finished the film, Pennebaker edited Godard's work together with his own behind-the-scenes footage to create *1 PM* (for "one parallel movie"), premiered in Berkeley in December 1969 and released commercially in 1972.[135]

Godard's interview with Cleaver (25:10) for *One A.M.* reveals the Black Panther leader's suspicion of Godard's methods and motives.[136] Around the time of shooting, Cleaver told the *Berkeley Barb* that "'this isn't going to be a movie; it's going to be a weapon. . . . It's going to be shown internationally,' he said, 'and we will reach millions of people with the ideology of the Black Panther Party.'"[137] The interview, however, reveals a much more guarded Cleaver, who acknowledges that "we agreed to make this with you," but warns about "all kind of sharks and cutthroats, man, who be coming over here with these fucking cameras, so that a lot of our cats now, man, they see a camera they want to kick the cat's ass and break his camera and all that." When Godard asks why the Black Panthers don't make their own films, Cleaver responds that "I don't want to fuck with no camera. If we want to do any shooting, the situation is so immediate that we have to shoot with guns."[138] Pennebaker claimed that Godard didn't have "the foggiest notion" about the Black Panthers, while James S. Williams argues that "Godard was clearly out of his rhetorical depth here."[139] Godard, always prone to self-criticism, told interviewers in 1970 that *1 PM* was "of no interest. It's of no interest to see Cleaver speaking like that. He would not be glad to see it. . . . Cleaver talked to us only because he knew at the time that we were sympathizers. He needed the money, so he accepted only for the money. And he was right to do so."[140] Both Godard and Pennebaker claimed that this money was what enabled Cleaver to escape the United States for Algeria shortly after his interview.[141]

Instead of the Rolling Stones, *1 PM* featured Jefferson Airplane, playing on the roof of the Schuyler Hotel in midtown Manhattan. Despite the band's interest in radical politics, they do not seem to have been particularly invested in Godard's film. Grace Slick remembered that "we met him in some office . . . and he could have been an insurance salesman. He was trying to impress us as a nifty filmmaker and we were trying to impress him as cool and bizarre musicians. It was an hour of pleasant bullshit."[142] Their rooftop performance (1:07:05) took place on the afternoon of November 19, 1968, as the crew filmed from Leacock-Pennebaker's tenth-floor office across the street. An offscreen voice that sounds like Marty Balin's screams "New York—wake up you fuckers! Free music! Make some free love!" as the band launches into an aggressive version of the apocalyptic "House at Pooneil Corners" (from *Crown of Creation*). Bystanders begin gathering in the street to listen and in nearby windows to watch the spectacle. *Variety* reported that "no permits had been sought for the concert or the filming."[143] In her autobiography, Slick recalled that the band "decid[ed] that the cost of getting out of jail would be less than hiring a publicist for the same 'volume' of public exposure."[144] Although "a delighted crowd in the street was shouting 'More! More!,'" police predictably arrived to put an end to the noise. In the ensuing argument, captured in part on camera, Rip Torn and David McMullin of Leacock-Pennebaker were arrested.[145] Slick remembered that "the film was meant to be a comedy of errors. . . . the incongruity of it combined with the illegality were enough to make the entire production a worthwhile farce—as far as I was concerned."[146]

Godard wanted more than farce from *One A.M.*, and he abandoned the project after deciding that there was no way to edit the footage into a politically valid result. Apologizing to Tom Hayden for involving him in the project, Godard said that "we had Cleaver of the Black Panthers, and then we went to some rock and roll, and we thought that putting that all together could bring something. But I was really progressing, because I just couldn't go to the end, even by instinct. So we stopped the movie."[147] Although Godard maintained an interest in Black Power—in 1970, for example, he made a speech at Yale Law School on behalf of Bobby Seale that was reported in the *Black Panther* newspaper—his flirtation with rock was over.[148]

Yet Godard's 1968 films remain intriguing if obscure essays on the radical and racial posturing of rock. Godard, whose revolutionary fervor was countered by his radical skepticism about simplified, supposedly transparent representations of politics, proposes a circumspect approach to this era. In an indirect but provocative way, *One Plus One* and *1 PM* suggest that historians and critics should approach rock, not as an unambiguous signifier of revolution, but rather as the elusive object of complex, often contradictory, representations of its political and cultural significance. As Godard tells Tom Hayden in *1 PM* (49:15), "to seem natural . . . is just to do something else. But art is not natural."

FIGURE 1. MC5, John Sinclair, and friends, Detroit, 1967. Back row, from left: Dennis Thompson, Rob Tyner. Middle row: Fred Smith, Steve Harnadek, Chris Hovnanian, Michael Davis, Wayne Kramer, John Sinclair. Front row: Becky Derminer, Pun Plamondon, Genie Plamondon. Photo by Leni Sinclair.

FIGURE 2. MC5 at West Park, Ann Arbor, 1969. From left: Rob Tyner, Wayne Kramer, Michael Davis, Dennis Thompson, Fred Smith. Photo by Leni Sinclair.

FIGURE 3. MC5 wearing White Panther Party pins, Ann Arbor, 1969. Clockwise from left: Fred Smith, Rob Tyner, Wayne Kramer, Dennis Thompson, Michael Davis. Photo by Leni Sinclair.

FIGURE 4. MC5 with emcee J. C. Crawford, Ford Auditorium, Detroit, 1969. From left: Rob Tyner, Wayne Kramer, Crawford, Dennis Thompson (behind drums). Photo by Leni Sinclair.

FIGURE 5. Amiri Baraka, 1980. Photo by Leni Sinclair.

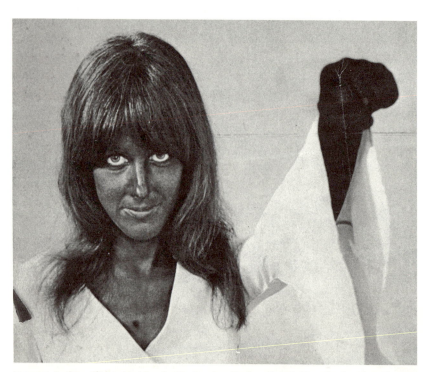

FIGURE 6. Grace Slick in blackface for *The Smothers Brothers Comedy Hour,* October 1968. Photo by Chuck Boyd.

FIGURE 7. A collage designed by radical group Up Against the Wall/Motherfuckers and printed in the *Berkeley Barb* (October 11–18, 1968: 13). Paul Kantner drew on this text in the lyrics of Jefferson Airplane's "We Can Be Together." berkeleybarb.net. Courtesy of the Berkeley Barb Project and the Berkeley Historical Society.

ELDRIDGE CLEAVER Welcome Here

The international Committee to Defend Eldridge Cleaver has asked all underground, movement, and radical papers to print this poster of Brother Eldridge and ask their readers to hang it up in a conspicuous place to show support for him.

The Fifth Estate endorses this effort and we urge all of our readers to participate in saluting his escape from the mother country police forces. We wish him luck wherever he may be and he *is* welcome here.

POWER TO THE PEOPLE!
BLACK POWER TO BLACK PEOPLE!

FIGURE 8. This poster appeared in the Detroit underground paper *Fifth Estate* (December 26, 1968–January 8, 1969, p. 3) while Cleaver was a fugitive from attempted murder charges. Jefferson Airplane displayed this or a similar sign outside their house in San Francisco. Courtesy of *Fifth Estate*.

FIGURE 9. Jean-Luc Godard, directing *One Plus One*, greets Rolling Stones bassist Bill Wyman as Mick Jagger strums his guitar. Olympic Studios, London, June 1968. Pictorial Press Ltd/Alamy Stock Photo.

FIGURE 10. Actors Frankie Dymon Jr. (left) and Bernard Boston on the junkyard set of Godard's *One Plus One*. London, August 1968. TCD/Prod. DB/Alamy Stock Photo.

FIGURE 11. Mick Jagger on stage with the Rolling Stones at Madison Square Garden, New York, November 27, 1969. © Amalie R. Rothschild.

FIGURE 12. Tompkins Square Park, New York, 1967. Photograph by Nathan Farb from the unpublished book *Summer of Love*.

FIGURE 13. The Motherfuckers satirize the MC5 in *Fifth Estate* (January 9–22, 1969, p. 5). Courtesy of *Fifth Estate*.

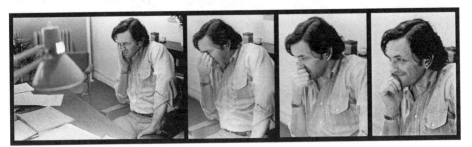

FIGURE 14. Bill Graham at Fillmore East, New York, 1970. © Amalie R. Rothschild.

FIGURE 15. Abbie Hoffman in Ann Arbor, 1969. Photo by Leni Sinclair.

FIGURE 16. Canned Heat on stage at Woodstock, August 16, 1969. From left: Harvey Mandel, Bob Hite, Larry Taylor. © Amalie R. Rothschild.

FIGURE 17. Jefferson Airplane on stage at Woodstock, August 17, 1969. From left: Paul Kantner, Grace Slick, Spencer Dryden (behind Slick), Marty Balin, Jorma Kaukonen, Jack Casady. © Amalie R. Rothschild.

FIGURE 18. Black Panther Party Chairman Bobby Seale flanked by bodyguards at the John Sinclair Freedom Rally, Crisler Arena, Ann Arbor, December 10, 1971. Photo by Leni Sinclair.

The Seats Belong to the People

The Battle of the Fillmore East
Lower East Side, Manhattan, December 26, 1968

On December 26, 1968, the MC5 waited backstage at the Fillmore East theater on Manhattan's Lower East Side as opening act David Peel (and his band, also called the Lower East Side) warmed up the crowd. The MC5's official New York debut had received much advance publicity, or, as cynical observers termed it, "hype," from both the rock press and the White Panther Party. A White Panther press release promised that "a heavy contingent of Panther officers" would accompany the band to New York "and will meet with freeks from all over the country to discuss plans and programs for the coming year . . . Brothers and sisters all over the country are urged to consider attending this monster get-together and toke-down."[1] In an effusive *New York Times* profile on November 24, critic Richard Goldstein claimed that "a new group from Detroit known as the MC 5 is shaking the walls of Motor City with the kind of poeticized intensity the Rolling Stones displayed in their early days. . . . they could restore to rock its lost mantle of disrespectability."[2] The MC5 did their best to live up to their disreputable reputation. According to bassist Michael Davis, at the Fillmore East the band "spent an enormous amount of time in the dressing room preparing for the performance by drinking and smoking pot beyond reasonable standards, even those of the day."[3]

Meanwhile, trouble was brewing outside. The show was the latest in a series of "free nights" that the Fillmore East's impresario, Bill Graham, had agreed to host after a protracted conflict with a pugnacious neighborhood collective who called themselves the Motherfuckers. The Motherfuckers were notorious for their violent rhetoric. Since September, they had confronted Graham repeatedly to demand that he grant "the Community" free access to the Fillmore.

The Motherfuckers and the MC5 had already met, not in New York but in Boston, where the band played at the Boston Tea Party concert hall from December 12 to 14. One of the Motherfuckers' leaders, Ben Morea, had been arrested for allegedly stabbing a serviceman, and the Motherfuckers asked if they could make an appeal to the audience during the MC5's show. The MC5 agreed to allow the Motherfuckers on stage during their set. When the Motherfuckers "got the spotlight, however, they told the crowd they were being ripped off by the Tea Party and launched into the then common cry that music should be 'free.' Don Law [the Tea Party's manager] was less than amused. He banned the MC5 from the club."[4] MC5 guitarist Wayne Kramer believes that "there may even have been some violence out in the crowd because of their speech."[5] Despite this setback, the MC5 accepted the Motherfuckers' invitation to perform at a Fillmore East free night on December 18.[6] Fights broke out within the audience, but the MC5 redeemed the evening with what one reviewer deemed a "wild and improvisatory and breathtaking" performance, although not before "Ron Levine, the 5's equipment guy, cleared the stage with hard body blocks."[7]

The December 26 Fillmore East concert was also a "free night," but it was sponsored by a well-known record company rather than the Motherfuckers. Both David Peel and the MC5 were signed to the Elektra label. Peel's debut album *Have a Marijuana*, which featured counterculture anthems such as "I've Got Some Grass" and "Up Against the Wall," a song that anticipated the MC5 and Jefferson Airplane by prominently featuring the word "motherfucker," had been released in March 1968. The MC5's *Kick Out the Jams* had been recorded live at Detroit's Grande Ballroom in late October and Elektra was promoting it in advance of its release.[8] Later, Elektra A&R executive Danny Fields looked back skeptically at the label's marketing strategy: "Jac Holzman [Elektra's founder] thought, Wouldn't it be a great idea if we present [the MC5] at the Fillmore and give all the tickets away free! The 'people's band'! This way the Fillmore gets a lot of publicity and we can promote the show on the radio and everyone will be happy!"[9] A glowing review of the MC5 in the December 20 *East Village Other*, which described the group as "the vanguard of a positively-vibrated era of guerilla [sic] rock bands," explained how to obtain free tickets to the Fillmore show but also proposed a simpler plan: "just smash the fuckin doors down."[10] A surly crowd showed up prepared for action. In the underground paper *Rat Subterranean News*, reporter Ken Pitchford wrote (after the fact) that "the community . . . knows that this will be the first chance for the Motherfuckers to show their displeasure with Graham's cancellation. Everyone arrives uptight. The vibes are so bad that they could easily asphixiate [sic] a whole [George] Wallace rally of TPF [Tactical Patrol Force] cops—except that to do that, the vibes would have to be focused and beamed in some one direction rather than bouncing around within the crowd and setting people one against the other."[11]

The bad vibes soon focused and beamed against Bill Graham. Fields fumed that "to placate the Community five hundred tickets were given to the Motherfuckers to distribute to their fat, smelly, ugly people. Then we found out later the tickets were locked in Kit [*sic*] Cohen's desk. The tickets never left his desk!"[12] Kip Cohen, the Fillmore East's manager, explained shortly afterward that "fearing trouble, we didn't want to give the tickets away. . . . At the last minute, we decided that it would be safer to give out the tickets and get all of that energy—both creative and hostile—inside of the theater rather than at the doors trying to get in."[13] John Sinclair helped force this decision by insisting that the MC5 would not play unless the crowd was allowed in.[14] Sinclair told a radio interviewer that "at the last minute, the Fillmore came up with two or three hundred tickets which they had [ironic tone] 'misplaced' recently."[15] As the theater filled to capacity, however, a group of over fifty people on the sidewalk continued to demand entry.[16] According to Cohen, "we insisted on order and kept the doors closed. The crowd was very angry. It wasn't an ego trip or a contest of wills, it was a *demand* for order on *our* premises because of *our* risks."[17] Wayne Kramer remembered admiringly that "Graham was not the kind of guy to back down to intimidation, so he stood out in front of the theater and held the Motherfuckers off with sheer heart and moxie."[18]

Finally, violence erupted. Osha Neumann (then Tom Neumann, one of the Motherfuckers) recalls that "the crowd chanted, yelled, and pushed. Bill himself stood in the doorway, blocking the entrance. Suddenly, Israel, one of the Puerto Rican street kids who hung out with us, slashed a bicycle chain across his face. Blood began pouring from his nose. Bill fell back."[19] Abruptly, the attack on Graham ceased. Cohen explained that "a strange thing happened. The minute that they saw the blood on Bill's face, there was a strong reaction from the crowd, and these hundreds of people who had been swarming on top of him, backed away. A lot of people were very disgusted, and it seemed to be a turning point in the whole thing."[20]

Inside the Fillmore, the MC5's show went ahead as planned, although according to Michael Davis they went on "about an hour and a half past the scheduled stage time."[21] Later, the performance received mixed reviews, with *Variety*'s headline opining "Rock Sinks to a New Sexual Low" while *Billboard* declared the band "simply the most electrifying, exciting, and inciting rock riot in America."[22] More pressing in the moment was the Motherfuckers' response. Davis recalled that "J. C. [Crawford] tried to introduce us, but was booed, yelled at, and drowned out by the noise. I heard people yelling, 'Where the hell were ya?' Our absence during the early confrontations had not simply been noticed. We had been expected to be out there, fighting the man for free tickets like the rest of them."[23] The MC5's flashy psychedelic style didn't help their credibility. Davis recalled that "we were dressed in colorful spangly outfits, sequined and satined to the tens. Most unrevolutionary in every respect, we must have appeared to be a huge target to the rabble that called themselves Motherfuckers, much like the aristocrats appeared to the revolutionary rabble that stormed the Bastille."[24] Kramer remembered that "the stage wings were crowded with Motherfuckers waiting for us to give the word to burn the place down. Of course we weren't about to give any such command and their anger started to turn on us."[25] In this anxious situation, Rob Tyner made a tactical error. According to Kramer, "Rob Tyner sometimes had the uncanny ability to put his foot in his mouth. . . . So he gets up onstage at the Fillmore and tells the audience, 'We didn't come to New York for politics, we came to New York for rock & roll!' Of course all the Motherfuckers go, 'GRRRRRR!'"[26] Sinclair wrote that "this really pissed off all the 'political' people in the place, especially the street-fighting dreamers who wanted to do pitched battle with the whole pig power structure of New York City right there that night."[27]

As the MC5's set concluded, a "coalition of Motherfuckers, Puerto Rican Black Cats, and bikers" took over the stage and kicked Dennis Thompson's drums in as the band ran for cover.[28] A reporter for the *New Haven Register* implicated the MC5's "guerrilla" image in the Motherfuckers' attack: "The insurgents, some still shouting, continued forward. They had responded to MC5's call. And no guerrilla, no matter how heroic, enjoys the possibility that he is about to get zonked."[29] Davis remembered that "amid mixed boos and cheers, the band retreated to the safety of the upstairs dressing rooms and bottles of whiskey, our New York entourage crowding in to witness our reaction to what had just happened."[30] The extent of the ensuing violence inside the theater is unclear, but Cohen claimed that before the night ended "someone was hit over the head with a microphone and hospitalized, a young Puerto Rican boy was stabbed, and one of our ushers had his arm fractured with a metal pipe. In addition to that, one thousand dollars worth of equipment was damaged or stolen and the asbestos stage curtain slashed by knives."[31]

The MC5's escape was short-lived. Dennis Thompson remembered the Motherfuckers surrounding the MC5 in "the middle of the theater" and engaging them in "revolutionary banter": "This is the time for revolution. You guys are either gonna be the real thing or if not, we're gonna kill you."[32] When one of their critics pulled out a knife, the entire band fought their way to the street, only to discover what Kramer calls "the greatest blunder in record business tactics imaginable": "two limousines show up to carry the band back to the hotel. The revolutionaries saw red! 'Limos!' The symbol of capi-

talist imperialism. . . . The Motherfucker women were screaming and weep-
ing about how we had sold the revolution out. They were smashing our records against the cadillac limos tail fins."[33] Pitchford proclaimed that "these
45's were r.p.m.'s, not calibers—black saucers of resentment slicing through
the icy midnight air, resentment that someone assumed we could be bought
so easily—and with just a little sprinkling of revolutionary bullshit."[34] Later,
Fields expressed regret: "I didn't anticipate how the image of a limo was going to affect these loathsome people. You can imagine, a bunch of people
that would call themselves the 'Motherfuckers,' what they would be like."[35]
Kramer, realizing that "if this idea that we were just a revolutionary hype took
hold, we would be finished as a credible band," tried to talk his way out: "So
there I stood, in the middle of an angry mob trying to explain White Panther/
MC5 political theory, while Motherfuckers are agitating the speed freaks and
street nuts into taking swipes at me with their knives. Finally, two Motherfucker lieutenants pick me up and cover me with their bodies to get me out of
the crowd and down Second Avenue to safety."[36] Davis realized that "it came
down to this: If we got into those limos, we were the Enemy. No matter. As
calmly as I could, I walked to the closest limo and got in. Wayne and Jesse
[Crawford] weren't far behind."[37] As Thompson remembered: "So we finally
escape and we're all going like, 'OOHHH! What are we doing? Fuck this revolution shit. We should have just stayed in Detroit.'"[38]

The chaos at the Fillmore East reveals clearly that rock's role in radical
politics was the subject of controversy and dispute rather than an unques-
tioned source of countercultural unity. Even those musicians and activists
emphatically committed to the revolutionary promise of rock music found it
difficult to agree about how a rock community should be constituted. But historical accounts of the 1960s often stress instead music's importance in unifying the counterculture. Terry H. Anderson, for example, writes that for the
counterculture music "forge[d] a hip community . . . challenged the establishment and liberated freaks from the older generation."[39] Scholars of popular
music have been more skeptical, often questioning the extent to which rock
helped forge a countercultural community during the 1960s. Ron Eyerman
and Andrew Jamison believe that the rock community, while genuine, proved
fleeting. They argue that during the 1960s "music could, for a brief period of
time, provide a basis of common understanding and common experience for
a generation in revolt. It worked only briefly, when the conditions allowed it;
when the contextual factors that shaped it disappeared, the music was 'incorporated' into more established channels."[40] Peter Wicke takes a more severe
view, contending that the notion "that rock music presented a realm of experience which allowed teenagers to feel themselves to be a community in spite of

all social differences was just as much of an illusion as the political aspirations with which it was linked."[41] And Simon Frith, who dismisses the "Woodstock Generation" as a "vacuous concept," stresses that in "the development of rock as a mass medium . . . fantasies of community (drawn from images of the streets and lower-class city life) were sold to middle-class youth."[42]

Here, I will argue that race, as well as class, was central to debates over the rock community. The combatants at the Fillmore East, although they were predominantly white, were deeply invested in the rhetoric of African American radicals as part of their public personae and as a source of political ideology. As they fought over their status as representatives of a revolutionary community, they also competed to claim the most authentic connection to a militant Black identity. While the Fillmore East conflict was particularly dramatic, it was only an intensified version of debates over race, community, and culture that took place in the rock press and at performance venues throughout the late 1960s.

The New Bohemians and the Lower East Side

The Fillmore East was a key venue in a neighborhood known as a countercultural hub. By 1966, recent arrivals had transformed the Lower East Side (or the "East Village," as its northern section was increasingly called) into what journalist John Gruen termed a "New Bohemia."[43] These new residents, mainly white, appeared just as many African American artists "began to leave the East Village (and other parts of the Village) and their frustrated hopes of an ideal, integrated community behind," some moving to Harlem to pursue their work in a predominantly Black community.[44] Some of the new bohemians started independent businesses such as psychedelic shops, bookstores, and coffeehouses. They also founded underground newspapers including the *East Village Other* (or *EVO*) and *Rat Subterranean News*, whose title reflected its obsessive coverage of urban squalor. A lively music scene flourished in the neighborhood throughout the mid-to-late 1960s, including avant-garde jazz clubs such as Slug's (or Slugs) Saloon (which began featuring jazz in 1966), rock clubs such as the Electric Circus (opened 1967) and the Dom (opened ca. 1964), and eventually larger rock venues such as the Anderson Theatre (which began featuring rock in 1968) and the Fillmore East (opened March 8, 1968).[45] A significant, if less formal, music venue was Tompkins Square Park, where hippies hung out and played guitars and hand drums. The park also featured occasional rock concerts.[46]

The Lower East Side's cheap rents attracted the counterculture. Ed Sanders, poet and co-founder of the Fugs, recalls that "living expenses were tantalizingly low during those years when the World War II rent controls were still firmly in place, so a person could become obsessed with a creative project for a couple of weeks, then surface to scrounge for rent and electricity for a few days, succeed, then dive back to the art."[47] Just as significantly, the Lower East Side's image as "the symbolic antithesis of postwar suburban society" drew bohemians.[48] The neighborhood's reputation "as both marginal and (perversely) alluring" dated to the turn of the twentieth century, when photographer Jacob Riis exposed the filth of its tenements and journalists such as Hutchins Hapgood celebrated "the everyday culture of immigrants."[49] Sanders was attracted to the neighborhood's long-standing tolerance of nonconformity. The Lower East Side, he writes, "had been discovered over and over for two hundred years by the beaten-down, the broken, the rebellious, the radicals, the socialists, the anarcho-syndicalists, the suffragettes and feminists, the Trotskyites, and in our time by the bards and pot-heads, the jazz hips, those into psychedelics, and those just passing through on the way to the gold-paved streets of the American Dream."[50] This sense of possibility encouraged bohemians to endure the less romantic aspects of the neighborhood. Sanders remembers that "the Lower East Side in the 1960s, before the ultra high rents and the gentrification, WAS a slum, with garbage-strewn sidewalks, apartments without adequate heat, and certain blocks you learned not to walk down day or night. There was police corruption, and plenty of junkies trying to break into pads."[51]

Bohemians often argued that they were simply the next wave in the Lower East Side's long history of immigration. Allan Katzman, editor of *EVO*, wrote in 1966 that the neighborhood was "a slum occupied by divergent groups: Puerto Rican, Negro, Ukranian [*sic*], Russian, Polish, Hassidim, Beatnik, Artist, Creep, Bar Fly, Bum and Policeman." Its newest arrivals sought refuge "from the New World of broken lives, broken homes and broken myths."[52] In 1967, *EVO* writer Lionel Mitchell conflated the backgrounds and motivations of the neighborhood's disparate residents: "People are here in the East Village because they could no longer make it in Harlem or Poland or Russia or Eastern Europe or Suburbia or Puerto Rico or what have you."[53] *Rat* reporter Margie Stamberg explained in 1968 that the Lower East Side housed four main groups of "ghetto-ized people": "Puerto Ricans, Blacks, Hippies, and Ukrainians."[54] The solidarity between bohemians and other local communities that such rhetoric implied was occasionally realized at such events as the Tompkins Square Smoke-In, which attracted a "mixed group of hippies, Puerto Ricans, Negroes, and straights" on July 23, 1967.[55] Sanders recounts that although "every group tended to leave other groups alone. . . . there was great cross-cultural mingling of groups in the many bars of the Lower East Side during the 1960s. The Ukrainians of course had a church, and a big presence on, say, East 7th between 2nd and 3rd Avenues. I used to wear flowered Ukrainian shirts at early Fugs shows I had made by an Ukrainian seamstress in the L.E.S."[56] In *1968: A History in Verse*, Sanders remembers Tompkins Square Park as a place "where all the races, cultures and factions came together / There was very little open strife."[57]

Yet other reports contradict Sanders's description of a placid, tolerant neighborhood. Sanders himself clashed with "a kind of Puerto Rican street gang on East Tenth near my bookstore. I had friction with one member because I refused to allow use of my tools to repair a zip-gun."[58] Sociologist Christopher Mele writes that "despite the 'Gentle People's' platitudes of inclusiveness and identification with the Lower East Side locals, differences between the old-timers and newcomers were apparent."[59] Mele argues that Tompkins Square Park was divided into segregated sections by "hippies, white ethnics, and Latinos" and thus represented not peaceful coexistence but rather "a microcosm of the neighborhood that clearly signified the social and cultural distance between the three dominant groups."[60] Tension between these groups led to violence on June 1, 1967, when "a melee broke out between the hippies and a crowd of Puerto Ricans and Negroes who hurled bottles and debris on the hippies and sought to strip one young woman of her clothes."[61] In his firsthand account, novelist Ronald Sukenick reports that a disagreement over music sparked the conflict: "I was in Tompkins Square Park listening to some live music from the bandshell when a hip-rock group came on and started playing. Right away the Puerto Ricans in the crowd clutched their heads and started yelling bloody murder. Wha kina noise's this? They call this music? Pretty soon a few bottles hit the stage. Local conga drums struck up a loud counterpoint. The kids pulled up several oil drums and started pounding on them with sticks to drown out the musicians."[62] Police reinforcements were called in to quell the incipient brawl, a teenager was arrested, and a thrown bottle injured a police officer.[63] A more notorious instance of violence occurred in October 1967, when young white bohemians Linda Fitzpatrick and James "Groovy" Hutchinson were murdered by two Black men in the basement of a tenement. Sensationalist coverage of the murders helped establish a popular conception of the Lower East Side as a "predatory ghetto" unsafe for middle-class whites.[64]

Bohemians hurt by hostile reactions to their cultural expressions and their very presence in the neighborhood sometimes declared themselves more authentic Lower East Siders than longer-standing residents. Emmett Grogan of San Francisco activist group the Diggers describes a Lower East Side community meeting at which hippies complained that "Puerto Ricans and blacks were prejudiced against them solely because of their long hair and life-style, making them the country's 'new niggers.'"[65] Such presumptuous claims of oppression offended the hippies' neighbors, who often resented middle-class, predominantly white bohemians for assuming "voluntary poverty" in what historians have called a "fantasy ghetto."[66] A 1967 New York Times piece suggested that the racist attitudes of some bohemians, as well as economic disparities, fueled this resentment: "For the Negroes, Puerto Ricans and elderly Ukrainian, Polish and Jewish families in the area, the influx of the hippies has meant higher rents, an increase in panhandling and narcotics pushing, a 'running down' of the neighborhood and, for some, a source of irritation over their strange customs . . . 'The hippies really bug us,' one young Negro said, 'because we know they can come down here and play their games for a while and then escape. And we can't.' . . . 'Everybody is very paranoid about the Spades (Negroes),' said a young girl named Suzie, who is a member of the Diggers, a sect that runs a free store and gives out food in the park."[67] Grogan writes that "the sight of a pair of well-fed hippies walking through the neighborhood, panhandling change against a backdrop of desperate bleakness may have appeared farcical to strangers, but to the people who lived their entire lives in the area, grew up there, it was a mockery, a derisive imitation of their existence and it got them angry."[68] In his 1968 book The Hippie Trip, sociologist Lewis Yablonsky quoted a "non-hippie cab driver who lived in the neighborhood" who protested that "we have to live in this shit. They don't. I don't understand these young punks."[69] Shared dislike of bohemians sometimes led to unpredictable ethnic alliances. The Times reported that "it seems . . . many Negroes don't mind the white, hirsute bongo drummers in Tompkins Square Park, and some Lower East Side Slavs side with Puerto Ricans in harassing hippies."[70]

In this volatile environment, a new institution opened on March 8, 1968: the Fillmore East at East 6th Street and Second Avenue, founded by Bill Graham. Graham began his entertainment career as manager of the San Francisco Mime Troupe and started presenting rock musicians at San Francisco's Fillmore Ballroom in 1965.[71] At the San Francisco Fillmore, Graham sought to foster an inclusive, communal atmosphere, in his words "always looking for ways to make the place more *haimish*."[72] Historian Charles Perry notes that Graham always "had balloons and a tub of free apples in the hall in the hope that having something to hold would make newcomers or outsiders feel less self-conscious."[73] Journalist Ralph J. Gleason, one of the Fillmore's biggest boosters, reassured square middle-class parents that their teenage children would find a wholesome environment at the Fillmore dances, which he described as "utterly harmless and a great deal of fun."[74] Some parents, he noted, even brought their toddlers to the dances with no apparent ill effect.[75] In 1966 a *Berkeley Barb* critic praised "the sense of your own people on the bandstand" and "the vast common ground between artist and audience" at the Fillmore.[76] Immersive, disorienting light shows and loud amplification similarly helped blur the boundaries between participants, creating what Richard Alpert (later Ram Dass) described as a communal sense of religious ecstasy.[77] During 1967's Summer of Love, Graham kept the Fillmore open six nights a week, which made it possible for regular patrons to drop in almost any evening they liked.[78] The Rolling Stones' Keith Richards remembered the Fillmore as "a community joint . . . where people virtually lived."[79]

But some Haight-Ashbury bohemians were suspicious of Graham, a so-called "hip capitalist" who provided a valuable venue for the counterculture but was unabashed about his desire to make a profit.[80] By 1967, some critics had begun to argue that the Fillmore's shows increasingly elevated rock stars above their audience, and that for Graham the bohemian community was merely a resource to be exploited. Hunter S. Thompson wrote that "genuine, barefoot, freaked-out types" couldn't afford the door charge at the Fillmore, which was populated instead by "borderline hippies who don't mind paying for the music and the light shows."[81] Graham's foil was the idealistic promoter Chet Helms, whose Avalon Ballroom was widely upheld as a more authentic alternative to the Fillmore. Graham remembered that "the pure hippie of the day thought of the Avalon as the *real* church. Mine was the commercial church."[82] Benefits that Graham staged for such worthy local causes as the Haight-Ashbury Free Clinic and the Diggers failed to fully counteract this perception.[83]

Many Lower East Side bohemians eagerly anticipated the opening of the Fillmore East. Allan Katzman of *EVO* wrote that "Graham's new venture in New York will be a great boon to the East Village which has too long suffered from shysters, Euster's, and tasteless producers in the area of good solid rock & roll and blues."[84] While the venue was an immediate success, comparatively high ticket prices made some Lower East Side residents feel excluded. *EVO* critic Jules Freemond complained in April 1968 that "the audience at the Fillmore is looking more and more like an upper-Eastside shopping tour."[85] The *New York Times* described a view increasingly common within the counterculture: "Graham, 'with all his money,' many sneer, stole his ideas from the community, made them a commercial formula, worked the formula for personal profit—and in the process killed the vibes."[86] Although Graham continued to host political benefits for such groups as the Black Panthers, some radicals questioned Graham's uneasy status as both free-market capitalist and left-wing benefactor.[87]

Total War on the System

Graham's most vociferous critics were a Lower East Side collective who called themselves The Family, Up Against the Wall Motherfucker, UAW/MF, or simply the Motherfuckers.[88] The Motherfuckers succeeded Black Mask, an anarchist group co-founded in 1966 by Ben Morea, a jazz vibraphonist from New York who had become a painter while serving a prison term for heroin possession. Black Mask's name "referenced both Frantz Fanon's canonical anticolonial book, *Black Skin, White Masks*, and the anarchist identification with the color black," as well as the black balaclavas the group wore during street demonstrations.[89] As art historian Gavin Grindon points out, "Black Mask," a reversal of Fanon's title, also evokes blackface as well as the group's desire "to echo the style and organization of the Black Panthers."[90] During the early months of 1968, Morea and other Lower East Side artists founded the Motherfuckers as a loosely affiliated chapter of Students for a Democratic Society.[91] According to Osha Neumann, the group comprised "ten to fifteen fully committed regulars" along with "a group of fellow travelers."[92]

While the Motherfuckers advocated "total war on The System" with such actions as hurling bags of cows' blood at guests arriving at a banquet for Dean Rusk, Lyndon Johnson's secretary of state, they most often targeted cultural institutions.[93] Morea took a strong interest in artistic movements, such as Futurism, Dadaism, and the avant-garde theater of Julian Beck and Judith Malina, that sought to confront audiences and to blur the barrier between art and everyday life.[94] On February 12, 1968, during a strike by sanitation workers, the Motherfuckers hauled piles of trash to Lincoln Center, declaring their action to be "A CULTURE EXCHANGE (garbage for garbage)."[95] Less whimsically, the Motherfuckers expressed support for Valerie Solanas immediately after she shot Andy Warhol on June 3, 1968, describing her as "the Sweet Assassin" and "the true vengeance of DADA."[96] The Motherfuckers also regularly printed full-page spreads of manifestos and collage art in *Rat Subterranean News*. An August 1968 page quoted Malcolm X in explaining that "we are going to have to defend ourselves and our communities by any means necessary." The page also included a picture of a revolver with the caption "We're looking for people who like to draw" copied from a well-known Famous Artists School magazine advertisement.[97] In all, the Motherfuckers aspired to what Conor Hannan terms "a refined synthesis of art and everyday life based on political activism, community relations and neighbor-hood welfare."[98]

The Motherfuckers' politics and tactics were strongly influenced by the Black Power movement. The group took its name from Amiri Baraka's poem "Black People!," which, as we have seen, helped make "up against the wall, motherfucker!" a revolutionary catchphrase during 1968.[99] Neumann ex-plains that "our name had the advantage that it could not be spoken in polite company. That which could not be spoken, could not be co-opted."[100] The word "motherfucker," as I have argued, was a common way for white radicals to signal their emulation of Black activists. Neumann remembers that "the Motherfuckers, under Ben's leadership, insisted that Whites must take the same risks as Blacks."[101]

Morea employed extreme and at times presumptuous rhetoric in claiming revolutionary commitment and an experience of oppression equal to that of African Americans. In a 1968 essay in which he quoted Stokely Carmichael, Morea asserted that "the question of 'Nigger' transcends race and becomes one of class. Obviously, at this point in America, that class is most clearly black (with some white drop-outs) but hopefully it will spread—Mexican-Americans, Puerto Ricans, and finally poor whites."[102] In an interview the same year, Morea declared that "hippies are niggers. Like the black man, they are insulted, harassed, beaten and arrested."[103] This insensitive false equivalence was intended to underline a critique of whiteness. Caitlin Casey argues that "though the Motherfuckers defended the possibility of white radicalism, they rejected white society—precisely that structure against which they revolted. According to Morea, they never imagined themselves as white, which they saw as 'a state of mind, and a privilege.' Instead, they sometimes called them-selves *lights*, as in 'light-skinned brothers.'"[104] Although the Motherfuckers' antipathy toward "white society" was sincere, their ostensibly "hip" deploy-ment of racial slurs and their assumption that they could divest themselves of white privilege simply by reimagining themselves reveals the arrogance and pretension that often informed their actions.

The Motherfuckers sometimes expressed direct support for Black radi-cals, for example by passing out flyers pledging solidarity at the Black Pan-thers' Fillmore East benefit.[105] Their credibility received a boost from El-dridge Cleaver, who in August 1968 "told the [Berkeley] BARB that the Up Against the Wall Motherfuckers struck him as the most 'profound' group at the P&F [Peace and Freedom Party] national convention" recently held in Ann Arbor. "'Those cats are out of sight,' he said."[106] Gavin Grindon argues that "though often problematic in imagery and representation," the Motherfuckers' engagement with Black politics "was more an honest, if at times clumsily fetishizing, attempt to build solidarity than an appropriation."[107] But in white radical circles, the line between solidarity and appropriation could be thin, if not invisible.

Community and Culture

None of the main adversaries at the Fillmore East were Black. The entire conflict, however, hinged on the rhetoric and ideology of the Black Power movement, and particularly that of commentators on music such as Amiri Baraka, from whose poetry the Motherfuckers took their name. The warring factions, even when they seemed utterly irreconcilable, shared at least a common notion of the issues that they were fighting over.[108] Two concepts fundamental to Black Power politics proved equally central to the Fillmore East battle: community and culture.

In January 1969, shortly after their attacks on Graham and the MC5, "The Reclaiming Project," a full-page screed composed by the Motherfuckers, appeared in *Rat Subterranean News*.[109] The Motherfuckers followed a polemical account of the previous months' events with a manifesto justifying their actions:

> Out of our experiences emerge A CULTURE / A PEOPLE / A VISION / Which have attracted the media / the money / A New Business is born: the business of stripping life from our culture and selling the husk / And they try to tell us the husk is the whole fruit and now the musicians who used to play for us play for them and money and plastic week-enders. Spaces where we found each other, danced stoned, dug lights, and moved now turned to "Music Palaces" where the dead sit specticalized [*sic*]. WE WANT IT ALL BACK.

The Motherfuckers concluded with a vague threat: "WE WILL TAKE WHATEVER IT TAKES TO STRENGTHEN OUR COMMUNITY IN ITS STRUGGLE / THE RECLAIMING PROJECT SPREADS TILL LIFE ITSELF IS OURS." Although the Motherfuckers found it unnecessary to define their terms, readers today might wonder: which "community"? Who were "we"?

The Motherfuckers idealized the notion of the community. They spelled it with a capital *C* in their leaflets, and made grand statements on its behalf, such as "WE WILL TAKE WHATEVER IT TAKES TO STRENGTHEN OUR COMMUNITY IN ITS STRUGGLE." What they meant by "community," however, varied. At times, the group employed the term in a local sense to refer to the "Lower East Side Hip Community," a group comprising counter-cultural residents of the neighborhood.[110] In March 1969, the Motherfuckers defined "community" explicitly as "the collection of families, communes, and tribes within one local geographical space."[111] Often, however, the Motherfuckers posited a community united by shared values rather than a particular location. The Motherfuckers' page in the November 15–28, 1968, *Rat* claims that "the Hip Community exists because we have abandoned the institutions of this so-called society: home/family, school, job, army, etc. We are all runaways. Wherever we are the Hip Community exists: the street, the pad, the park, the subways—all night, the pawnshops, the coffee shops, Gem's Spa— the place doesn't matter."[112] While this might still describe a community limited to New York, other Motherfucker publications suggested that the community could be defined more broadly. In January 1969, the Motherfuckers argued that "Hip Communities throughout amerika face a constant struggle for survival and growth. Although we are dispersed, we are one community, one people . . . our experiences affecting each other."[113] As Conor Hannan points out, this sense of community was inspired in part by the Black Arts Movement, which emphasized "the practical uses of art as a conduit for community identity and dialogue."[114]

But what made the "hip community," whether local or national, hold together? The Motherfuckers' answer to this question was culture. In her study of the Motherfuckers, Caitlin Casey argues that "those who trivialized the cultural aspects of the revolution, Morea said, were mistakenly equating culture with 'western-bourgeois culture'—the type of culture trapped in museums and art books. In fact, he claimed, everyone was fighting for their own culture," including the Vietnamese people, anticolonialist Africans, and Black Power activists.[115] The Motherfuckers employed "culture" in a quasi-anthropological sense, claiming that "we are a tribal culture" and celebrating a distinctive way of life supposedly authentic to the entire "hip community."[116] To some extent, this rhetoric reflected the fetishization of Native Americans common among the counterculture; one Motherfucker broadsheet featured a large image of Geronimo with a rifle.[117] It also, however, echoed the Black Arts Movement's rejection of an autonomous art that stood apart from life, what Baraka termed "that junk pile of admirable objects and data the West knows as *culture*."[118]

Just as Baraka saw blues and related musics as authentic to African Americans, so did the Motherfuckers claim rock as the authentic music of the predominantly white counterculture. Rock, in its pure form, was neither a bourgeois high art nor mass-mediated entertainment but rather a kind of organic folk music. A Motherfucker manifesto declared that "music is in the people / & the people are in the streets / Move to the natural rythms [*sic*] / Move to the rythms inside / WE ARE OUR MUSIC."[119] If rock was the expression of an entire culture, then it belonged collectively to all members of that culture, and marketing it was a form of theft. As Simon Frith argues, for many members of the counterculture rock "was a folk form not despite commercialism but in conscious opposition to it, and musicians' claims to 'represent' their communities were thought to be compromised by involvement with the capitalist organization of the record industry."[120] Morea told *Rolling Stone* that "we're not a business—we're a people who feel we have a culture which we want access to, that's been taken from us, and that's being used to make money for other people."[121] The Motherfuckers described Graham as a "hippie entrepreneur, who has made money from our music, but claims the right to his property for himself."[122] For the Motherfuckers, "culture" and "commodity" were mutually exclusive concepts.

This argument paralleled that of Black critics such as Baraka, who asserted that African American music and culture had been appropriated and marketed by whites. Baraka dismissed "integration" as "the harnessing of Black energy for dollars by white folks, in this case in the music bizness."[123] The Motherfuckers similarly accused the music business of sapping their culture's energy. They proclaimed, for example, that "if the music you make to listen to isn't to be limited by commodity demands it must lead toward that energy— that free spirit that will express itself as it feels itself."[124] The Motherfuckers' analogy between Lower East Side bohemia and Black radicals persuaded some members of the "hip community." Ken Pitchford, for example, wrote that "as quoted by the *New York Times*, Graham previously considered us Lower East Siders to be 'pus.' Now he talks about the ideals of a new generation and tries to imply that he thought we were beautiful all along. This is precisely the same change in tone that came over whites when they first discovered that blacks meant business—from nigger to Negro overnight."[125]

Yet the striking distinctions between an African American musical heritage rooted in a long history of resistance to oppression and the culture of a self-selected community of disaffected white youth rarely entered into the arguments of the Motherfuckers or their supporters.[126] Nor did the uncomfortable fact that the rock musicians prized by the counterculture were often the same musicians accused of theft and inauthenticity by Baraka and other Black commentators. As we have seen, Baraka was critical of the Beatles and the Rolling Stones, and he cited Lower East Side celebrities the Fugs, who performed at the November 13 free night, as an example of "white kids playing around."[127] The Motherfuckers' desire to emulate the seriousness and intensity of Black protest entailed that they overlook or conceal such contradictions.

Bill Graham's own idea of rock as culture differed sharply from that of the Motherfuckers. While the Motherfuckers defended rock as a folk tradition,

Graham promoted it as culture with a capital C: an ultimately serious, albeit fun, fine art that he was helping advance. Graham believed that by booking the best musicians and presenting them with professionalism, he could convince a larger audience to take rock seriously. Pushed by *Rat* interviewer Jeff Shero, who asked "what do you do to create change?," Graham responded: "There are a lot of things in this society I don't like. . . . There should be more hospitals, more schools, more books, higher literary standards. There shouldn't be ghettos. Fine. I am not qualified to be in all these areas. The one area in which I am involved is in the public's taste in music."[128] Graham rejected Shero's grandiose claim that rock was "a revolutionary expression of a new generation," arguing instead that rock was simply "following along progressively. Why wasn't it said when be-bop came in or modern jazz or the modern jazz quartet began, or when [Gábor] szabo plays or coltrane. . . . . in the 30's didn't Kurt Weil [sic] express certain feelings about his generation? We're talking about an art form for this generation. And there was one for the last one and for the last one."[129] Here, Graham rejects the apocalyptic visions of cultural revolution that inspired the Motherfuckers, instead portraying rock as a modern art that had evolved logically from its predecessors. This version of rock as culture was not inconsistent with the notion of rock as commodity, which justified Graham in aggressively marketing the music and taking pride in the commercial success he achieved.

Graham accordingly held a less utopian view of "the community," viewing it as a market at best and a threat at worst. Graham sometimes displayed open contempt for the Lower East Side counterculture. In the *New York Times* profile cited by Pitchford, Graham indeed called the "New York scene" "pus," and went on to say "it's a jungle, full of every kind of speed freak, hop head, wino and scum imaginable."[130] In a *Rolling Stone* interview, he called the Motherfuckers "filthy, low-life scum."[131] While such statements were aggressively insulting, Graham often expressed more measured skepticism about the community's ability to unite successfully or restrain its more unruly members. In his autobiography, Graham remembered that at one Motherfucker protest "some kid started tearing his seat out. I said, 'Hold it. Hold it. There's going to be *no* dialogue unless that stops. . . . Until we decide what's going to happen, that's one of your people, *you* control him.'"[132] For Graham, the clash between the MC5 and the Motherfuckers was further evidence that the "community" could not manage itself: "the people's band had all their equipment stolen. By the *other* people, I guess."[133] In June 1969, Graham was still angry, telling interviewer Howard Smith that "there is no community in the East Village" and that the Fillmore East was "not a sanctuary."[134]

The underground press, like the Motherfuckers, denigrated Graham's unabashed desire for profit, describing him as a "robber baron" or calling the Fillmore East a "psychedelic counting house."[135] Even the more approving *New York Times* reported that Graham "sounds like a 19th-century industrial titan, glorying in having carved out a business that depends solely on himself."[136] In a letter responding to the *Times* profile, Graham protested what he felt was a "cartoonish description of me as a raving Scrooge McDuck" and argued that "our prices are dictated by economic fact, not greed."[137] In a *Rat* interview, Graham patiently explained that "what the public doesn't realize . . . is that in order to survive you must show profit" and asked "who would pay the artists on stage?" if the theater became free. He also revealed a deep frustration with his critics, describing their position as "I give you: I'm love. I don't give you: I'm capitalistic. Fuck you."[138] Graham had supporters in the rock press: *Rolling Stone*, for example, pointed out that "no dance or concert promoter in recent entertainment history has yet to pay a band $10,000 a night and give the tickets away free."[139] Graham struggled constantly, however, to convince the counterculture of his integrity, even as many of his critics continued to patronize his venues.

One Nite a Week or the Sky's the Limit

The feud between Graham and the Motherfuckers brought their competing notions of community and culture into dramatic opposition. Reconstructing the story is not a simple task, because the participants gave widely divergent accounts even as events transpired. (*Rolling Stone* reporter Paul Nelson, piecing it all together in February 1969, invited readers to "play *Rashomon*" with him.)[140] According to a chronology that the Motherfuckers published in *Rat* in January 1969, the quarrel began in September 1968, when "Members of the Lower East Side Hip Community (including Motherfuckers) approach[ed] Bill Graham and demand[ed] the use of the Fillmore East FREE one nite a week for the Community."[141] In his autobiography, Graham describes a relatively civil discussion, in which the Motherfuckers explained that "they wanted their own night at the Fillmore to 'express themselves.' They said, 'You know, Bill, you always say you're part of the community, man. *Prove it.*' I said, 'Fine. Every Wednesday night is yours. You respect the building and we'll operate it. You can use it that night but only under our jurisdiction."[142] Osha Neumann remembers, in contrast, that the meeting with Graham "did not go well." During the discussion, depending upon whose memory one believes, Graham compared the Motherfuckers to Nazis, Morea made a veiled death threat, and either Graham or the Motherfuckers tried to intimidate the other by displaying bullets.[143] Despite this less-than-productive negotiation, Graham appears to have briefly relented. A free "COMMUNITY FREAK OUT" at Fillmore East scheduled for Wednesday, October 9, was announced in *Rat*, in an advertisement proclaiming that "THE SEATS BELONG TO THE PEOPLE" and adding that "IT SHLD BE FOR FREE ALWAYS FOREVER AND EVER BUT FOR NOW WE'LL TAKE ONE NITE."[144] According to the Motherfuckers, Graham then backed out, canceling the free night two days before it was to take place.[145] The group sought publicity, "dar[ing] Graham *not* to give them the hall" in pamphlets and announcements on community radio station WBAI-FM.[146]

The Motherfuckers decided to take over the Fillmore East themselves rather than wait for Graham's permission. On October 22, the venue hosted "Up Against the Wall Theatre," a benefit for the Columbia Legal Defense Fund.[147] Although the Motherfuckers later disparaged the event as a "Benefit for . . . the respectable Movement," Ben Morea was scheduled to speak, and an *EVO* article claimed that part of the proceeds would go to Morea's defense fund for the assault charges he faced in Boston.[148] *Rolling Stone* reported that "the theater was about half full when one of the acts, Julian Beck's Living Theater, began (in cahoots with the Motherfuckers) to hand out the remaining tickets in the street."[149] In the *Village Voice*, Richard Goldstein described a diverse audience including "speed-freak saints," "West Side liberalatti," "Black Panthers," "earth mothers," and "media men."[150] This eclectic audience saw a series of avant-garde performances by troupes including the Open Theatre and the Pageant Players, as well as speeches by activists Bob Collier, Ray Brown, and Abbie Hoffman.[151]

The event peaked as the Living Theatre performed *Paradise Now*, an emotionally charged performance piece that involved nude, pot-smoking actors directly confronting the audience, all creating a carnivalesque atmosphere ideal for the Motherfuckers' purposes.[152] Neumann writes that beforehand Morea conferred with the Living Theatre's Judith Malina and Julian Beck "and together they agreed that at the end of the performance the audience would stay and hold the theater. We seeded the audience with contingents of our followers. As the play reached its conclusion, we joined the actors on stage."[153] The *New York Times* reported that "leaflets were spewed out into the seats, proclaiming 'Tonight the people return this theatre to themselves . . . the seats belong to the people.'"[154] The audience then became the show as over two hundred of its members took over the stage. According to the *Times*, the Fillmore was "rocked by shouts of 'To the Streets!' 'Revolution Now!' and 'Up Against the Wall!'—interspersed with obscene words." Audience members "whirled paper gliders through the air, applied matches to old newspapers and ran up and down the aisles. A hidden musician blew on a ram's horn somewhere deep in the cavernous premises."[155]

The night culminated in an onstage showdown between the Motherfuckers and Graham. According to an *EVO* report, Graham expounded "on the facts of his owning the Fillmore and on how he disliked the do-nothing scum of the Lower East Side (in general)," to which the "Motherfucker representative gave no answer, stunning silence prevailed, and then burst out with: Shoot-bomb-kill! And Graham told him to get the hell out of his place."[156] Both sides employed violent rhetoric, the Motherfuckers in what one reporter called "a kind of Black Panther shorthand, impaired only a little by whitey inflection."[157] Morea threatened to burn down the Fillmore, to which Graham replied that "the Fillmore was his, and if they thought they were going to take it from him, they'd have to shoot him."[158] Fortunately for Graham, nobody took him up on this challenge, and according to Neumann, "well after midnight, Bill took a microphone and announced that if we would leave the theater he would agree to hold a town meeting on our proposal the following Wednesday."[159] The Motherfuckers celebrated by bringing their mimeograph machine on stage and printing a flyer asserting that "Bill Graham, hippie entrepreneur . . . may tonite have been a little liberated, or he may not. Next Wednesday will tell. . . . One Nite a Week or the Sky's the Limit."[160] As Peter Doggett points out, "the sky's the limit" was a phrase borrowed from the Black Panthers, who employed it as a threat in their "Free Huey Newton" campaign.[161]

After a contentious "town meeting" on October 30, the first official free night took place on November 13, with music by the Group Image and the Fugs.[162] Neumann remembers: "from our point of view it was an enormous success. The theater was packed. It felt as if 2nd Avenue had tipped on its side and deposited its entire contents—animate and inanimate—in the theater. Discarded sandwiches, cigarette butts, cans and bottles littered the carpets. Much wine was drunk, much dope was smoked. The program, such as it was, proceeded amidst a chorus of boasts, threats, brags and rambling fantasies shouted out from every corner of the auditorium. . . . Carpets were stained. Seats were broken. Toilets clogged and overflowed."[163] The Motherfuckers celebrated the evening as "up to 1200 people smoking-giving-dropping STONED and the music of Hip Culture our culture free culture—and we are Together."[164] What the Motherfuckers upheld as "our culture," however, Graham condemned as chaos and destruction. In his autobiography, Graham complained that "the first Wednesday night, people came in and brought their babies. They messed up the floor and peed on the walls and put their feet on the chairs and brought in their cooking utensils so it became like an overnight shelter for the homeless."[165] Ben Morea admitted later that "there was free use of dope, or fairly free. The police became very uptight because they knew they couldn't come in there and stop it because there were, like, a thousand people *acting freely*."[166]

The crowd's spirit of community and its seeming immunity to police repression were briefly threatened, however, when a fight started outside the Fillmore, "where some people were standing to get fresh air and rap."[167] According to *Rat*'s Jonathan Moore, "the fight was broken up by the crowd itself," but police nonetheless intervened, giving the "community" a chance to display its solidarity. "As one cat was being dragged into a car by a cop three or four hip people went over to try and free him. The cop drew his gun on them. Meanwhile the word went back into the Fillmore and several hundred people rushed out. 'Pigs, Pigs!' 'Let him go!' A bottle flew from the crowd and smashed itself against a patrol car. Sirens, more cars."[168] When the police attempted to enter the theater, "a crowd masse[d] yelling 'Out! Out!,' and coming forward. Discretion being the better part of valor, the cops withdraw. No further incidents that evening."[169] After the night's music concluded, a large group stayed inside the theater for a discussion that "center[ed] around police harassment of the hip community, made real by what occurred just hours before. . . . A concensus [sic] is reached to hold a meeting the next day at the Common Ground Coffee House [at 338 East 6th Street] to explore setting up a patrol to prevent police brutality."[170] The street patrol was successfully organized, and in December *Rat* reported approvingly that "the patrol shows a surprising vitality considering how basically impotent it is stacked up against the police."[171] In all, the evening had been a great success for the Motherfuckers, both as a freewheeling celebration of drugs and music and as an opportunity to demonstrate and reinforce a sense of community.

The Motherfuckers' street patrol recalls the Black Panther Party, founded in 1966 to monitor police in Oakland.[172] The Lower East Side group's insistence on unfettered, spontaneous action, however, clashed with the values of their Black role models. The Black Panthers observed strict, written rules about personal and organizational discipline.[173] The Motherfuckers, in contrast, advocated a utopian libertarianism derived from cultural theorists such as Norman O. Brown and Herbert Marcuse, who drew on Freud and Marx to argue for a less repressive, more openly erotic society.[174] While the Motherfuckers' talk of "liberated space" had a militant ring, this space was not to be used for conventional political action, but rather for the free exploration of fantasy and energy. One UAW/MF flyer contended that "the community needs free space. It needs it to survive, grow freaky, breathe, expand, love,

struggle, turn on."[175] At the Fillmore East, this attitude was evident in the un-
restrained sex, drug use, and overall messiness typical of the free nights. Osha
Neumann later critiqued his own opposition to "The System" as "revel[ing] in
the power of excrement": "treating 'no-trespass' signs as invitations, shoplift-
ing from supermarkets, turning over garbage cans, hurling muck and rocks
and invective, I became a human dirt ball."[176] The Motherfuckers' tactics on
behalf of the community were a volatile fusion of belligerent rhetoric and
willfully undisciplined activity.

Free nights continued on November 20, December 11, and December 18,
featuring local bands including Sirocco and Children of God as well as the
MC5 in their first Fillmore East appearance.[177] The next UAW/MF event at
the Fillmore was planned for Monday, December 23. *Rolling Stone* reported
that "according to Morea, the Motherfuckers had asked to use the hall that
night 'not as a free night, but to discuss the use and non-use of dope in connection with the whole problem.'"[178] On the scheduled date, however, Graham canceled the event and released an "open letter" announcing that police
complaints about drugs and violence had forced an end to the free nights.[179]
The Motherfuckers responded by "post[ing] an announcement on the Fillmore doors saying that since Graham and the police won't allow free nights,
then the community must see to it that pay nights are also ruled out."[180] The
Motherfuckers now faced public pressure to live up to their militant rhetoric. "Some outsiders milling about to read both announcements regard the
Motherfuckers blast as a declaration of war and somebody says that the
Motherfuckers will have to make good on this escalation or lose face in the
community."[181]

The violent climax to the conflict arrived when all parties involved followed their irreconcilable notions of community and culture to their logical
conclusions. The Motherfuckers were prone to aggressive statements such
as "TO LIVE ONE MUST LOVE / TO LOVE ONE MUST SURVIVE / TO
SURVIVE ONE MUST FIGHT!"[182] Graham's apparent rejection of "the hip
community" required a strong response. Graham, in turn, felt entitled to pro-
tect his property from a community that had not paid for its use: "I work
and I bought this theater and I have my rights."[183] The MC5 found themselves
trapped between competing notions of culture, as both a self-proclaimed
"people's band" and professional recording artists whose career aspirations
precluded providing free music for the community. As Jeff A. Hale points out,
John Sinclair justified the MC5's position within the entertainment industry
as an opportunity to undermine the capitalist establishment "parasitically
from within."[184] Rob Tyner's onstage insistence that the band simply wanted
to play music, however, had more in common with Graham's notion of rock

as fine art than it did with the revolutionary propaganda of the White Panthers. Some commentators saw the band as hypocrites who employed radical rhetoric insincerely as a marketing ploy. In a generally favorable review, *Village Voice* columnist Sandy Pearlman argued: "what with American flags carefully hung on their Marshall cabinets and all, you might think the MC-5 political. But really they're some great Cosmic Show. . . . politics is merely one of their inspirational phases."[185] *Rat*'s Ken Pitchford asserted more pointedly that at the MC5's December 26 show "it was obvious to all that they were copping out of a chance to actually put their revolutionary rhetoric on the line. . . . it's a great big surprise, baby, when you come on with a lot of White Panther talk and the naming of Ministers of This and That and then show a whole audience that it's only a new comercial [sic] gimmick to sell your product."[186] Pitchford was especially bothered by the band's appropriation of Black radical style: "there are a lot of people who could end up being highly pissed off at someone taking over the external without being willing to pay the dues. Because blacks have bought and paid for the style, man, with blood, death, imprisonment, and exile."[187]

There Is No Unity

"The Fillmore debacle," as Caitlin Casey explains, "split the Lower East Side into pro- and anti-Motherfucker factions."[188] The conflict captivated the underground press, which published both soul-searching essays and angry invective. *Rat*, in a sympathetic account of the October 30 "town meeting," proclaimed that "without authority, panels, leaders, or programs, 500 of the most independent and alienated people in New York were trying to find the way to create a revolutionary community and free space to maintain it."[189] Other observers were more ambivalent, expressing support for the ideal of community but questioning the Motherfuckers' tactics or commitment. Ken Pitchford, who was generally supportive of the Motherfuckers, nonetheless argued that while "their rhetoric . . . calls for unity, for joining together against the common enemy, such as the police or Graham. . . . everybody senses that this message isn't getting through—there is no unity."[190] San Francisco's *Rolling Stone*, which sympathized with Graham, criticized what it called "the amorphous 'community,' a coalition of various factions without any duly appointed leadership" that "seems to reject any collective responsibility."[191]

But much criticism of the Motherfuckers was more pointed. Dean Latimer of *EVO*, incensed by a UAW/MF flyer accusing the paper of siding with Graham, took perhaps the harshest approach: "'Community,' **bullshit**. Those cretins, they wouldn't know a community if it tarred and feathered them. Creeps, brain-farts, shit-mouthed fascist assholes . . ."[192] (The Mother-fuckers fired back with a letter to the editor calling the *EVO* staff "counter-revolutionary two-bit capitalist ass-holes.")[193] Others expressed admiration for Graham. Emmett Grogan told an interviewer that "the so-called revo-lutionary take-over of the Fillmore East by the Motherfuckers was nothing more than a fun fest with one usher being smacked by a few lushed sidewalk bikers. Even though Bill Graham is small time, he could have had Ben Morea's legs broken for two bits if thought that the situation was actually as serious as the pop-revolutionaries led the newspapers to believe. As it turned out, Graham went along with the hoax and won hands down and the MF'ers were content with their press notices."[194] Frank Zappa insisted, "I like Bill Graham. I respect him because he's an honest businessman . . . If those guys in the East Village really want to impress everybody about asserting themselves and do-ing a takeover why don't they go up and take over Lincoln Center."[195] Patricia Kennealy of *Jazz and Pop* argued that "Bill has done more good for the com-munity than all the radical groups put together: maybe that's what they're really pissed off about."[196]

Several observers looked beyond the contested Fillmore East to point out that the counterculture the Motherfuckers presumed to represent was only one part of the greater Lower East Side community. *EVO* editor Allan Katzman asserted that "it is time the community at large, which the Mother-fuckers claim to speak for, make their own lifestyles felt. I propose a board representing various members of the community; from Negroes to Puerto Ricans, to Ukrainians, to Hippies, Yippies and Motherfuckers . . . Let them run the free nights at the Fillmore East."[197] The Motherfuckers responded in a letter to the editor, "what the hell has EVO ever done for the Ukes, the P.R.s, and the Negroes on the Lower East Side?"[198] To that, reader Pat Henry retorted: "I'd guess that fewer people trust UAW/MF than before they under-took the Glorious Struggle . . . I'll bet that the 'Ukes, PR's, and Negroes' still don't give a shit."[199] Some bohemians recognized that the utopian dreams of such groups as the Motherfuckers, like the rock culture represented by the Fillmore East, held little relevance for many of their Lower East Side neigh-bors. Such arguments were confined largely to the pages of the underground press, however, and Katzman's vision of a multicultural advisory board for the Fillmore East was never realized.

Critics sometimes contrasted the Motherfuckers with their Black role models. Discussing fights within the audience at the December 26 MC5 show, Pitchford asked, "Can you imagine black militants in a ghetto letting *their* community meetings get torn apart by one or two bullies who happened to drop by? I can't. But that only goes to show that white militants have got some pretty hard thinking and doing ahead of them. We'd beter [sic] stop this crap of mistaking death-dealing chaos for life-giving anarchy. . . . I don't blame black militants for laughing at us, for doubting our seriousness. We can look damn silly."[200] More succinctly, Dean Latimer speculated, "could you imagine if these shits were **black** and they pulled this noise down here? The Tack Squad would have had all **kinds** of fun."[201] A letter from reader Maxene Fabe to the editor of *Rat* quoted Eldridge Cleaver: "We have the courage—the good sense—to defend ourselves, but we are not about to engage in the kind of random violence that will give the pigs an opportunity to destroy us." Concerned that the Motherfuckers' "irresponsible fucking around" was hindering more rational forms of protest, Fabe demanded, "were you glad, Crazies, when you saw Bill Graham's nose get broken with a chain? . . . What's to become of us when the rest of us sit back, picking our noses, watching a bunch of strong-arm, bullying, loudmouth, infantile, elitist, egotripping fascists take over our movement?"[202]

It is striking that even the Motherfuckers' most emphatic critics rarely questioned the fundamental premise that the Fillmore East, as opposed to City Hall or the New York Stock Exchange, formed the ideal site for a radical occupation in support of a self-proclaimed community. What made the Motherfuckers' provocation at the Fillmore East seem worthy of reasoned debate rather than outright condemnation or dismissal? One possibility is that the Motherfuckers' actions looked like the logical extension of the ideas of community that Graham had successfully established at the San Francisco Fillmore.[203] If the San Francisco Fillmore offered free apples for all, why couldn't you cook at the Fillmore East? If toddlers were welcome at the original Fillmore, why not change diapers on the Fillmore East's seats? If there was no true separation between bands and audience, why pay to hear music? If people "virtually lived" at the Fillmore, why couldn't they actually live at the Fillmore East? In short, if a rock venue both depended upon and represented the culture of your "community," why did you ever have to leave?

The conventional capitalist answer, that the hall's availability depended on Graham's willingness to take financial risks and patrons' willingness to compensate him, threatened to expose the entire ideal of rock-as-community as merely cynical, commercial hype. Graham, who had helped create this ideal, found himself disparaged by those who adopted it as dogma. When Graham announced in 1971 that he was closing both Fillmores, he explained that he was tired of the abuse he had received in "the role of 'anti-Christ of the underground.'"[204]

In the end, there were no winners in the battle for the Fillmore East. The transformation from rhetorical to physical violence was disconcerting to at least one of the Motherfuckers. Osha Neumann, reflecting decades later, remembers that the evening led him to reassess his commitments: "I had watched Bill get hit with the chain and felt a door open between our violent rhetoric and reality. I did not want to walk through it. The vulnerability of the flesh of my opponent gave me no pleasure."[205] Graham, surprisingly, continued to negotiate with the Motherfuckers even after he was attacked, but the free nights were finished.[206] Beyond his broken nose, Graham emerged comparatively unscathed from the fight, remaining one of the most successful promoters in rock until his death in 1991. For Graham, however, the counterculture's criticism rankled for years afterward. In 1971, in his office at the Fillmore East, he told a reporter, "I can do all this, present the best shows in the business, but if one kid yaps 'capitalist pig,' it blows the whole thing for me."[207] In retrospect, one irony of this battle is that each side needed the other: the Motherfuckers, despite their avowed anti-capitalism, depended on Graham's capital and his organizational skill for the very existence of the Fillmore East, while the pragmatic Graham required the Motherfuckers' visions of a utopian rock culture in order to sell the music as a liberating, transformative art form.

The MC5, who had done their best to stay out of the Fillmore East fight, found their career derailed by it. Kramer laments that "we were on the same side, but they turned their revolutionary zeal against us."[208] Bill Graham, convinced (almost certainly incorrectly) that it was Rob Tyner who had hit him with a chain, took revenge. Danny Fields remembers that Graham "blackballed the MC5, and he had the power because he controlled every market. He put out the word to other promoters across the country, 'Watch out for this band. Don't have anything to do with them or any of their ilk.'"[209] At the same time, the band "found themselves criticized and ridiculed in the rock press because they had failed to demonstrate true political commitment."[210] After the Fillmore conflict, the Motherfuckers launched their propaganda against the MC5, describing the band as a "'revolutionary' rock promotion scheme" and decrying "cute, little Rock and Roll groups who preach revolution at a profit."[211] A page, likely designed by the Motherfuckers, in the January 9–22, 1969, issue of Detroit's *Fifth Estate* featured a photo of the MC5 with the caption "Pull Out the Plugs Brothers and Sisters" ("Motherfuckers" is crossed out) in a satire on Elektra's censored version of *Kick Out the Jams*, a still from *The Battle of Algiers* with characters labeled "Pseudo-Hip Merchant," "Media Freak," and "Dead Opportunist," and a poem charging that "Rock dares to say / it is something more than five competent white musicians / playing the blues and getting $10,000 per set."[212] In an impassioned letter to John Sinclair, poet Marilyn Lowen Fletcher wrote that she "was following closely the happenings at the fillmore, etc." and explained:

the lower east side is an exploited community. the resident blacks and puerto ricans used to despise the hippies—those voluntary poor folk who always seemed to get let off by local police supt. SGT. Fink for little things like grass while the tercer mundo brothers were getting their heads opened by Sgt. Fink's boys for walking the streets they were born and grew up on. Naturally, the natives are pissed when out of town white musicians who are MAKING it come into their territory that they have struggled and yes BLED for without wanting to join with them or understand them—only to ENTERTAIN them.[213]

As Sinclair summed it up, the Fillmore battle "finished us off with Bill Graham and the pop star world, and with the 'political movement' at the same time."[214] The MC5, who parted ways with the White Panthers in 1969, suffered a further series of commercial setbacks until their eventual breakup in 1972.[215] Michael Davis concluded ruefully that "it was because we had made such a fuss about being revolutionaries that we brought this type of scrutiny upon ourselves. Revolutionaries are always subject to purges."[216]

Was there a rock community? At first glance, the Fillmore conflict suggests not. Within the microcosm of the Lower East Side, rock's musicians, promoters, and devotees were unable to come together without exchanging bitter insults and senseless violence. On the other hand, the intensity and earnestness of their arguments about community and culture indicate that the opponents in the conflict at least shared a passionate belief that rock music could form the foundation of a better society. The rock community was neither a clearly defined group of people nor a utopian delusion, but rather a shared obsession, constantly contested by various factions who vied to determine its form and significance. At the Fillmore East, these factions sought to demonstrate their credibility by applying Black Power ideologies of cultural authenticity to rock, often in insensitive or misguided ways. Both the Motherfuckers and the MC5 competed to display signifiers of Black radicalism that would establish their group as genuine revolutionaries. In the moment, their desire to win this competition outweighed ideals of community.

Declare the Nation into Being

Woodstock and the Movement
Woodstock Music & Art Fair, White Lake, NY, August 15–18, 1969

In August 1969, the White Panther Party's fortunes looked dim. On July 28, "Detroit Recorder's Judge Robert J. Colombo sentenced John Sinclair to nine and a half to ten years in prison for his third marijuana offense. . . . Rubbing salt in the wound, Judge Colombo refused to set bond, arguing that Sinclair displayed 'a propensity and a willingness to further commit the same type of offenses while on bond.'"[1] Shortly thereafter, the MC5, growing skeptical of the politics of what they called "romantic adventurism" and realizing that an imprisoned manager could not do them much good, began breaking away from the White Panthers. They announced that Danny Fields would take over as manager, but that a percentage of their earnings would go to Sinclair's defense fund.[2] Leni Sinclair wrote to the imprisoned John that she was considering whether to "give up Trans-Love & everything in it, and use the 15% from the MC5 for your defense except for what I + Sunny [their daughter] need, just like Wayne [Kramer] suggested."[3]

But there was still hope. The Woodstock Music & Art Fair, which had been publicized aggressively in the underground press, was expected to draw large crowds to upstate New York. Surely the rock community would pitch in to help their imprisoned brother? On August 13, Pun Plamondon wrote to John to report that a group including Pun's partner Genie Plamondon and Leni were driving toward Woodstock, with Pun following by plane the next day. Abbie Hoffman had sent the group $200 to cover gas for the trip.[4] The White Panthers were optimistic about opportunities for fundraising. "We felt," Plamondon explained, "that we had to take a killer squad up to Woodstock to be the most effective, I want to come away from there with a bout [sic] $20,000, maybe that's to [sic] high, but lets [sic] hope we get at least $5,000."[5]

The MC5's erstwhile nemeses, the Motherfuckers, also planned to attend, and since the Fillmore East conflict they had resolved their differences with the band and the White Panthers. The MC5 had praised the Motherfuckers in interviews and appeared with them at benefits for "street people" and marijuana legalization.[6] More recently, Ben Morea and others had stayed with the White Panthers in Ann Arbor on their way from New Mexico to Woodstock. Plamondon reported that the Motherfuckers had joined John's "list of supporters," and expressed admiration for "Crazy Ben" Morea: "that brother has got his shit together to be able to do what he has doen [sic] in the conditions they have tolive [sic] in." According to Plamondon, the differences between the Motherfuckers and the White Panthers were largely a matter of political theory: "I talked to Ben a long time and he really loves us, he [sic] just scared about parties, what he doesn't understand is the organic formation of the White Panthers, I tried to impress that on him, and he may be seeing the picture now, however he admits being a nationalists [sic], and wanting to work just for the heads, right on Ben!" This suggests that Morea shared John Sinclair's belief in "cultural nationalism," the notion that countercultural youth comprised a separate and distinct nation. Plamondon proposed that a benefit for Sinclair could be arranged at the Fillmore East, possibly in conjunction with the East Side Service Organization, a Lower East Side activist group.[7]

Woodstock's producers, contrary to the hopes of the White Panthers and the Motherfuckers, intended the festival to be apolitical. Producer Joel Rosenman remembered that "we certainly didn't want political statements," both "stylistically" and "because we felt that it greatly heightened the potential for violence."[8] Rosenman's position irked Abbie Hoffman, who arranged a meeting in New York including Woodstock's producers as well as the Motherfuckers and other Lower East Side groups. Producer Michael Lang recalled that "the Lower East Side community of activists, radicals, and politicos thought we were trying to rip off the counterculture—at least that's the position they chose to take."[9] Hoffman threatened to sabotage the festival unless the producers gave him $10,000, a demand that they met with the suggestion that the money be used to print a "survival sheet" for festivalgoers.[10] Shortly thereafter, at a public meeting held at New York's Village Gate, the organizers and the audience decided that "politics, while represented in booths and in distributed literature in an area called Movement City, would not be part of the onstage proceedings."[11] Hoffman contributed an essay to the official festival program that addressed the upcoming Chicago Eight trial and encouraged readers to "visit Movement City at the Festival to rap with the activists about getting your community together."[12]

Movement City's booths attracted an array of countercultural groups. Critic Tom Smucker, a member of Movement for a Democratic Society, re-

ported that "I was there, Abbie Hoffman was there, SDS, MDS, Mother fuckers, Peaceniks, Swamis, Meh[e]r Babaites, the Hot Chow Mein truck guys, we
were all there, trying to pick up on it, but nobody got all the energy. Not even
the performers."[13] Security head Wes Pomeroy allowed Hoffman to "park his
truck right near the gate with a printing press and crank up anti-establishment
and maybe anti-Woodstock stuff all this time—that was O.K.—in exchange
for his diffusing the real wild guys from New York City."[14] But in the end,
Smucker writes, "the booths were never used. The scene was so far-out people
started leaving right away. Literature got rained on or was never distributed.
The plates for the printing press never showed up, so it couldn't be used."[15]

While the Motherfuckers, along with "a coalition of radical underground
newspapers . . . had reserved one of the booths adjoining the bazaar to promote
'the inevitable revolution,'" they bridled against their relegation to Movement
City.[16] Shortly before the festival, the group distributed a leaflet pointing out
that the off-duty New York police hired as security would be unarmed and
easily identifiable in red T-shirts; the implied threat threw festival planning
into disarray when the police commissioner responded by banning officers
from working at Woodstock.[17] Caitlin Casey writes that the Motherfuckers
"arrived at Woodstock armed with pliers and dismantled a large section of the
fence to create a 'ticket optional' entrance,'" a gesture that proved meaningless
when overwhelming gate-crashing led the producers to declare Woodstock
a "free festival."[18] On Saturday, the group attacked the festival's food stands
(run by a concession named Food for Love) with a promise to "liberate the
food." The Motherfuckers "accused Food for Love of everything from selling horsemeat hamburgers at a premium to making a 300-percent profit on
a 35-cent hot dog to purposely not paying for fuel so the People would have
to eat cold meat." That night, the Motherfuckers burned down some of the
food stands (either two or twelve, depending on the report).[19] Casey describes
this as a "truly Motherfucker kind of action; they used legitimate complaints
about the politics of space and communal living to justify fundamentally illegal actions."[20] Tom Law, a member of the Hog Farm commune who provided
security for the festival, assessed the action more succinctly as "some crazy
radicals trying to fuck up a nice thing."[21]

Meanwhile, the White Panthers struggled in vain to raise money for John
Sinclair's defense. Movement City's location proved less than ideal. Leni Sinclair remembers that "you had to go through the woods over planks—they
put kind of a path through the woods—and in the next valley they let the
movement people put up some booths. The White Panthers had a booth . . .
that we built ourselves . . . And nobody came! It was just the movement people that were there talking to each other."[22] An Underground Press Syndicate

report confirms that although "the White Panthers were able to appeal openly for a bail fund for John Sinclair . . . few of the crowd showed any interest."[23] In his memoir, Pun Plamondon recalls remorsefully that although "Leni, standing in the rain and mud with strands of hair washed over her tired face, was exhausted, crying, and looking like a flood victim or war refugee," he was too "spaced out" on acid to help her try to collect money.[24] On August 18, White Panther Darlene Pond reported to John that "Leni and the rest haven't been allowed to use the loudspeaker, have made almost zero money, and the UhHaul [sic] towed back to NYC to get repaired, so they won't be back until Thursday."[25] On August 19, Leni wrote a despondent letter to John:

> Going to the pop festival was a huge mistake. We only collected about $300—we talked to some bands, but most of them copped out on us, esp. the Grateful Dead. Country Joe & Canned Heat said they'd do benefits when they came back from Europe. Paul Butterfield will do one, but we still didn't get a date from them. The whole thing was so incredibly ridiculous, it's impossible to describe. On one side you have musicians being flown in by helicopter & champagne flowing. On the other side kids kneedeep in cold mud without food, water or shelter for days. The movement was a myth.[26]

Leni's letter was written on the stationery of the Bergen County Sheriff's Office in Hackensack, New Jersey. The unlucky White Panthers had once again been busted for pot possession, this time by police on the lookout for "hippie types" returning from Woodstock.[27]

It's Not Really the Time

The White Panther Party's misfortunes at Woodstock epitomize a trend that many radical observers noted in 1969—rock's increasing distance from political engagement. More specifically, the party's association of rock with Black radicalism was falling out of vogue. Although Woodstock's white musicians continued to imitate Black performers, they avoided references to Black political causes. After the festival, as white radicals began to embrace Woodstock itself as a symbol of youth culture, they too began to turn away from the model of Black Power politics.

Leni Sinclair's letter from New Jersey provides one of the earliest accounts of a famous moment at Woodstock: "Abbie [Hoffman] just flipped Sat. night. He went on stage + grabbed the mike away from the WHO + started rapping about you. Peter Townsend [sic] hit him on the head w. his guitar and flattened Abbie out. He split for N.Y. right after that."[28] An audio recording reveals that Hoffman only had time to yell "I think this is a pile of shit! While

John Sinclair rots in prison!" before Townshend shouted "Fuck off! Fuck off my fucking stage!" to the crowd's approval.[29] Despite his earlier conflict with Woodstock's organizers, Hoffman had until this point played a valuable role at the festival, assisting with medical services and helping in the Hog Farm's "trips tent" to calm people panicking from the effects of LSD.[30] Yet he was unwelcome on stage. Lang remembered telling Hoffman, "It's not really the time. Nobody really wants to hear that right now. There's an act on stage and it's just not the time for it."[31] Leni Sinclair recalls that "after that we had to run home with our tails between our legs because we were not wanted. Anybody who disrupts the Who set is not a friend of the masses who were there to see the Who. It was the wrong thing to do."[32]

For many observers, Townshend's attack on Hoffman neatly symbolized rock's divorce from political activism; historian Peter Doggett describes it as "a mythic encounter between rock and the revolution."[33] Critic Susan Willis, shortly after Woodstock, reported that "Peter Townshend hit Hoffman with his guitar, which is more of a commentary on the relation of rock to politics than all of *Rat*'s fuzzy moralizing."[34] Decades later, rock scholar Thomas M. Kitts argued that the conflict "perhaps more than anything else at Woodstock indicates the increasing disconnectedness of rock music and politics and points the way to Altamont."[35] Townshend himself later admitted that Hoffman might have had a point: "My response was reflexive rather than considered. What Abbie was saying was politically correct in many ways. The people at Woodstock really were a bunch of hypocrites claiming a cosmic revolution simply because they took over a field, broke down some fences, imbibed bad acid, and then tried to run out without paying the bands. All while John Sinclair rotted in jail after a trumped-up drug bust."[36]

Others decrying rock's lack of political consciousness pointed instead to the festival's racial exclusivity. Historian Craig Werner's argument that "nothing at Woodstock asked the overwhelmingly white nation to extend its boundaries" was anticipated by perceptive critics immediately after the festival.[37] A letter to the *New York Times* published August 26, 1969, asserted that "it is curious that in your extensive coverage of the Woodstock Festival no mention is made of the fact that at that fantastic outpouring there was an almost total absence of Negro youth. . . . Is there latent in the 'youth' scene the racism of which the elders are accused?"[38] Tom Smucker pointed out that "we were all out in the country around nothing but white middle-class kids (notice that intentional lack of soul acts or more proletarian acts up there)."[39] Journalist Craig McGregor was scathingly critical: "Hardly a black face in that massive come-together. A few black performers, but then Louis Armstrong played the Jim Crow circuit. The cruelest paradox of the Woodstock nation is that it has been liberated, primarily, by the black race from which it has borrowed its music, dance, language, style and much of its sense of brotherhood—but that so far it has done little to free those who freed it. Yet, finally, young white America has to free black America if the Woodstock ethic and everything it stands for is to survive at all; in a slave state, nobody's free. Otherwise, Mailer and Cleaver are right: There's a hurricane in the wind."[40] McGregor's claim that "nobody's free" ignores the considerable advantages that whiteness conferred upon the young people who dominated Woodstock, but his point that the counterculture sought to generate a "sense of brotherhood" by imitating African Americans applies neatly to the White Panthers or the Motherfuckers, both in attendance at the festival.

Like its audience, Woodstock's musicians were primarily white. Notable exceptions included two Black performers who bookended the festival with political statements. Richie Havens, the opening act, sang his anti-war anthem "Handsome Johnny" and concluded with the improvised "Freedom," which incorporated the spiritual "Sometimes I Feel Like a Motherless Child." Jimi Hendrix closed the festival with a set including his storied take on "The Star-Spangled Banner."[41] Hendrix's new band, Gypsy Sun and Rainbows, showcased his ongoing collaboration with Black musicians such as Juma Sultan and Billy Cox.[42] Although at Woodstock Sly and the Family Stone did not perform overtly political material such as their provocative recent release "Don't Call Me Nigger, Whitey," they nonetheless, as Rickey Vincent argues, "symbolized the potential for community that so many disaffected, idealistic youth were striving for: women musicians were empowered and treated onstage as equals to men; blacks and whites worked together and sang, danced, and played complex, exhilarating music that exploded the standards for black music presentation."[43] White folk and folk-rock musicians who expressed political views focused on Vietnam. Country Joe McDonald's "I-Feel-Like-I'm-Fixin'-to-Die Rag," for example, mordantly skewered pro-war propaganda, while Joan Baez told the story of her husband David Harris's arrest for draft evasion and capped her set with the civil rights anthem "We Shall Overcome."[44]

But much more typical at Woodstock were those white musicians, almost exclusively men, who imitated Black music without articulating a position on racial politics.[45] A significant number of these performers, such as Johnny Winter, Paul Butterfield, and Ten Years After, were associated with the blues revival that had recently become central to rock. As Ulrich Adelt demonstrates, by the end of the 1960s, "in the larger context of the burgeoning counterculture, audiences for blues music became increasingly white and European" even as "blackness, in particular black masculinity, remained a marker of authenticity."[46] The MC5's attempts to tie blues to Black Power politics made them an exception to what Adelt terms "a depoliticized and commercially charged blues culture" that sought the "nostalgic re-creation of a safe black-ness that predated the civil rights movement."[47] This nostalgia was uninten-tionally (but nonetheless tellingly) evoked at Woodstock at the conclusion of Ten Years After's set, when singer-guitarist Alvin Lee, just having completed his frenetic blues showcase "I'm Going Home," hoisted a watermelon onto his shoulder and carried it off stage.[48] Jefferson Airplane gestured toward the blues revival with Jorma Kaukonen's draft protest "Uncle Sam Blues," a con-ventional 12/8 slow blues built around the traditional line "Uncle Sam ain't no woman, but you know he sure can take your man." Although the song alludes to contemporary concerns about Vietnam, its musical language looks to the past. The band's take on "Come Back Baby," most commonly associated with Ray Charles, deviates further from blues tradition with loose, improvisatory playing by the rhythm section and Kaukonen's acid-rock guitar style, with its unpredictable string bends and his signature wide vibrato.[49]

A band more central to the blues revival was Canned Heat. The group's founders, Bob Hite and Alan Wilson, were known for what drummer Fito de la Parra terms "their encyclopedic knowledge" of the blues tradition.[50] De la Parra describes them as "two white suburban kids who loved black coun-try blues, who collected so many obscure records and listened to them for so many hours that the music just began spilling back out of them like over-filled bathtubs."[51] While this analogy implies an approach to Black music that was instinctual rather than calculated, other comments suggest that the band thought of themselves as innovators (or, in de la Parra's terms, as "totally whacked-out hippies" rather than "purist nerds").[52] De la Parra argues that "we were messing around with the songs of old country blues artists, changing them into something different and new," and adds that "we deliberately left 'blues band' off the name Canned Heat. We didn't want to be labeled as a bunch of white kids copying the old black masters."[53] The band's cover versions, for example, were "the kind of thing the old blues masters performed with only a lone guitar. We wanted to keep the primitive feel, but to appeal to our audi-ence; we added distorted rock guitars and a heavy R&B style rhythm section."[54] Canned Heat's music reflected both their immersion in blues history and Wil-son's dedication to what de la Parra terms "forging keys that would make the blues safe for white people, that would give them—and a lot of blacks too—the knowledge to appreciate and savor this raw art that he loved."[55]

The band's set at Woodstock paid homage to several different styles of blues.[56] "Going Up the Country," which had been a hit single earlier in 1969, adds a new set of lyrics and an electric rhythm section to Henry Thomas's

"Bull-Doze Blues," recorded in 1928. The studio recording features a flute imitating Thomas's quills, a melodic line that Alan Wilson sings at the beginning of the Woodstock performance. "A Change Is Gonna Come" is not Sam Cooke's well-known civil rights anthem, but rather a 12/8 shuffle blues that closely resembles Elmore James's "Dust My Broom." The set's centerpiece, "Woodstock Boogie," is an extended jam based around a one-chord groove in the style of John Lee Hooker, with whom the band later collaborated on 1971's *Hooker 'n Heat*.[57] It comprises a string of solos, from Wilson's slide guitar to Harvey Mandel's overdriven lead guitar to Larry Taylor's bass. De La Parra plays a long drum solo, a practice pioneered in blues-rock by Cream drummer Ginger Baker's "Toad" (1966), and Hite sings conventional blues lyrics that were likely improvised. As an encore, the band plays their single "On the Road Again," derived from recordings by blues singers Tommy Johnson and Floyd Jones. In all, Canned Heat achieved their goal of combining faithful curation of older blues styles with a contemporary, accessible approach.

But as de la Parra's description of blues as "primitive" and "raw" reveals, Canned Heat's obsession with the music, like that of the MC5, was linked to a romantic yet condescending vision of the transgressive, macho bluesman. Hite claimed that "to sing the blues, you have to be an outlaw. Blacks are born outlaws, but we white people have to work for that distinction."[58] But unlike the MC5, Canned Heat did not connect their "outlaw" image to a political program.[59] For some critics, "Canned Heat" became shorthand for an unreflective white appropriation of Black music. Ralph J. Gleason, for example, wrote in *Rolling Stone* that some radicals "wrap themselves in the Panther rhetoric and attitudes and pretend that they are oppressed and exploited like the genuinely oppressed and exploited black people, but they are simply political Canned Heat, that's all."[60] This serves as an implicit criticism of groups like the White Panthers, who remain unnamed, but also as an attack on Canned Heat for feigning an authentic relationship to blackness. Robert Christgau of the *Village Voice* singled out Hite's singing in a review of the Canned Heat album *Hallelujah*: "as usual, it is dominated by Bob 'Rastus' Hite, who must have been responsible for *Rolling Stone*'s suggestion that the next Canned Heat album be called *Yassuh Boss*. He is most offensive on one of those 'introducing the band' jams ('Henry shoah does have the feelin', yeah') and on another exercise in solipsism called 'Canned Heat.'"[61] These critics viewed Canned Heat's music as appropriation or minstrelsy, a position not contradicted by the band's silence on racial issues.

Other white musicians at Woodstock were influenced more by soul, R&B, and jazz than by blues revivalism. These included the Keef Hartley Band, Blood, Sweat & Tears, and Janis Joplin's Kozmic Blues Band, which each had a horn section. Joplin's band featured Black baritone saxophonist Cornelius "Snooky" Flowers, whom Joplin had insensitively described as a "great big ugly spade cat" in a *Rolling Stone* interview earlier in the year.[62] These bands, like the blues revivalists, continued to draw on African American music as a perceived source of authenticity as well as a musical influence.

One of the most celebrated performers in this soul style at Woodstock was Joe Cocker. Cocker's greatest influence was Ray Charles, which French audiences noted as early as 1965 when they called Cocker "Le Petit Ray Charles" or "Joey Charles."[63] At Woodstock, Cocker performed renditions of Charles's "Let's Go Get Stoned" and "Don't Need No Doctor" (both songs were written by Nick Ashford and Valerie Simpson and recorded by Charles in 1966). Cocker makes it clear that his "Let's Go Get Stoned" is about marijuana rather than alcohol—Charles's "bottle of gin" becomes "a little lid"—but the performance is fairly faithful to Charles's original with the exception of a cadenza in which Cocker addresses the size of the Woodstock crowd in pentatonic, unmetered vocal lines that evoke a stereotypical Black preacher. "Doctor," a twelve-bar blues, borrows its driving straight-eighth rhythm from Charles's record but changes the tonic chord from minor to major. After another "preaching" section (in which Cocker exhorts listeners to eat fruit instead of hamburgers so that they won't "need no doctor"), the song concludes with a six-minute jam on the tonic. Throughout, Cocker's band highlights driving electric guitars and electric piano rather than imitating the more subdued organ and acoustic piano of Charles's "Stoned" or the horn section and backing vocals (by the Raelettes) of Charles's "Doctor." The most famous song in Cocker's set, his cover of the Beatles' "With a Little Help from My Friends," similarly draws Charles's vocal style into a "heavy" rock context that recalls Vanilla Fudge's slowed-down version of the Supremes' "You Keep Me Hangin' On." Cocker seems to vacillate between divergent approaches to his Black influences, sometimes indulging in stereotypes and sometimes creating surprising juxtapositions between conventional elements of soul and rock.[64]

Not everyone was persuaded by Cocker's take on R&B. *Rolling Stone*'s Jan Hodenfield reported that "Sunday's marathon was opened by Joe Cocker, his fingers epileptic butterflies, his voice harsh and driving, but grey rather than black, driving home the absence of R and B artists. As with most of the festivals, white was right. No Sam and Dave. No Wilson Pickett. No Stevie Wonder. No Aretha. No Temptations. No Fats Domino. Which is perhaps understandable when the audience itself is largely white. But it is not explicable, when a darkie show such as provided by Cocker is offered as the forgivable alternative."[65] For Hodenfield, Cocker's act amounted to minstrelsy rather than a creative new variant of soul music.

Perhaps in response, A&M Records ran a full-page advertisement for Cocker's new album (the eponymous *Joe Cocker!*) in the December 13 issue of *Rolling Stone* to defend him from charges of appropriation.[66] At first, the ad seems to attack Cocker's competitors as inauthentic: "Today a lot of frustrated young white boys are trying to sing black men's blues. Every month their albums come pouring into the local record stores . . . packaged in 'Dem' witty fold-out photos of 'Hip' down-home shacks, 'Groovy' ghetto tenements and all the other plasteo-agonized symbology of the 'funk' they think they're into. It's pure shuck and everybody knows it." This suggests that inexperienced white "boys" falsely claim an authentic connection to blues by invoking stereotyped Black "men" who supposedly pay their dues in shacks and tenements. But the next sentence rejects that idea, explaining that "the blues is not black, it's human . . . truth human. You can't cover your skin with chocolate syrup and call it bar-b-que . . . no matter how good the syrup is. You don't need to." This is a confusing analogy. Perhaps chocolate syrup represents the artifice of blackface and "bar-b-que" authentic blackness, but if so the writer proposes that some racial artifice can be "good," which seems to contradict the ideal of a "human" music in which race does not matter at all. The ad concludes that "Joe Cocker is a perfect example" (of what is unclear). "He doesn't cover up anything. On his new album from A&M Records, you'll simply hear a 24-year-old Englishman singing his guts out . . . nothing else. Nothing else because there's nothing left . . . and that's exactly why Joe Cocker is probably the greatest white male blues singer alive today." To the extent that the ad had a message at all, it was that Cocker was authentic because he expressed himself, a self that just happened to be white and male. This presentation of Cocker betrays an incoherent concern about race even as it argues for colorblindness. Notably, despite its reference to "ghetto tenements," it does not address the fractious racial politics of the present and how Cocker might fit into them—instead, it falls back on humanistic rhetoric that effaces racial conflict. Although claims about authenticity and appropriation had entered the commercial discourse of rock, here they were reduced to a jumble of hip signifiers rather than a coherent position on race.

In his autobiography, Ray Charles does not mention Cocker specifically, but his discussion of his own 1972 recording of "Look What They've Done to My Song, Ma," written by white singer-songwriter and Woodstock performer Melanie, might point in Cocker's direction:

> I was saying—in my own way—that the whites had taken a lot from me and from the soul community. I wasn't bitter or angry; I was just telling the truth.
> For thirty years, I had seen my records—and the records of other black

musicians—taken over or imitated by whites. They mutilated the songs, and they still wound up selling more by accident than the black versions sold on purpose. I remember that when I went to England to do the Tom Jones TV show I didn't even have to take my arrangements out of my suitcase. The band already had them.[67]

Speaking to the Congressional Black Caucus in 1971, comedian Bill Cosby put the matter simply: "Ray Charles can't make the money he used to make because Joe Cocker's doing it."[68]

A Separate Nation of Freeks

In the afterglow of Woodstock, activists such as John Sinclair and Abbie Hoffman saw the possibility of using the festival's mystique to promote their causes. As John Street puts it, Hoffman "spun" Woodstock, "promoting the event's claim to a radical agenda" despite the "many conflicting ideologies" the festival represented.[69] In embracing the rhetoric of "Woodstock Nation," radicals continued to explore and celebrate values of community and culture even as they began to retreat from Black Power as a central source of inspiration.

Despite the radical skepticism toward "hip capitalism" that motivated groups like the Motherfuckers (and which had forced the cancellation of San Francisco's planned Wild West festival shortly before Woodstock), the immediate reaction to Woodstock in the underground press was generally positive.[70] Even before the festival concluded, many in the counterculture had begun to promote it as the harbinger of a new society. The *East Village Other*'s festival coverage is a case in point. Editor Jaakov Kohn opined that "it was a weekend when the magic, cosmic vibrations of sounds, love and laughter, emanating from half a million grooving, loving, laughing people doing their thing in total freedom and care for all, hit uptight America right in the face and left it in wonder and disbelief." He added that "a year after Chicago, it has become more evident than ever before that the high vibes of sounds, love, and laughter are our real tools and only weapons."[71] John Hilgerdt, reporting from the festival, asserted that "we now know we can live together as we had only done previously in our fantasies. No one will leave here the same person that existed before. For a few days we were all in a beautiful place. Can we do it again? All I know is I don't want to leave here. I feel like I've come home."[72] These writers glorified Woodstock as the spontaneous, inspirational manifestation of a prefigurative politics.

On August 25, Leni Sinclair, now back at home in Ann Arbor, wrote John in prison with strategic reflections on Woodstock.[73] She argued that "by abondoning [*sic*] the staight [*sic*] forward wording of our program, 'dope, rock n'roll, etc.' & giving in to the BPP too much, I think we lost a lot of potential support. I became aware of this more than before at Woodstock. There was 500,000 actively engaged in our 3-point program ['rock and roll, dope, and fucking in the streets']. That's the future. The MC5, as they were about the time they recorded their first album, would have carried the audience by a storm. There was no other band there that was as far out as the kids."[74] Abbie Hoffman, meanwhile, had hit upon a slogan for the new movement. On August 30, Leni reported that "Abbie called last night. His book is finished and will be published in 3 weeks. The title is 'The Woodstock Nation.'" She added that "your suggestion of a WPP-Yippie merger really makes me think that you'll dig the idea of th [*sic*] Woodstock Nation" because it "will give us proper credit for what we are/hade hone [*sic*] so far: being the most important communications center for the new cu;ture [*sic*] in the country. Except before nobody besides us was hip to it."[75]

Shortly thereafter, Hoffman wrote John Sinclair directly with some practical suggestions for the new nation. Contrary to the title of his forthcoming book, Hoffman expressed concern that "the nation needs another name than Woodstock it needs a name that comes out of the collective consciousness of the tribes that gather." But he also suggested "many theater ideas" for the Nation, including "issue our own passports," "TAX all rock groups & everyone making bread," and "Apply to U.N. ask recognition from Cuba etc." He proposed as well that the "Colors of Nation" be "GREEN (land, grass, peace) + BLACK (anger, defiance anarchy)." Although the Motherfuckers would presumably get involved, Hoffman expressed concern that "the NATION thing could be fucked up by motherfuckers & anti-media attitude. I don't know solution. Ben is a beautiful cat but gets pissed if everybody doesn't play by his rules." But Hoffman also praised the Motherfuckers' slogans: "TO LOVE WE MUST SURVIVE / TO SURVIVE WE MUST FIGHT! / ARMED LOVE stuff good."[76] In his response, typed on Marquette Prison stationery on September 22, 1969 ("Coltrane's birthday!," he noted, was the next day), John Sinclair wrote: "I still feel WOODSTOCK NATION is a useful name at present since it has the constant reference to Woodstock, which has to be kept in front of the people so they can relate back to it at all times . . . the one thing is to create an image that kids can relate to in their hippiness and fear of 'the political.'"[77]

Sinclair raised a legitimate concern. Woodstock Nation had been inspired by rock musicians and an audience who were largely apathetic toward revolutionary politics and might not appreciate the nation founded in their name. To employ "Woodstock" as a symbol of countercultural togetherness required radicals to grapple with the commercial, apolitical aspects of the festival.

Sinclair worried, for example, that Hoffman's idea of taxing bands to support Woodstock Nation could fail because rock musicians "are for the most part . . . a bunch of capitalist pigs who are wallowing in self-righteousness and hate anything 'political' except capitalism as they partake in it." The MC5, Sinclair complained, "lost it all when they started getting the capitalist press attention and the money from the New York rock and roll imperialists. Now they won't even give my old lady any money to pay the rent." Rock fans, for their part, were impressed by stardom rather than radical ideology. Without the proper guidance, Sinclair explained, "the kids would pant and say, wow, man, that was PETER ****TOWNSHEND Creator of the magnificent ROCK OPERA ***TOMMY*** It's WAY UP ON THE CHARTS man and I saw them at Woodstock when he bashed that funny-talking dude over the head for trying to mix up politics (ugh) with the ***MUSIC****."[78] In a letter to Abe Peck of the *Chicago Seed* written a day later, Sinclair elaborated: "I don't know, Abe, but all I think about in here is how to develop better programs so that more of these kind of kids can relate to what's happening so they can save their asses, you know?" While he once thought that the "band scene" was the best approach, he now saw that the MC5 "was too close to the pig culture to overcome it."[79] It fell to activists such as Sinclair and Hoffman to lead the new Nation into political engagement.

This project would require a radical coalition. On September 25, John wrote again to Leni with detailed ideas about "the make-up of the Nation and the political arm, the Youth International Party," which he proposed should be modeled on the party systems of China or North Vietnam. The White Panther Party was to merge with YIP and serve as "the guerrilla force, active in the streets and cities; the YIP is the NLF, the political arm for negotiation and other dealings with govts of other nations, and the Nation itself is the people, with its own representative Councils and all, carrying on daily activity and striving for recognition as a sovereign nation." Ben Morea could serve as "Minister of Propaganda" or "Minister of War," while figures such as Tom Hayden (Foreign Affairs), Abbie Hoffman (Interior), and Ed Sanders (Propaganda) could also be folded into the organization. As usual for the White Panthers, these appointments were both entirely serious and a grand put-on. Sinclair explained, "the way I see it this stuff has to be done for its value not only as a media ruse but as a foundation for the people's provisional revolutionary government when the time comes, and plus if we're going to be talking about going to the U.N. and really trying to get recognition as a sovereign nation from our allies we'd better have a recognizable political structure that they can relate to and deal with." He proposed that "we should declare the Nation into being" on October 1, followed by a press conference October 2.[80]

Perhaps coincidentally, the White Panthers in Ann Arbor had already planned a meeting for October 2 inspired by Woodstock. In a letter "mailed to about 50 people" on September 24, they explained that "the festival at Woodstock convinced all, or many of us, that we, and our people, are the potentially greatest force ever to storm the planet. Many feel that what is needed now, is the forming of this energy into something fierce and formidable, some feel that we need machinery that will enable us to deal with large masses of people, organizing, educating, etc." In response, members of the White Panther Party, the Motherfuckers, YIP, and "other Cultural Revolutionaries and Madmen" were to gather, "starting with a celebration of John Sinclair's birthday on Thursday, October 2 at the Grande Ballroom in Detroit" and continuing through the weekend at the White Panther house in Ann Arbor. "THIS IS DEFINITELY NOT A MEDIA RUSE," they added (unwittingly contradicting Sinclair's letter). "This organic gathering is being planned only to TAKE CARE OF BUSINESS!"[81] The age of Woodstock Nation was at hand.

But what distinguished Woodstock Nation from predecessors such as the White Panther Party or the Yippies? John Sinclair and other White Panthers discussed the question in their correspondence, just as Hoffman did in his hastily written book *Woodstock Nation*, published the week of September 26.[82] Their new direction included a move away from Black Power as a model as well as an increasing skepticism about the utopian potential of rock.

Both Sinclair and Hoffman continued to equate the struggle of the white counterculture with that of Black Americans. Hoffman argued with his typical presumption that the establishment has "used pot busts as an excuse to attack WOODSTOCK NATION. Nixon's three biggest enemies right now are the Vietcong, blacks and drugs. Drugs means us and he treats us like the country has always treated its VIETCONG NIGGERS. He aims to kick our ass."[83] In "On Youth Culture: Proposal to the Central Comm[ittee]," a typescript dated January–February 1970, Sinclair used more theoretical language to draw a parallel between Black Power and the white counterculture. Citing Cleaver and Newton's "theory that the black masses in the United States constitute an oppressed colonial population within the mother country," Sinclair posited that "the great masses of young people in the United States . . . also constitute an oppressed colonial population within the mother country, and that the role of the youth revolutionary vanguard is to lead the youth colony to rebel against the mother country ruling class and end its rule over the youth colony."[84] Colonized (and implicitly white) youth had benefited from learning from and reworking the culture of colonized Black communities. "Black music, black art, black language, black clothing styles, the whole black colonial experience in Amerika has been absorbed and transformed into something unique and almost equally vital by the youth culture, and has in its own turn exerted a strong influence over the course of that transformation." As a result, white youth had come to appreciate the problems faced by Black Americans, Sinclair argued, "and have entered into strong supportive relationships with the people of the black colony in their struggle for national liberation." The culture of youth, like that of African Americans, was now being co-opted by "the dominant plastic honko culture," raising awareness and sympathy toward young people within the mother country itself. Just as white revolutionaries such as the White Panthers had been inspired by Black music, so might "greater and greater segments of the broad masses" be radicalized by young, white rock musicians.[85]

Yet the White Panthers had begun to believe that while Black Power imagery and rhetoric had served an important purpose in organizing the youth colony, it was time for the new Nation to distance itself from them. In a letter to John Sinclair, White Panther Minister of Education Skip Taube argued that "we must learn from the objective reality of the bpp experience," which encompassed violent attacks by "the pigs" as well as the party's "internal structure of harsh lines and harsh disipline [sic]." "The bpp," Taube believed, "has served the people well but it has dealt with the pig power structure in the wrong way, i.e. to [sic] directly." In contrast, "400,000 people living at woodstock as a community of brothers and sisters, and millions more wanting to be there or working to recreate it in their locale is a revolutionary example that people [sic] of what the nation is—all that remains is to make it permanent."[86] In "On Youth Culture," Sinclair noted that "the radicals have concentrated on projecting a romantic revolutionary/street-fighter image to the broadest masses as well as to the yotuh [sic] masses, while the culture freek/activists have treid [sic] to promote a weird, paradoxical quasi-political but generally benevolent image to the broad masses." The latter approach better served the aim of "creating a huge mass response to a line that the masses can relate to, in order to draw more and more people into the movement and educate them through the process of the struggle itself." Sinclair argued that "we have to make it clear to ourselves as well as to all the masses of all the people that we are working in their interests—otherwise we have no revolution, otherwise we are just stupid adventurists posturing and posing for the news cameras, otherwise we might as well march en masse to the jails and penitentiaries."[87] Pun Plamondon remembers that in 1970 "we changed our public image from one of leather-jacketed militants to a less threatening one of leather-jacketed community organizers. This strategy not only reflected the broader changing political scene and the need for us to garner support from a wider base, but also aided our defense efforts by accentuating the positive and downplaying our militancy."[88] This suggests that the White Panthers' change of image was in part pragmatic—as Sinclair fought his conviction, it would have been bad strategy for his party to appear dangerous and violent.

Instead, Sinclair emphasized Native Americans rather than the Black Panthers as models for Woodstock Nation, drawing on countercultural notions of Indianness, which, as Philip J. Deloria demonstrates, could signify both "social harmony" and "radical individual freedom" as well as "an identity as a critic of empire."[89] Sinclair wrote to Hoffman that "there are so many great metaphors in the Native American heritage that are pertinent to present youth Nation. E.g. Tecumseh (Michigan Chief) speaking of his Nation: the 5 Tribes are like the 5 fingers of a hand." The Motherfuckers, whose propaganda included "that great photo of crazed Red Chief with a rifle across his chest," had already gestured in this direction. Group structures could be based around Sinclair's notion of Native American political organization: "it seems to me (I don't know if I wrote this in my last letter) that we should use the tribal-native American-psychedelic mix and focus as much as possible, so the meetings can be called Councils, the different groups tribes . . . and the permanent Council members Chiefs or Elders or both." At the same time, however, "I don't see why we don't use RED GREEN & BLACK as in the black nationalist flag too . . . it adds to confusion in mass media when we use same colors as black groups and also makes alliances with them more easily negotiated when they see (as with White Panthers) that we are sympathetic to even their symbols as welll [sic] as their programs." In the end, Sinclair proposed mixing the two: "maybe a National flag with red green and black with a fist clutching a peace pipe superimposed on it, stuff like that."[90] By combining symbols of Black nationalism with a clichéd emblem of Native American culture, Sinclair implied an equivalence between the two based primarily on their distance from whiteness.

Hoffman's writing also reflected ambivalence about his relationship to Black Power. In an open letter to US attorney general John Mitchell included in *Woodstock Nation*, Hoffman mentioned that "we would also make some suggestions about the BLACK NATION and the rest of what we call the Free World (although I believe you call them something else). You, of course, realize you must negotiate independently with them."[91] Hoffman continued to describe Black radicals as an inspiration for white revolutionaries but also indicated here that the "BLACK NATION" was on a political course independent of Woodstock Nation. Biographer Jonah Raskin argues that while Hoffman viewed himself as "a hippie nationalist: the countercultural counterpart to black nationalists, who had sprung up all across American ghettoes and who espoused the gospel of separatism," this did not imply a shared mis-

sion; critic of "flower power" H. Rap Brown, Hoffman felt, "ought to direct
his comments to ghetto youth and leave the white dropouts and longhairs to
white organizers like himself."[92] Like Sinclair, Hoffman increasingly invoked
Native American metaphors, as when he asserted at the Chicago Eight trial:
"I live in Woodstock Nation . . . It is a nation of alienated young people. We
carry it around with us as a state of mind in the same way as the Sioux Indians
carried the Sioux nation around with them . . . It is in my mind and in the
minds of my brothers and sisters."[93] Hoffman's "Sioux nation" represented a
metaphysical vision of community rather than an attempt to forge alliances
with Native Americans.

But it was Woodstock itself, an event consciously designed to showcase
rock while transcending politics, that had inspired the new nation. As scholar
Michael J. Kramer puts it, the idea of the "Woodstock Nation" presented in
Hoffman's book "was equal parts sophisticated conceptual theory, simplistic
political slogan, and effective marketing tagline, but what is easy to forget is
that the idea of Woodstock Nation arose most of all from Hoffman's musings about the relationship between rock music and citizenship."[94] Hoffman
reveals Sinclair's influence by crediting Black music for his development as a
revolutionary. He recalls that during the 1950s he listened avidly to rhythm
and blues 45s as well as radio DJs, such as Symphony Sid and Alan Freed, who
brought African American music to white audiences. His investment in this
music, he claims, turned him against white "Culture-Vultures" such as the
Crew Cuts and Pat Boone who began "ripping off black-ass rock-and-roll and
dressing it up with white bucks! WHITE BUCKS! Stepping on punks' white
bucks as they came home from school was in fact among my first political
acts . . . Nothing else more than that rip-off of black music made me more
ashamed of being white than anything, not even the 'woman who came in on
Thursdays.'" Like Eldridge Cleaver, Hoffman views Elvis Presley as a crucial
figure in bringing authentic blackness to whites: "he was a tough-ass motherfucker and he sang from the inside out and yet he was white." "Back then,"
Hoffman writes, "Elvis spoke the words of POWER TO THE PEOPLE, to
the fringe ones, the visitors that came to taste of freedom." Telling the story
of Elvis's influence, in turn, allows Hoffman to "talk to the folks who live in
WOODSTOCK NATION. It helps to get the message out."[95] For Hoffman,
like Sinclair, rock and roll served as both a source of inspiration and a medium for propaganda.

But Woodstock itself had failed to live up to the promise that Hoffman
had heard in early rock and roll. Hoffman recounts his conflicts with the festival organizers as well as with Ben Morea, "the Morea-Eel of the Motherfuckers, whose role I sometimes think is just to chew me out."[96] With the

exception of the Hog Farm commune, whom Hoffman admires for their pragmatism in providing free food and medical services at the festival, he dismisses Movement City "lefties," who "packed up their leaflets or abandoned them and headed out of WOODSTOCK NATION still thinking it was a festival, or worse, a concentration camp. Those that stayed are better for it all, including me."[97] Apolitical musicians, sequestered backstage in their "uptown plastic dome," were another problem.[98] Hoffman tries to settle the score with the Who, annotating the lyrics to their song "We're Not Gonna Take It" with such comments as "Peter, how can we follow you when you admire Hitler?" and "How can we forsake John Sinclair?" and "How can we touch you Who you're in the helicopters, way up there . . ."[99] Hoffman gives other Woodstock performers backhanded compliments, praising their music while denigrating their lack of political commitment: "Janis is all fuckin right even if she don't know from California grapes and freeing John Sinclair . . . Sure it'd be nice if Sly and the Family Stone stopped playing once and looked out at PIG NATION and said 'Oh, by the way we're Communists,' God that would blow a lot of fuckin holes in 'His Master's Voice.' Yeh, but maybe that's unfair because on the other hand we politicos don't sing too good."[100] Hoffman praises the White Panthers' militant stance while criticizing Woodstock's slogan, "3 Days of Peace & Music": "In Ann Arbor and in other places like that around the country they ain't into peace and music, they're into WAR and MUSIC and Right on! Music can make the walls shake but you need an army to take the city and artists to rebuild it. Rock music will provide the energy but the people will provide the power, for only with power can we defend what beauty we create."[101]

John Sinclair, although he had been prevented from attending, also found Woodstock disappointing. The only bright spot, argued Sinclair, were "revolutionary culture freeks . . . busy serving the people in very down-to-earth ways—the hospital, the free food line, the bad-trip counseling center, security, etc." This category presumably included Hoffman as well as the Hog Farm. "Advanced revolutionary elements," in contrast, "failed to make use of this unprecedented opportunity to propagandize among the masses and educate them as to what was happening." This category likely encompassed the Motherfuckers and other Movement City radicals, as well as the White Panthers themselves. Worst of all were the performers, who "took advantage of the opportunity to segregate themselves from the masses of the people who were sleeping in the mud while the pop-stars were drinking champagne and flying back and forth in helicopters and counting their paychecks." Drawing young people into "revolutionary political struggle," Sinclair believed, would require "educating the pop-stars and entertainment figures who have access to the youth masses and enlisting them in the struggle.... if Peter Townshend or someone of his ilk were to endorse and support the people's vanguard the masses would find it easy to add their support and even to take an active role in the movement." Woodstock thus represented a missed opportunity. "As brother Pun Plamondon wrote to me when he returned from Woodstock, 'If someone would've gotten on the stage and said "We are a People! We are a Nation!" that would've been the heaviest political scene in the country.'" Instead, "very little was done to give the masses any sort of revolutionary political education at Woodstock—although Abbie has done a beautiful job since with his book WOODSTOCK NATION."[102]

Hoffman and Sinclair thus proposed a Woodstock Nation that transcended, or perhaps simply contradicted, what actually happened at Woodstock.[103] Woodstock was valuable primarily as a symbol of nationhood itself, as the vast, generally peaceful mass at the festival demonstrated the possibility that a self-sufficient youth culture could unite to create political change. Sinclair contended that at Woodstock, where "the spectre of the alternative culture was clearly visible to every person in the United States," the youth colony had demonstrated its viability as a nation. Although the mass media focused on "the sensational aspect of our culture (mass use of dope, public nudity, traffic jams, deaths, sickness, etc.) . . . there were so many people at Woodstock, and they were all so together, that the image of peace/love that the pig power structure had been trying for a year to obliterate from the public consciousness was once again forced foremost into the public mind."[104] In short, "Woodstock was so important for the youth masses because they were able to see and feel the possibility of community, of the revolutionary life-style as a fact—they know after Woodstock that they are part of something different from the dominant pig-death culture, that they do indeed belong to a separate and distinct Nation of free people." For participants in the "dominant pig-death culture," moreover, the festival served as an invitation to reconsider their values: "everyone, even the severest critics of youth culture, could see that the youth were having a much better time than the rest of the people and that there might be something to this phenomenon, something of use to them, after all."[105] Woodstock displayed youth culture as both self-reliant and inspirational to others.

This optimistic view was reflected in the pages of the White Panther newspaper *Sun/Dance*, published twice during 1970. Alongside the expected references to "pigs" and to Black Power leaders such as Cleaver, Newton, and Malcolm X were appeals to a hippie vision of Native American culture and tradition and an increased emphasis on nation-building over protest. John Sinclair wrote that "we have to define ourselves as the POSITIVE thing we are, and we have to destroy the negative definitions of us advanced by the established order." "Woodstock Nation" is an appropriate name for the "New people," he continued, "because it is rooted deep in our national experience" and because it honored the Seneca people of New York, whose culture Sinclair claimed was "rooted in communalism, peace, justice, equality, and harmony."[106] Sinclair proposed a "National symbol" that combined "three elements—the guitar, the gun, and the peace pipe full of weed" into a shape that evokes both a teepee and peace sign.[107] A stylized version of the symbol appeared on the cover of *Sun/Dance* no. 1 surrounded by a sunburst and the word "NATION."

With the MC5's defection from the White Panther Party, the Up, managed by John's brother Dave Sinclair, became musical propagandists for the new Nation, combining a continued emphasis on militant rhetoric with exhortations to the audience to pull together as a people. John wrote to journalist Abe Peck that "my brother's band the UP is coming up now and they've learned a lot from the [MC]5's experience and are starting to relate to the real needs of the people and not just their own little existence."[108] Lead singer Franklin Bach's essay "Rock for Our People," published in *Sun/Dance*, promoted a platform similar to John's: "every musician that really knows what's going on and is doing something positive about it is a guerrilla fighter in the revolution. If you can dig that."[109] The program for a March 20, 1970, concert at Michigan's Jackson Armory recalled the MC5 in its blend of libidinous originals ("I'm Looking for Some Skin," "Be My Tootsie Roll") and covers of songs by Black men including Hendrix, Howlin' Wolf, and Sun Ra. Explicitly political songs included "Hassan I Sabba[h]," which portrays the eleventh-century Persian warrior as "the old man of the hills who used to sit back with his band of assassins and lots of hash and check out the scene in the nearby cities and towns. When the rulers started mistreating people Hassan I and his boys would swoop down on the punks and take care of business, if you know what we mean." The program's cover, inspired by the band's song "Just Like an Aborigine," presents a cartoon caricature of an indigenous Australian with a nose piercing and an elongated neck smoking a pipe. That the image is ostensibly playful makes it no less offensively primitivist. The same can be said of the song, which juxtaposes intentionally silly lines about fleeing kangaroos and tearing off one's clothes with the more earnest "The soil is my mother ... The hot sun's my father ... The trees are my brother" over thunderous distorted power chords. The program declares "Just Like an Aborigine" "a tribal song, the song of our people. Yes, we are a people, all of us are people of a new Nation ... we have our own way of talking, our own way of acting, our own way of having a good time, our own rock and roll music. We live just like the aborigine, together as in the music, free as the energy that holds us close. United with our selves, nothing can stop us, we can do anything we want to do . . . WE ARE THE FUTURE, and we know it!!!" The program touts the 45-RPM release of "Just Like an Aborigine" as "a product of Woodstock Nation!"[110] While the theme of liberating the body through music recalls Sinclair's utopian rhetoric about avant-garde jazz, "Just Like an Aborigine" no longer relied on African American models either musically or thematically, and the "aborigine" represented a stereotype of "tribal" hedonism and connection to nature rather than a specific political stance.[111]

By 1971, both Abbie Hoffman and the White Panthers had revised their views of Woodstock Nation. In an epilogue, "The Head Withers as Body Grows," written for a new edition of *Woodstock Nation*, Hoffman wrote that "somewhere deep inside of the monster born at Bethel also lay the kernel for its destruction."[112] Inspirational musicians Janis Joplin and Jimi Hendrix were dead, and rock stars now seemed increasingly distant from their audiences: "the walls around the stars get higher and electric fences and police dogs guard their mansions."[113] Yet Hoffman believes that "Woodstock Nation ain't dead at all": "there is no community in the land without a vast number of communes, food conspiracies, alternate universities, violent underground, dope-dealing networks, people's rock groups, switchboards and newspapers. That is the Woodstock Nation."[114] John Sinclair had become more skeptical about Woodstock's value as an organizing theme. In a "Draft Statement for the Movement" dated April 12, 1971, he charged that the party had "effectively lost contact with the young masses in our local 'free area' of Ann Arbor/Detroit and increasingly concentrated on trying to advance our 'Woodstock Nation' thesis among the rest of the movement in an insane attempt to create a 'separate nation' of freaks all on paper and in our heads." The party blamed its members' "infantile adventurism" for a recent disaster, the July 23, 1970, arrest of Pun Plamondon, who had gone underground after being indicted for the 1968 bombing of a CIA office in Ann Arbor.[115] In his memoir, Plamondon recalls his resistance to the name "Woodstock People's Party," proposed by Sinclair: "after all, Woodstock was a capitalist venture that was ill-prepared to deal with the consequences of its own advertising. It was a great cultural event, but not one I'd want as the image for a revolutionary party."[116] By 1972, Sinclair disparaged Woodstock as "something we produced out of our own national genius and energy . . . but the mother-country record companies and movie companies and vampires of all kinds swooped down on it and grabbed it and took it into their factories and cooked the reality of Woodstock down into records and movies and shit which they now sell back to us at $3.50 and $12.00 a shot. We control no part of it, yet it's entirely produced by us."[117]

While the 1970 *Woodstock* film, as Gina Arnold points out, celebrates a new "nation" of "freaks," it ultimately reconciles "the counterculture and the opposition" to provide "the assurance . . . of America as a united nation."[118] What had seemed like the possibility of a new social form had been tamed by hip capitalism.

In April 1971, the Central Committee of the newly named Rainbow People's Party announced the dissolution of the White Panther Party. According to Leni Sinclair, there were several reasons for the change. The central core of the party could no longer keep up with the loosely affiliated White Panther chapters that had sprung up around the United States and the world. After the split with the MC5, Sinclair recalls, "we lost our poster child," making it more difficult to promote the party. The term "White Panthers" sometimes gave the misleading impression that the group was a white supremacist organization.[119] But the new name also reflected a new emphasis on diverse influences (albeit still often filtered through stereotypes) and local action. The party declared that "we call ourselves 'Rainbow People' because that is what we are, first of all—the culture that defines us is not a 'white' culture at all, but a true Rainbow Culture borrowing from many different peoples—our music comes from black culture, our sacraments (marijuana, peyote, mescaline) from brown and red (American Indian) cultures, our philosophy and sciences from yellow (Eastern) culture, our clothing from red culture. And our vision of the future is that of a free and beautiful Rainbow Nation that includes all of the people on the planet."[120] The Rainbow People's Party made it clear that while they had "not abandoned or repudiated the Black Panther Party. . . . the best way we in the Rainbow colony can contribute to the liberation of our natural brothers and sisters in the black colony—and all oppressed peoples—is by organizing ourselves in our own communities and moving in an organized fashion against our common oppressor."[121] Leni Sinclair asserts that "when we changed from the White Panthers to Rainbow, we stopped being a national organization—we were going to concentrate on Ann Arbor and trying to serve the people, as we called it, in Ann Arbor, and that's what we did. In fact, that led to us helping to elect two people to the city council and transform the politics of Ann Arbor for a while."[122] Historian Jeff A. Hale describes the new party as "a nonmilitant, grassroots organization whose activities mirrored the Movement's entrance into mainstream politics after 1970."[123] But while the Rainbow People's Party's aims were more practical and less grandiose than the White Panthers' had been, Sinclair believes that the new group was actually "more radical": "What's more radical than feeding people and having a daycare center for free . . . and a dental clinic and the People's Ballroom and the food co-op—you know, that's all taking care of the people."[124] While the party continued to promote rock musicians such as Mitch Ryder through its "production and management company," Rainbow Multi-Media, music formed only one part of a larger mission.[125]

As the White Panther Party became the Rainbow People's Party, they moved away from militant revolutionary politics and toward a more pragmatic, less utopian notion of political engagement. As part of this change in strategy, they reconsidered their obsession with the political potential of rock and the "black magic music" that informed it, embracing instead a broader range of goals and inspirations. Rock, meanwhile, continued to thrive as a form of commercial entertainment built on white imitation of Black musical practices but characterized by apathy toward racial issues. If, as Abbie Hoffman contended, Woodstock Nation persisted into the 1970s, it did so sundered from the engagement with Black music and politics that had once inspired it.

Epilogue

Black Culture is cool, but black issues sure aren't huh?

AZEALIA BANKS TO IGGY AZALEA, 2014[1]

You're in videos with black men, and you're bringing out black women on your stages,
but you don't want to know how black women feel about something that's so important?

NICKI MINAJ TO MILEY CYRUS, 2015[2]

We take all we want from black culture, but will we show up for black lives?

MACKLEMORE, 2016[3]

As this beat backspins, it's like we're drifting back in / To the sixties—having black skin
is risky

EMINEM, 2017[4]

During the 1980s, Dave Sinclair, John's brother, wrote a poem memorializing the Rainbow People's Party that speaks both to the playful, joyful side of their activism and to the very real difficulties the group faced.

> There was a flower of folly there,
> fit perhaps for laughter;
> but it was fearful what it took to fertilize;
> and still less funny, what it took
> to pluck it.

He concludes:

> There went my outsized heart, for one, utterly spent:
>
> not so important, indeed; but still,
> not a seemly subject for any second
> guesses
> but our own.[5]

Sinclair reminds his readers that with the benefit of hindsight, it is a simple matter to pass judgment on decisions, whether political or musical, that were necessarily complex and improvisatory in the moment. But even if second guesses are unseemly, perhaps there are still lessons to learn. What conclusions can be drawn from this book's stories about white rock musicians' engagement with Black music and politics?

Perhaps it all amounts to a cautionary tale of shattered hopes and lost innocence.[6] It is a convention of rock history to contrast Woodstock with Altamont, the notorious free concert of December 6, 1969, where, as Robert Christgau put it:

> On America's ultimate frontier some three hundred thousand bohemians come together with their chosen images, five formerly lower- to middle-class Englishmen who fuse Afro-American music with European sensibility. Denouement: An Afro-American bohemian is murdered by a lower-class white Hell's Angel while the Englishmen do a song called "Sympathy for the Devil."[7]

The murder of Meredith Hunter unmasked the apathy of a hedonistic counterculture who lacked courage and commitment. At Altamont, "Berkeley radicals . . . circulated with buckets collecting money for the Black Panthers' legal defense fund . . . and met with indifference and even hostility from the solidly anti-political rock audience."[8] Critic Ralph J. Gleason asked: "Is this the new community? Is this what Woodstock promised? Gathered together AS a tribe, what happened? Brutality, murder, despoliation, you name it."[9] Gleason, famously, blamed the Rolling Stones, charging that "the name of the game is money, power and ego . . . and money is first and it brings power. The Stones didn't do it for free, they did it for money, only the tab was paid in a different way."[10] Critic Sandy Darlington targeted instead Jefferson Airplane's Altamont performance: "It pissed me off that the Airplane kept playing during one fight. It pissed me that Jorma wore a big iron swastika around his neck. Oh yes it's a sun symbol. And we're only in it for the music. They ended their set with a song about revolution. Horseshit."[11] A tragic narrative might follow both bands into the 1980s and conclude with the Rolling Stones' massive arena tours and Jefferson Airplane's eventual transformation into Starship, one of the most maligned "corporate rock" bands of the era.[12] In this account, any connection that either band had to either African American music or political radicalism sinks into a mire of greed and cynicism.

Or one could write a happier ending that highlights moments of interracial solidarity in rock. This uplifting conclusion might start by noting a display of courage at Altamont: Jefferson Airplane's Marty Balin jumped offstage to help a Black man (possibly Hunter) being beaten by Hells Angels and was beaten unconscious himself.[13] Darlington acknowledged that "Balin was brave. Or foolish? Yes, but there were few fools that brave that day."[14] Then the story could leap ahead to December 10, 1971, when the John Sinclair Freedom Rally attracted 15,000 to the University of Michigan's Crisler Arena to hear music by artists including John Lennon and Yoko Ono, Stevie Wonder, and Bob Seger and speeches by Abbie Hoffman, Bobby Seale, Jerry Rubin, and John Sinclair himself "over the loudspeakers by way of a telephone hookup direct from Jackson Prison."[15] Three days later, Sinclair's bond was granted and in 1972 the Michigan Supreme Court overturned his conviction. In the same year, the Rolling Stones paid tribute to activist Angela Davis, then on trial for murder, with their song "Sweet Black Angel" (the feel-good version of the story obliges one to downplay the issues raised by Jagger's exaggerated "black" locution and his presumably "ironic" use of the N-word).[16] One could listen for echoes of White Panther principles a few years later in the Rock Against Racism movement, inspired in reaction against a bigoted onstage rant by Eric Clapton, a prominent white interpreter of songs by Black musicians including Robert Johnson and Bob Marley. Between 1976 and 1982, RAR sponsored carnivals and tours highlighting British punk and post-punk musicians such as the Clash, themselves noted adapters of Jamaican music.[17] Turning to the 1980s, and glossing over criticism of Paul Simon as an appropriator of South African popular music, one could highlight the role that his *Graceland* album played in raising international awareness of apartheid.[18] In the 1990s, interracial rap-metal group Rage against the Machine pulled hip-hop and grunge together in such songs as "Wake Up," which cites the murders of Martin Luther King Jr. and Malcolm X and includes a recitation from COINTELPRO documents.[19] Without proposing a direct chain of influence, a historian might point to these moments as evidence that white rock musicians have repeatedly, if sporadically, taken an interest in anti-racist causes.

It is difficult, however, to trace either of these stories past the turn of the millennium, simply because rock is no longer hegemonic within the world of popular music. As Jack Hamilton puts it, "I don't actually think hardcore rockism exists anymore as a viable critical disposition."[20] Because rockism typically benefits and promotes straight, white, cisgender men, its dethroning marks a positive step toward greater inclusivity in popular music. It also means that critics no longer look primarily to rock for evidence of popular music's political engagement. When John Mellencamp "takes a knee" in solidarity with protesting NFL quarterback Colin Kaepernick or Green Day's Billie Joe Armstrong sings "no Trump, no KKK, no fascist USA" at the American Music Awards, these gestures stand out as exceptions within a genre now viewed as largely apolitical.[21] Punk bands such as the trans, queer, femme hardcore band G.L.O.S.S., whose anti-white-supremacist "Fight" proclaims

"Wave your flag / For your fucked-up race / If you don't take flight / You'll take a brick to the face," continue to address racial issues, but voices such as theirs remain marginalized in rock.[22] In 2016, Corin Tucker of Sleater-Kinney argued that rock "has long been replaced as the standard-bearer of social consciousness. 'We're already in an incredible time in the United States for protest music, but it's all happening in a lot of hip-hop and R&B tied to the Black Lives Matter movement.'"[23] Kendrick Lamar's "Alright" or Beyoncé's "Freedom," not rock, form the movement's soundtrack.[24]

Hip-hop and R&B, central to anti-racist protest today, also have become fundamental to debates over white appropriation of Black music, debates that have shifted away from rock as the genre has become less dominant. Moreover, the terms of debate have changed. Hip-hop and R&B are widely understood as Black genres, and white performers are concerned less with adapting them into new forms than with claiming the right to perform them at all.

Take the controversy over Miley Cyrus, who, as Kyra D. Gaunt puts it, "used YouTube twerking as an ethnic marker to transform her brand identity" toward hip-hop in the 2013 video for "We Can't Stop" and, more notoriously, at the 2013 MTV Video Music Awards.[25] In both performances, Cyrus appeared with Black women, "actors-for-hire" who "seem to symbolize a generalized and authentic black female identity of girlfriends."[26] Rather than pointing out twerking's roots in Black dance practices, instead "the media's spin machine . . . de-racialized the dance in a day," declaring Cyrus "the new twerk queen."[27] Trinidadian American hip-hop star Nicki Minaj lectured Cyrus for her thoughtless appropriation: "Come on, you can't want the good without the bad. If you want to enjoy our culture and our lifestyle, bond with us, dance with us, have fun with us, twerk with us, rap with us, then you should also want to know what affects us, what is bothering us, what we feel is unfair to us. You shouldn't *not* want to know that."[28] Or consider the popular success of white Australian rapper Iggy Azalea, whose vocal imitation of "a downhome Atlanta girl" seems to contradict her claims "that she only rap[s] about incidents that were true to her life experiences" and has been likened to "verbal blackface."[29] African American rapper Azealia Banks argued that Azalea's music is "like a cultural smudging, is what I see. And when they give those Grammys out, all it says to white kids is 'Oh, you're great, you're amazing, you can do whatever you put your mind to,' and what it says to black kids is 'you don't have shit, you don't own shit, not even the shit you created for yourself.' And it makes me upset."[30] As James McNally points out, Azalea consistently takes a colorblind stance in response to charges of appropriation, "play[ing] down the advantages she received as a white woman" and asking "why is it such a big deal? This is the entertainment industry. It's not politics."[31] These examples reveal that white engagement with Black music has not necessarily become more self-aware since the 1960s.

Other white hip-hop artists, such as Macklemore and Eminem, have assumed a more "woke" public image by addressing both Black struggle and their own racial privilege. In 2014, Lanre Bakare of the *Guardian* described Macklemore's appearance at a Seattle Black Lives Matter rally as "one of the most bizarre moments of the US street protests" surrounding the failure to indict police officer Darren Wilson for the killing of Michael Brown in Ferguson, Missouri. "It was something you saw but didn't quite believe. Was that him? No way. What? Was that really the rapper Macklemore . . . on the frontline of the Seattle protest talking about solidarity with Brown's family?"[32] Macklemore's action seemed to contradict his reputation as a figure who "has often been accused of appropriating hip-hop from black musicians, and of stealing song ideas from black musicians. There has also been controversy over his success in popular music, the argument being that he was able to ascend to the 'top' so quickly, and win so many prestigious awards in the music industry, because of his whiteness."[33] At the same time, some critics gave Macklemore credit for not adopting an inauthentically Black voice. Brittney Cooper describes him, along with the Beastie Boys and Eminem, as "white men who've been successful in rap in the last 30 years and generally . . . don't have to appropriate Blackness to do it."[34]

In 2005, Macklemore demonstrated awareness of these issues in a song called "White Privilege," in which he asks "Where's my place in a music that's been taken by my race / Culturally appropriated by the white face?" In 2016, Macklemore, producer Ryan Lewis, and singer Jamila Woods released a sequel, "White Privilege II," that specifically addresses the Black Lives Matter movement. The sprawling track, over eight minutes long, comprises (in *Pitchfork*'s summary) "four rap verses, internal monologues, a sung outro, chants, cinematic segues, keys both twinkling and ominous with no baseline [*sic*], horn solos, and disembodied voices."[35] Macklemore's first verse is an account of his own uneasiness at a Black Lives Matter protest. He asks himself "is this awkward? Should I even be here marching?" and "am I in the outside looking in, or am I in the inside looking out?" Later in the song, in lines that also seem to be directed at himself, he charges that "you're Miley, you're Elvis, you're Iggy Azalea / Fake and so plastic, you've heisted the magic." Macklemore concludes with a question—"we take all we want from black culture, but will we show up for black lives?"—before unidentified voices talking about the Black Lives Matter movement give way to Black singer Woods asserting that "your silence is a luxury / Hip hop is not a luxury" as the beat steadies and the piano's harmonies change to an uplifting major-key progression.[36]

Eminem preceded Macklemore in finding a place in hip-hop without imitating conventional signifiers of blackness. Certainly, the violent misogyny and homophobia of Eminem's lyrics, delivered in what Carl Hancock Rux calls a "nasal, white-boy, horror-rap cadence," places him in the tradition of white men who seek to assert an unfettered, transgressive masculinity through Black music.[37] On the other hand, as Loren Kajikawa puts it, "parodying common understandings of whiteness, Eminem advanced a white identity both at ease with black culture and humble before it." This persona relies on class politics rather than racial mimicry: "by focusing on his class identity and various unflattering and outrageous images of whiteness, Eminem positioned himself as an underdog."[38] Although this strategy suggests that interracial alliances might be formed along class lines, it also risks creating the impression that "because a single white rapper growing up in black Detroit had to struggle for acceptance, it is whites who are equally disadvantaged by U.S. society."[39] Eminem is a complex figure, respected and respectful within a Black art form while still reaping the advantages of whiteness.

Eminem's "Untouchable" takes a more sardonic approach than does Macklemore's "White Privilege II." Provocatively, Eminem's first two verses take the point of view of a racist white police officer who chants "Black boy, black boy, we don't like the sight of you" (in a satirical take on the theme song of the TV reality show *Cops*) and assures himself that "no matter how many lives you ruin / It's for the red, white, and blue." The second half of the song assumes the perspective of an African American who argues that "we just want a safe environment for our kids / But can't escape the sirens" and adds that "we're trapped in these racial biases / That plague our society which makes our anxiety levels raise." By shifting between these voices, Eminem does not suggest a moral equivalence between them, but rather creates a sense of drama and interpersonal conflict reinforced by the musical setting. The first half of "Untouchable" is built somewhat surreally on samples from Cheech and Chong's 1974 hard-rock parody "Earache My Eye," which associates the white cop character with the "rockist" crunch of electric guitars as well as with lines like "my mama talking to me trying to tell me how to live" that mark him as unreflective and antisocial. In contrast, a tense minor-key ostinato played by piano, bass, and drums backs the Black narrator's verses, reinforcing their assertions of fear and anger. Eminem's serious message is underpinned by an unpredictable and at times playful musical texture that mirrors the song's shifting personas.

Both "White Privilege II" and "Untouchable" sparked debate among musicians and critics. Some Black musicians and activists tweeted praise for Macklemore's song—Ice T called it "so NEEDED," while DeRay Mckesson declared the song "important" (although he added that "all art, including his song, is open to critique").[40] When Iggy Azalea took offense at her depiction in the song, rapper Talib Kweli Greene retorted that "if you can find the time to be offended when Macklemore suggests that black lives matter, u can find the time to say they do."[41] *Billboard* celebrated Eminem for trying to "kill stereotypes" with his "intricate lyrics" in "Untouchable."[42] But other critics pointed out that even while showing solidarity with African Americans, these rap stars were talking mainly about themselves. In *The Atlantic*, critic Spencer Kornhaber argued that "Macklemore never explicitly asks you to feel sorry for him, the rich white rapper bedeviled by his own conscience, but you still walk away feeling as though he has."[43] Azealia Banks similarly argued, "just know that Macklemore 'admitting' his white privilege is about to eclipse the REAL conversation about Blacks & Entertainment."[44] NPR's Gene Demby described Jamila Woods as "the little-known black female singer brought in to lend her talents, her thoughts, and yeah, *her blackness*, to what will inevitably be seen as *his* project."[45] Eminem came in for similar criticism for what Tshepo Mokoena called his "entry-level musing on whiteness."[46] *Pitchfork* explicitly compared Eminem to Macklemore, writing that "there's a level of Mackling to a white celebrity rapper" stating "'and I admit there have been times where it's been embarrassing to be a white boy,' as if Marshall Mathers' mortification is of any import here."[47]

A welcome distinction between the 1960s and today is that these critiques are frequently intersectional, drawing issues of gender and sexuality into discussions of white appropriation, and that the critics and musicians at the forefront of the debate are often Black women. Brittney Cooper, for example, points out that Black men such as rapper and producer T.I. were complicit in Iggy Azalea's rise to stardom, and charges that "by riding for white female rappers to the exclusion of Black women, Black men collude with the system against Black women, by demonstrating that our needs, aspirations and feelings do not matter and are not worthy of having a hearing."[48] Allison P. Davis writes satirically that "Macklemore is all of my woke ex-boyfriends," such as "my super-woke white summer-camp ex-boyfriend whose last name was also Davis, who told me, 'You know, I know my family owned slaves, and I want to apologize.'"[49] And Kyra Gaunt reminds readers that "the mainstream media surge" surrounding Miley Cyrus's twerking "didn't include any references to the origins of twerking or its association with cis- and trans-gender bounce queens from New Orleans."[50] These critics provide crucial perspectives often absent from or marginalized within mainstream media and academia during the 1960s.

Today, the conversation around "woke" white musicians is no longer as utopian as during the 1960s, but rather levelheaded and pragmatic, fore-grounding critiques of inequality and misrepresentation. White musicians continue to benefit from systemic racism that amplifies their voices over those of others. Yet many white musicians today also continue to grapple with their own role in African American political struggles as well as the opportunities and responsibilities created by Black music. Is it better for white artists to speak up and risk turning the conversation to their own confusion rather than Black Americans' exclusion? Or is it better to stay silent at the risk of remaining complicit in ongoing injustice? These difficult questions demand a search for answers regardless of how elusive those answers may be.

In this book's introduction, I suggested that the white musicians discussed here promoted a prefigurative politics. In embracing Black music and engaging with Black politics, white radicals of the 1960s sought to invent and model an interracial solidarity largely absent from the world around them. But what did 1960s rock actually prefigure? White musicians and audiences continue to take all they want from Black culture while showing up only rarely for Black lives. Although white rock musicians' earnest attempts at performing Black music during the 1960s did not solve this problem, these musicians insisted that Black culture and Black lives are connected and believed that performance of Black music carried a moral responsibility. Michael Denning argues in another context that recordings of popular music "were not utopian in the classic sense; they rarely projected a perfected world . . . rather the records often prefigured the contradiction to come."[51] As white musicians and activists attempt to find ethical, respectful approaches to racial politics in our current "age of contradiction," efforts made during the 1960s can provide both inspiration and a sense of perspective. Or, as the MC5's Wayne Kramer puts it, "we lost the revolution . . . but I can't look at it as a failure."[52]

Acknowledgments

Many wonderful people helped and inspired me in countless ways during the years that it took me to write this book. I'll do my best here to thank everyone, and I apologize to anyone I've left out.

My research was made possible by the expert guidance of librarians and archivists. These include Valerie Love, Betsy Pittman, and Melissa Watterworth Batt at the Thomas J. Dodd Research Center, University of Connecticut; Malgosia Myc at the Bentley Historical Library, University of Michigan; and Andy Leach at the Rock and Roll Hall of Fame Library and Archives. I also thank the librarians and staff at the New York Public Library's Schomburg Center for Research in Black Culture and Library for the Performing Arts as well as those at New York University's Fales Library. And above all I thank Brad Short, Paul Hahn, Karen Olson, Mark Scharff, and others at Washington University's Gaylord Music Library as well as Ted Chaffin at Olin.

At Washington University in St. Louis, I benefited from the support of Department of Music chairs Todd Decker, Dolores Pesce, and Peter Schmelz and gifted administrators Kathy Carmody, Kim Daniels, Jessica Flannigan, Jen Gartley, and Pat Orf. Graduate research assistants Kelsey Klotz and Sarah Luehrs brought order (temporarily) to the chaotic piles of paper on my desk. Paige McGinley, with whom I co-directed the Race and Popular Music initiative within Wash U's American Culture Studies program, deserves special thanks for her encouragement and insights. I also thank the other members of the Voice and Sexuality Working Group—Cynthia Barounis, Anna Bialek, Denise Gill, Dana Logan, Jasmine Mahmoud, Paige McGinley, Amber Musser, and Rhaisa Williams—for thoughtful and incisive comments on an earlier version of chapter 2.

Beyond Wash U, I have been granted many valuable opportunities to share my work with colleagues. These opportunities included invited lectures at Berklee College of Music, Saint Louis University, the University of Illinois, the University of Oslo, and the University of Wisconsin–Madison, as well as presentations and panels at the conferences of the American Musicological Society, the International Association for the Study of Popular Music–US, Music and the Moving Image (NYU–Steinhardt), the Performa Conference on Performance Studies (University of Aveiro, Portugal), the Society for American Music, the Society for Ethnomusicology, and the Revisiting the Summer of Love conference hosted in San Francisco by Northwestern University.

Less formally, I've had the good fortune to discuss my work with convivial and generous colleagues, mentors, and friends, including Saher Alam, Christina Baade, Andrea Bohlman, Daphne Brooks, J. Dillon Brown, Kevin (J.) Burke, Jerome Camal, Eric Drott, Tom Duckworth, Gerald Early, Luis-Manuel Garcia, Maya Gibson, Claire Gilbert, K. Goldschmitt, Katie Graber, Ben Harbert, Katie Kinney, Stephanie Kirk, Marshall Klimasewiski, Michael J. Kramer, Maureen Mahon, Wayne Marshall, Bill Maxwell, Jeffrey McCune, Edward McPherson, Karl Hagstrom Miller, Ingrid Monson, Fabien Montcher, Ron Radano, Guy Ramsey, Griff Rollefson, Tim Rommen, Ruth Rosenberg, Jessica Rosenfeld, Sherry Smith, Gabriel Solis, Chris Stark, Alex Stefaniak, Paul Steinbeck, Matt Sumera, John Turci-Escobar, Steve Waksman, Gayle Wald, and Rafia Zafar. If you like this book, they deserve much of the credit for helping shape my thoughts and gently correct my misconceptions. (If you don't like it, it's not their fault.) During 2013–2014, I worked on the book as a guest scholar in the Department of Musicology at the University of Oslo, where I thank Anne Danielsen especially for her hospitality.

Wayne Kramer, Ed Sanders, and Leni Sinclair graciously took the time to answer my questions about their experiences. Photographers Nathan Farb, Amalie R. Rothschild, and Leni Sinclair contributed beautiful and evocative illustrations. I also thank Raquel Scherr and Gar Smith of the Berkeley Barb Project and Peter Werbe and Robby Barnes of *Fifth Estate* for providing images from these important underground papers.

At Chicago, I have been supported by a remarkable group of editors. The late Doug Mitchell, who initially brought the book under contract, was endlessly enthusiastic and encouraging. Elizabeth Branch Dyson and Mollie McFee guided the manuscript toward publication with great skill, insight, and care, and it's been a pleasure to work with both of them. I also thank production editor Caterina MacLean and copyeditor Marianne Tatom for their meticulous and thoughtful work.

Finally, I thank my family. My parents, Frank and Diane Burke, introduced me to 1960s rock music and have unfailingly supported my aspirations. I dedicate this book to them. My sister Amy and the Henderson clan, Kevin, Walter, and Teddy, as well as my in-laws Gary, Martin, Kelly, Lila, Kali, and the late Sandra Haug, provided a necessary sense of perspective and fun. Most of all, I thank Flannery, who took time from her brilliant scholarly career to read innumerable drafts and provide innumerable pep talks, and Kevin, who as I worked somehow transformed from an inquisitive preschooler into a kind, funny teenager and reliable late-night movie companion. You two are my favorite and best.

✶

My research and writing were funded by generous grants, including a Sigmund Strochlitz Travel Grant, Thomas J. Dodd Research Center, University of Connecticut; a Rock and Roll Hall of Fame Library and Archives Research Fellowship, Center for Popular Music Research, Case Western Reserve University; and a National Endowment for the Humanities Fellowship. (Any views, findings, conclusions, or recommendations expressed in this book do not necessarily reflect those of the National Endowment for the Humanities.)

The introduction and chapter 2 incorporate material first published in "Tear Down the Walls: Jefferson Airplane, Race, and Revolutionary Rhetoric in 1960s Rock," *Popular Music* 29, no. 1 (January 2010): 61–79. Chapters 1 and 3 include elements of "Rock, Race, and Radicalism in the 1960s: The Rolling Stones, Black Power, and Godard's *One Plus One*," *Journal of Musicological Research* 29, no. 4 (Fall 2010): 275–94. Chapter 4 draws on "The Fugs, the Lower East Side, and the Slum Aesthetic in 1960s Rock," *Journal of the Society for American Music* 8, no. 4 (November 2014): 538–66.

Notes

Introduction

1. Amiri Baraka [LeRoi Jones], "The Changing Same (R&B and New Black Music)" (1966), in Baraka, *Black Music* (New York: William Morrow, 1967), 187.

2. Albert Goldman, "Why Do Whites Sing Black?," *New York Times*, December 14, 1969.

3. Introduction to MC5, *Kick Out the Jams* (Elektra EKS 74042, 1969, recorded October 30–31, 1968).

4. Jefferson Airplane, "We Can Be Together," *Volunteers* (RCA Victor LSP-4238, 1969).

5. Frederick Douglass, "The Hutchinson Family—Hunkerism," *The North Star* (October 27, 1848); also see Douglass, "Gavitt's Original Ethiopian Serenaders," *The North Star* (June 29, 1849); Brittney Cooper, "Iggy Azalea's Post-Racial Mess: America's Oldest Race Tale, Remixed," *Salon* (July 16, 2014), https://www.salon.com/2014/07/15/iggy_azaleas_post_racial_mess_americas _oldest_race_tale_remixed/, accessed March 17, 2019.

6. Baraka, "Changing Same," 183.

7. Baraka, "Changing Same," 184.

8. Baraka, "Changing Same," 186–87.

9. Baraka, "Changing Same," 205.

10. Baraka, "Changing Same," 207, 185. Joel Rudinow labels the two complementary aspects of Baraka's position summarized here the "Experiential Access Argument" and the "Proprietary Argument" (Rudinow, "Race, Ethnicity, Expressive Authenticity: Can White People Sing the Blues?," *Journal of Aesthetics and Art Criticism* 52, no. 1 [winter 1994]: 129). Black social critic Harold Cruse, addressing Baraka's work in 1967, asserted that "Afro-American folk music became the aesthetic ingredient, the cultural material, the wealth exploited by white American cultural imperialism" (Cruse, *The Crisis of the Negro Intellectual* [New York: William Morrow, 1967], 108); see also Cruse, *Rebellion or Revolution?* (New York: William Morrow, 1968), 119. For similar arguments by a white critic, see Ralph Gleason, "Can the White Man Sing the Blues?," *Jazz & Pop* 7, no. 8 (August 1968): 28–29.

11. Goldman's contradictory language here reveals the ambiguities of racial impersonation: if Joplin is "creole," racial hybridity is essential to her identity, but if she is a blackface minstrel, she can presumably remove her mask at will.

12. As historian Jack Hamilton argues, for Goldman "white access to soul music had

emancipatory potential, and the white practice of 'singing black' held a moral-even spiritual-component. Black music, in this telling, was the path to white racial transcendence and redemption" (Hamilton, *Just around Midnight: Rock and Roll and the Racial Imagination* [Cambridge, MA: Harvard University Press, 2016], 181).

13. Goldman, "Why Do Whites Sing Black?"

14. Hamilton, *Just around Midnight*, 220. Hamilton is discussing a 1968 essay by critic Richard Goldstein. On Joplin, also see Hamilton, *Just around Midnight*, 191.

15. Ingrid Monson, "Fitting the Part," in *Big Ears: Listening for Gender in Jazz Studies*, ed. Nichole T. Rustin and Sherrie Tucker (Durham, NC: Duke University Press, 2008), 269.

16. For a popular account of the year's events, see Mark Kurlansky, *1968: The Year That Rocked the World* (New York: Ballantine, 2004).

17. Dominick Cavallo, *A Fiction of the Past: The Sixties in American History* (New York: St. Martin's, 1999), 186–88.

18. Robert Christgau, *Going into the City: Portrait of a Critic as a Young Man* (New York: Dey St., 2015), 175.

19. Christgau, *Going into the City*, 176.

20. Christgau, *Going into the City*, 176; Charles Perry, *The Haight-Ashbury: A History* (New York: Wenner, 2005), 254; Terry H. Anderson, *The Movement and the Sixties* (New York: Oxford University Press, 1995), 253.

21. Anderson, *Movement and the Sixties*, 241.

22. Anderson, *Movement and the Sixties*, 217–19.

23. Perry, *Haight-Ashbury*, 133, 241; Nadya Zimmerman, *Counterculture Kaleidoscope: Musical and Cultural Perspectives on Late Sixties San Francisco* (Ann Arbor: University of Michigan Press, 2008), 26–30.

24. Parke G. Burgess, "The Rhetoric of Black Power: A Moral Demand?," *Quarterly Journal of Speech* 54, no. 2 (April 1968): 133.

25. Doug Rossinow, *The Politics of Authenticity: Liberalism, Christianity, and the New Left in America* (New York: Columbia University Press, 1998), 259.

26. Take, for example, Hoffman's slogan for the radical Diggers group, "Diggersareniggers" (Free [Abbie Hoffman], *Revolution for the Hell of It* [New York: Dial, 1968], 28).

27. Zimmerman, *Counterculture Kaleidoscope*, 33.

28. Christgau, *Going into the City*, 184.

29. William L. Van Deburg, *New Day in Babylon: The Black Power Movement and American Culture* (Chicago: University of Chicago Press, 1992), 46.

30. Peniel E. Joseph, *Waiting 'til the Midnight Hour: A Narrative History of Black Power in America* (New York: Henry Holt, 2006), 219.

31. Joseph, *Waiting 'til the Midnight Hour*, 221, 236, 240.

32. Cruse, *Crisis of the Negro Intellectual*, 370.

33. Amy Abugo Ongiri, *Spectacular Blackness: The Cultural Politics of the Black Power Movement and the Search for a Black Aesthetic* (Charlottesville: University of Virginia Press, 2010), 62.

34. Ongiri, *Spectacular Blackness*, 69.

35. Ongiri, *Spectacular Blackness*, 72.

36. Elaine Brown, *A Taste of Power: A Black Woman's Story* (New York: Anchor, 1994), 209–10.

37. On the "rock revolution," see Patrick Burke, "Tear Down the Walls: Jefferson Airplane, Race, and Revolutionary Rhetoric in 1960s Rock," *Popular Music* 29, no. 1 (January 2010): 63–66.

38. Peter Doggett, *There's a Riot Going On: Revolutionaries, Rock Stars, and the Rise and Fall of the '60s* (Edinburgh: Canongate, 2007), 4.

39. Howard Brick, *Age of Contradiction: American Thought and Culture in the 1960s* (New York: Twayne, 1998), 114.

40. Hamilton, *Just around Midnight*, 85.

41. Gleason, "Can the White Man Sing the Blues?"

42. John J. Sheinbaum, "'Think about What You're Trying to Do to Me': Rock Historiography and the Construction of a Raced-Based Dialectic," in *Rock over the Edge: Transformations in Popular Music Culture*, ed. Roger Beebe, Denise Fulbrook, and Ben Saunders (Durham, NC: Duke University Press, 2002), 111.

43. Sheinbaum, "'Think about What You're Trying to Do to Me,'" 111.

44. Nelson George, *The Death of Rhythm and Blues* (New York: Plume, 1988), 92.

45. Brian Ward, *Just My Soul Responding: Rhythm and Blues, Black Consciousness, and Race Relations* (Berkeley: University of California Press, 1998), 299, 413–15; Pat Thomas, *Listen, Whitey! The Sights and Sounds of Black Power 1965–1975* (Seattle: Fantagraphics, 2012), 85–87; Brown, *Taste of Power*, 195–200; Rickey Vincent, *Party Music: The Inside Story of the Black Panthers' Band and How Black Power Transformed Soul Music* (Chicago: Lawrence Hill, 2013).

46. E. Patrick Johnson, *Appropriating Blackness: Performance and the Politics of Authenticity* (Durham, NC: Duke University Press, 2003), 227.

47. Hilary Moore, *Inside British Jazz: Crossing Borders of Race, Nation and Class* (Aldershot: Ashgate, 2007), 56.

48. Hamilton, *Just around Midnight*, 4.

49. On Black rock musicians, see Maureen Mahon, *Right to Rock: The Black Rock Coalition and the Cultural Politics of Race* (Durham, NC: Duke University Press, 2004); *Rip It Up: The Black Experience in Rock 'n' Roll*, ed. Kandia Crazy Horse (New York: Palgrave Macmillan, 2004).

50. Eric Lott, *Love and Theft: Blackface Minstrelsy and the American Working Class* (New York: Oxford, 1993).

51. Josh Kun, *Audiotopia: Music, Race, and America* (Berkeley: University of California Press, 2005), 17, 21.

52. Kun, *Audiotopia*, 23, 56.

53. My self-reflection here is inspired by Guthrie P. Ramsey Jr.'s call for white scholars of Black music to defamiliarize what he calls the "invisible white critical 'I'" by openly considering their own positions and motivations (Ramsey Jr., "Who Hears Here? Black Music, Critical Bias, and the Musicological Skin Trade," *Musical Quarterly* 85, no. 1 [spring 2001]: 40).

54. Ronald M. Radano, *Lying Up a Nation: Race and Black Music* (Chicago: University of Chicago Press, 2003), 3.

55. Radano, *Lying Up a Nation*, 113.

56. Radano, *Lying Up a Nation*, 276.

57. Ronald Radano, "On Ownership and Value," *Black Music Research Journal* 30, no. 2 (fall 2010): 367.

58. Radano, "On Ownership and Value," 369.

59. Hamilton, *Just around Midnight*, 7.

60. Guthrie P. Ramsey Jr., *Race Music: Black Cultures from Bebop to Hip-Hop* (Berkeley: University of California Press, 2004), 36.

61. Ramsey, *Race Music*, 38.

62. Ingrid Monson, *Freedom Sounds: Civil Rights Call Out to Jazz and Africa* (Oxford: Oxford University Press, 2007), 105.

63. Ingrid Monson, "On Ownership and Value: Response," *Black Music Research Journal* 30, no. 2 (fall 2010): 376. Greg Tate argues that "the same market forces that provided Caucasian imitators maximum access to American audiences through the most lucrative radio, concert, and recording contracts of the day also fed out whatever crumbs Black artists could hope for in the segregated American entertainment business" (Tate, "Nigs R Us, or How Blackfolk Became Fetish Objects," in *Everything but the Burden: What White People Are Taking from Black Culture*, ed. Greg Tate [New York: Broadway, 2003], 3). Hamilton, while skeptical of racial essentialism, writes similarly that "arguments for a defining, essential power in African American music have long been a powerful way of guarding said music against a white dominant culture that has repeatedly pillaged it, as well as a way of celebrating a cultural tradition whose legitimacy white America has long degraded, or simply denied" (Hamilton, *Just around Midnight*, 173).

64. Monson, *Freedom Sounds*, 105.

65. Monson, "On Ownership and Value: Response," 376–77.

66. Monson, "On Ownership and Value: Response," 377.

67. Radano, *Lying Up a Nation*, 10, 59; also see Samuel A. Floyd Jr. and Ronald Radano, "Interpreting the African-American Music Past: A Dialogue," *Black Music Research Journal* 29, no. 1 (spring 2009): 1–10.

68. Monson, *Freedom Sounds*, 251.

69. Tate, "Nigs R Us," 10.

70. Paul Gilroy, "Sounds Authentic: Black Music, Ethnicity, and the Challenge of a *Changing Same*," *Black Music Research Journal* 11, no. 2 (Autumn 1991): 124.

71. D. Soyini Madison, "Performance, Personal Narratives, and the Politics of Possibility," in *The Future of Performance Studies: Visions and Revisions*, ed. Sheron J. Dailey (Annandale, VA: National Communication Association, 1998), 276–77, 284; see also Johnson, *Appropriating Blackness*, 208–18.

72. As John Leland puts it, "hip can be a self-serving release from white liberal guilt, offering cultural reparations in place of the more substantive kind. This is white supremacy posing as appreciation" (Leland, *Hip: the History* [New York: Ecco, 2004], 6). On colorblindness, also see Monson, *Freedom Sounds*, 78–80.

73. Or, as Greg Tate reports, "African-American performance artist Roger Guenveur Smith once posed the question: Why does everyone love Black music but nobody loves Black people?" (Tate, "Nigs R Us," 4–5).

74. As Michael Rogin, in his influential work on blackface in film, asks, "if black-inflected white performance is to be proscribed, what is to be done with the white investment in black artists (the double meaning of investment, tying money to love, only hints at the problem), who themselves vary widely in the influences they felt and in their relations to white promoters and audiences?" (Rogin, *Blackface, White Noise: Jewish Immigrants in the Hollywood Melting Pot* [Berkeley: University of California Press, 1996], 67).

75. Johnson, *Appropriating Blackness*, 3.

76. Hamilton, *Just around Midnight*, 23.

77. Charles Perry, "The Sound of San Francisco," in *The Rolling Stone Illustrated History of Rock and Roll*, ed. Anthony DeCurtis and James Henke with Holly George-Warren (New York: Random House, 1992), 364; Geoffrey Stokes, "The Sixties," in Ed Ward, Geoffrey Stokes, and Ken Tucker, *Rock of Ages: The Rolling Stone History of Rock and Roll* (Englewood Cliffs, NJ: Rolling

Stone, 1986), 333; also see Philip J. Deloria, *Playing Indian* (New Haven, CT: Yale University Press, 1998), 154–80. Sherry L. Smith argues that Indians of All Tribes' occupation of Alcatraz, which began in November 1969, inspired many non-Indians, including the counterculture, "to turn their romantic, inadequate, and flawed ideas about Indians into tangible and significant support for substantive political change" (Smith, *Hippies, Indians, and the Fight for Red Power* [Oxford: Oxford University Press, 2012], 77).

78. Scott Prinzing argues that Robertson "initially proved himself an important songwriter and guitarist before using that platform to introduce the story of his own heritage" in the 1980s and 1990s (Prinzing, "Brothers of the Blade: Three Native Axmen: Link Wray, Robbie Robertson, and Jesse Ed Davis," in *Indigenous Pop: Native American Music from Jazz to Hip Hop*, ed. Jeff Berglund, Jan Johnson, and Kimberli Lee [Tucson: University of Arizona Press, 2016], 83). The Black quotation is from the Mothers of Invention, *We're Only in It for the Money* (Verve V6-5045X, 1968).

79. Ed Morales, *The Latin Beat: The Rhythms and Roots of Latin Music from Bossa Nova to Salsa and Beyond* (Cambridge, MA: Da Capo, 2003), 291; Roberto Avant-Mier, *Rock the Nation: Latin/o Identities and the Latin Rock Diaspora* (London: Continuum, 2010), 87–109.

80. Monson, *Freedom Sounds*, 276.

81. Jerry Rubin, "An Emergency Letter to My Brothers and Sisters in the Movement," in *BAMN (By Any Means Necessary): Outlaw Manifestos and Ephemera 1965–70*, ed. Peter Stansill and David Zane Mairowitz (Middlesex: Penguin, 1971), 244; Zimmerman, *Countercultural Kaleidoscope*, 35–36; Sue C. Clark, "Wexler: A Man of Dedication," *Rolling Stone* (September 28, 1968): 8, 10; Hamilton, *Just around Midnight*, 191.

82. My claim here recalls Monson's observation that within the 1960s jazz world "white fear of exclusion (by the excluded) [was] quite ironic" (Monson, *Freedom Sounds*, 246).

83. John L. Jackson Jr., *Real Black: Adventures in Racial Sincerity* (Chicago: University of Chicago Press, 2005), 13, 15, 18.

84. Monson, *Freedom Sounds*, 250.

85. Bobby Seale, *Seize the Time: The Story of the Black Panther Party and Huey P. Newton* (New York: Random House, 1970), 181–87.

86. Albert Murray, *The Omni-Americans: New Perspectives on Black Experience and American Culture* (New York: Outerbridge and Dienstfrey, 1970), 101–2.

87. Archie Shepp, "An Artist Speaks Bluntly," *Down Beat* 32, no. 26 (December 16, 1965): 11; also see Amiri Baraka [LeRoi Jones], "New Tenor Archie Shepp Talking" (1965), in Baraka, *Black Music* (New York: William Morrow, 1967), 155.

88. Robert Palmer, liner notes (1978) to Albert Ayler, *Live in Greenwich Village: The Complete Impulse Recordings* (Impulse CD IMPD-2-273), 18.

89. Nat Hentoff, "Archie Shepp: The Way Ahead" (1968), in *Giants of Black Music*, ed. Pauline Rivelli and Robert Levin (New York: Da Capo, 1979), 120.

90. George Lewis, *A Power Stronger Than Itself: The AACM and American Experimental Music* (Chicago: University of Chicago Press, 2008), 197; Steven L. Isoardi, *The Dark Tree: Jazz and the Community Arts in Los Angeles* (Berkeley: University of California Press, 2006), 96.

91. James Brown, *I Feel Good: A Memoir of a Life of Soul* (New York: New American Library, 2005), 156.

92. On Brown's political ambivalence, see Brown, *I Feel Good*, 154–65; James Brown with Bruce Tucker, *James Brown: The Godfather of Soul* (New York: Thunder's Mouth, 2002), 196–200.

93. Vincent, *Party Music*, 41, 208.

94. Carl Boggs, "Marxism, Prefigurative Communism, and the Problem of Workers' Control," *Radical America* 11, no. 6/12, no. 1 (November 1977–February 1978): 100.

95. Boggs, "Marxism," 119.

96. Wini Breines, *Community and Organization in the New Left, 1962–1968: The Great Refusal* (New York: Praeger, 1982), 95.

97. Rossinow, *Politics of Authenticity*, 292.

98. Breines, *Community and Organization*, 45.

99. Stuart Hall, "The Hippies: An American 'Moment'" (1968), in *CCCS Selected Working Papers*, vol. 2, ed. Ann Gray et al. (London: Routledge: 2007), 167; also see Michael J. Kramer, "Stuart Hall's Hippies," February 28, 2015, http://www.michaeljkramer.net/stuart-halls-hippies/, accessed March 29, 2019.

100. Johnson, *Appropriating Blackness*, 6.

Chapter 1

1. "Notes from a Yippizolean Era," *East Village Other* 3, no. 11 (February 16–22, 1968): 8; Jerry Rubin, "The Yippies in Chicago," *Chicago Seed* 2, no. 3 ([March?] 1968): 8; "Paper Radio," *Warren-Forest Sun* 1, no. 5 (March 1–14, 1968): 7. For a thorough account of the Yippies' planning for the convention, see David Farber, *Chicago '68* (Chicago: University of Chicago Press, 1988), 3–55.

2. Abbie Hoffman et al., "The 1968 Election?," *WIN* 4, no. 5 (March 15, 1968): 5.

3. "Walli Yippie" [Walli Leff], letter to John Sinclair, April 3, 1968, folder 30, box 2, John and Leni Sinclair Papers, Bentley Historical Library, University of Michigan [collection cited hereafter as JLSP].

4. John Sinclair, letter to Jann Wenner, May 7, 1968, folder 30, box AF8, Rolling Stone Collection, Library and Archives, Rock and Roll Hall of Fame and Museum [archive cited hereafter as RRHOF]. Despite Sinclair's complaint, Wenner attacked the Yippies days later in a front-page article (Jann Wenner, "Musicians Reject New Political Exploiters: Groups Drop Out from Chicago Yip-In," *Rolling Stone* 1, no. 10 [May 11, 1968]: 1, 22).

5. "Flash! MC5 Set to Kick Off Yippie Festival Chicago Sunday August 25!," *Sun* (Ann Arbor), no. 9 (August 7, 1968): 1.

6. Two Chicago bands, Home Juice and Conqueror Worm, played at a rally at the Coliseum on August 27 (advertisements, *Chicago Seed* 2, no. 12 [(August) 1968]: 10, 16; David Lewis Stein, *Living the Revolution: The Yippies in Chicago* [Indianapolis: Bobbs-Merrill, 1969], 100; Daniel Walker, *Rights in Conflict: The Violent Confrontation of Demonstrators and Police in the Parks and Streets of Chicago during the Week of the Democratic National Convention of 1968* [New York: Signet, 1968], 182). Walker mistakenly refers to the latter band as "Popular Worm."

7. John Sinclair, "Rock and Roll Dope," *Fifth Estate* 3, no. 9 (September 5–18, 1968): 15. On McDonald, see Stein, *Living the Revolution*, 53. Sinclair later claimed that the Up, another Ann Arbor band associated with the White Panthers, had just arrived in Chicago when the MC5, fleeing the park, told them "You gotta go back!" (Legs McNeil and Gillian McCain, *Please Kill Me: The Uncensored Oral History of Punk* [New York: Grove, 1996], 44).

8. McNeil and McCain, *Please Kill Me*, 45.

9. Wayne Kramer, "Riots I Have Known and Loved," *Left of the Dial*, no. 4 (2002), http://makemyday.free.fr/wk1.htm, accessed December 15, 2016.

10. Peter Doggett, *There's a Riot Going On: Revolutionaries, Rock Stars, and the Rise and Fall*

of the '60s (Edinburgh: Canongate, 2007), 140–41. Journalist Richard Goldstein, who helped recruit bands to play in Chicago, remembered in 1982 that "the Jefferson Airplane responded, in full sincerity, by pointing out that their equipment was too heavy to move easily, should the police converge. Other bands were simply bemused by the political process, or considered themselves beyond it" (Michael D. Cary, "The Rise and Fall of the MC5: Rock Music and Counterculture Politics in the Sixties" [DA diss., Lehigh University, 1985], 46).

11. Ochs, a close associate of the Yippies, was arrested with Jerry Rubin for disorderly conduct after he helped deliver Mr. Pigasus, the pig that the Yippies presented as their presidential candidate, to the Chicago Loop (John Schultz, *No One Was Killed: Documentation and Meditation: Convention Week, Chicago, August 1968* [Chicago: Big Table, 1969], 49; Stein, *Living the Revolution,* 47). Ochs sang at the rally at the Coliseum and in Grant Park, where he directed his songs to the National Guard (Farber, *Chicago '68,* 190; Stein, *Living the Revolution,* 101; Don Miller, "Leaders Aren't Needed on Michigan Avenue," in *Telling It Like It Was: The Chicago Riots,* ed. Walter Schneir [New York: Signet, 1969], 146). Peter, Paul, and Mary, in Chicago to support the candidacy of Eugene McCarthy, sang for protesters in Grant Park ("Convention Notes: Hungry Dems Please Cafes," *Chicago Tribune,* August 25, 1968; "Yippies Assemble for Protest March on Amphitheatre," *Chicago Daily News,* August 28, 1968; Farber, *Chicago '68,* 193, 202; Walker, *Rights in Conflict,* 301). According to David Lewis Stein, folk duo Jim and Jean were scheduled to follow the MC5, although the electricity was cut off before they could perform; they later appeared at the Coliseum (Stein, *Living the Revolution,* 72, 100). Firsthand accounts also reveal that amateur music-making—including hand drums, guitars, flutes, group singing of hymns and such songs as *America the Beautiful,* and in one instance the use of ceramic building tiles as percussion instruments—was common during the protests (Schultz, *No One Was Killed,* 81, 139, 148, 199; Stein, *Living the Revolution,* 134; Walker, *Rights in Conflict,* 114–15, 124, 167, 169–70, 189).

12. Farber, *Chicago '68,* 177; Free [Abbie Hoffman], *Revolution for the Hell of It* (New York: Dial, 1968), 124–26; Edward Sanders, *1968: A History in Verse* (Santa Rosa, CA: Black Sparrow, 1997), 184–85; Walker, *Rights in Conflict,* photo section following 148.

13. Ed Sanders, *Shards of God* (New York: Grove, 1970), 119.

14. Kramer, "Riots I Have Known and Loved"; also see Kramer's account in McNeil and McCain, *Please Kill Me,* 43–44. David Farber estimates that there were two thousand people in the park when the MC5 began playing, with "several thousand more" attracted by the music, while the Walker Report estimates a crowd of between three and five thousand (Farber, *Chicago '68,* 177; Walker, *Rights in Conflict,* 120).

15. Mathew J. Bartkowiak, *The MC5 and Social Change: A Study in Rock and Revolution* (Jefferson, NC: McFarland, 2009), 99; also see David A. Carson, *Grit, Noise, and Revolution: The Birth of Detroit Rock 'n' Roll* (Ann Arbor: University of Michigan Press, 2005), 172–73; Brett Callwood, *MC5: Sonically Speaking: A Tale of Revolution and Rock 'n' Roll* (Detroit: Wayne State University Press, 2010), 40–41.

16. McNeil and McCain, *Please Kill Me,* 44.

17. Norman Mailer, *Miami and the Siege of Chicago: An Informal History of the Republican and Democratic Conventions of 1968* (1968; repr., New York: New York Review Books, 2008), 142. Mailer claims that a "folk-rock group" (142) played before the MC5, but other sources do not corroborate this.

18. Mailer, *Miami and the Siege of Chicago,* 142–43. Walker reports that the crowd included "a few blacks, ranging from West and South Side teenagers to older militants from California,"

and photos of the MC5's performance appear to show a few Black listeners (Walker, *Rights in Conflict*, 120, photo section following 148).

19. Marty Jezer, *Abbie Hoffman: American Rebel* (New Brunswick, NJ: Rutgers University Press, 1992), 92.

20. Paul Krassner, "The Yippies Are a Community of Voluntary Niggers," in Schneir, *Telling It Like It Was*, 18.

21. Jezer, *Abbie Hoffman*, 42–70; Jonah Raskin, *For the Hell of It: The Life and Times of Abbie Hoffman* (Berkeley: University of California Press, 1996), 99, 108; "George Metesky" [Abbie Hoffman], "Diggery Is Niggery," *WIN* (September 15, 1967): 8–9.

22. Jezer, *Abbie Hoffman*, 123–24, 154–56; Farber, *Chicago '68*, 167. On the Black Panthers' use of "pig," see Bobby Seale, *Seize the Time: The Story of the Black Panther Party and Huey P. Newton* (New York: Random House, 1970), 404–7.

23. Farber, *Chicago '68*, 51–52. Jerry Rubin, however, had a supportive relationship with Eldridge Cleaver of the Black Panther Party, who asked Rubin to serve as his running mate during his 1968 campaign for president on the Peace and Freedom Party ticket (Farber, *Chicago '68*, 44).

24. Steve Waksman notes that "Rob Tyner had one of the most impressive afros to adorn any public figure in the 1960s and 1970s, especially among whites" (Waksman, *Instruments of Desire: The Electric Guitar and the Shaping of Musical Experience* [Cambridge, MA: Harvard University Press, 1999], 354). Kramer claims that "Rob Tyner was the first white boy with an Afro" (Wayne Kramer, *The Hard Stuff: Dope, Crime, the MC5 and My Life of Impossibilities* [New York: Da Capo, 2018], 61).

25. Both Wayne Kramer and Plamondon himself credit Sinclair's friend Lawrence "Pun" Plamondon with the inspiration for the White Panther Party (Kramer, *Hard Stuff*, 88; Pun Plamondon, *Lost from the Ottawa: The Story of the Journey Back* [Victoria, BC: Trafford, 2004], 117–19). What may be Sinclair's first recorded use of the term "'white panther' party" appears in Lou Cartier, "Hippie, Yippie, Beatnik, Sinclair Still an Enigma," *Ypsilanti Press*, September 26, 1968, clipping in folder "Legal and prison files, Red Squad and police files, MI state police files (2 of 2)," box 46, JLSP. Although, as their name suggests, the White Panther Party's membership was predominantly white, it had at least one Black member, Hiawatha Bailey (Matt Thompson, "Ann Arborite Hiawatha Bailey: Still Rocking," *Ann Arbor Observer* [July 2014], http://annarborobserver.com/articles/ann_arborite_hiawatha_bailey_full_article.html, accessed January 17, 2017). Leni Sinclair recalls that "Hiawatha was a hippie . . . and he really couldn't join the Black Panther Party—they were too militaristic and macho, you know" (Sinclair, interview with the author, March 22, 2019).

26. John Sinclair, "Our Program," *Fifth Estate* 3, no. 14 (November 14–27, 1968): 8.

27. Jeff A. Hale reports that at the time of their move from Detroit to Ann Arbor in May 1968, "the new Trans-Love Energies commune consisted of twenty-eight people, including three children and the MC5 members" (Hale, "The White Panthers' 'Total Assault on the Culture,'" in *Imagine Nation: The American Counterculture of the 1960s and '70s*, ed. Peter Braunstein and Michael William Doyle [New York: Routledge, 2002], 136).

28. MC5, *Kick Out the Jams* (Elektra EKS74042, 1969).

29. Hale, "Total Assault," 148. Sinclair's papers include a copy of a 1970 letter from J. Edgar Hoover to Gerald Ford, then House minority leader, in which he outlines the White Panther Party's activities and reports that "the FBI has this organization and its membership under active investigation" (photocopy of J. Edgar Hoover, letter to Honorable Gerald R. Ford Jr., Septem-

ber 25, 1970, folder "Legal and prison files, FOIA documents, FOIA correspondence, 1975–1977," box 46, JLSP).

30. Neil Nehring, "The Situationist International in American Hardcore Punk, 1982–2002," *Popular Music and Society* 29, no. 5 (December 2006): 528.

31. Hale, "Total Assault," 149–51. With hindsight, the group's former members have made similar arguments; Dennis Thompson, for example, described the band as "a representational model of a group of people who were willing to fight" rather than genuinely violent revolutionaries and suggested that much of their rhetoric was "tongue in cheek" (Bartkowiak, *MC5 and Social Change*, 90; Carson, *Grit, Noise, and Revolution*, 208; also see Callwood, *Sonically Speaking*, 60).

32. Hale, "Total Assault," 142.

33. Waksman, *Instruments of Desire*, 209–10; on the MC5's "machismo," also see Bartkowiak, *MC5 and Social Change*, 50. As Waksman correctly notes, the MC5's "crude notion of sexual liberation was decidedly pre-feminist if not anti-feminist" (209). Kramer later admitted: "we were sexist bastards. . . . We had all the rhetoric of being revolutionary and new and different, but really what it was, was the boys get to go fuck and the girls can't complain about it. And if the girls did complain, they were being bourgeois bitches—counterrevolutionary. Yep, we were really shitty about it" (McNeil and McCain, *Please Kill Me*, 47; also see Michael Davis, *I Brought Down the MC5* [Los Angeles: Cleopatra, 2018], 106–7).

34. Kramer, *Hard Stuff*, 88–89.

35. Waksman, *Instruments of Desire*, 219. Iggy Pop, whose Stooges were the MC5's "little brother band" in Ann Arbor, later pointed out the MC5's macho stereotyping of Black men, recalling that "the MC5 went beyond having a sense of humor about themselves, they were a parody. They just acted like black thugs with guitars" (McNeil and McCain, *Please Kill Me*, 48).

36. Jack Hamilton, *Just around Midnight: Rock and Roll and the Racial Imagination* (Cambridge, MA: Harvard University Press, 2016), 104.

37. Wayne Kramer, interview with the author, March 28, 2019.

38. Dennis Thompson, for example, has asserted that "ideologically speaking, I think we got more information from . . . the jazz music that we studied," while Wayne Kramer explains that "the militancy and anger of the black Free Jazz movement was the same anger we felt" (Bartkowiak, *MC5 and Social Change*, 92).

39. Scott Saul, *Freedom Is, Freedom Ain't: Jazz and the Making of the Sixties* (Cambridge, MA: Harvard University Press, 2003), 293–94; Hale, "Total Assault," 142. Saul argues that "Sinclair may have written more poetic tributes to jazz musicians than any other writer of the mid-1960s" and that "Sinclair was at home claiming the black avant-garde as his own usable tradition" (Saul, *Freedom Is*, 294–95).

40. David A. Carson describes the band's early influences (ca. 1965) as "James Brown, Chuck Berry, and the Rolling Stones, mixed in with some blues and Motown" (Carson, *Grit, Noise, and Revolution*, 102). On the influence of the Stones, the Who, and the Yardbirds, see Bartkowiak, *MC5 and Social Change*, 60; Callwood, *Sonically Speaking*, 22; Michael Simmons and Cletus Nelson, *MC5: The Future Is Now!* (London: Creation, 2004), 17–19; Waksman, *Instruments of Desire*, 210; Davis, *I Brought Down the MC5*, 50–51.

41. Waksman, *Instruments of Desire*, 212.

42. James Smethurst, "'Pat Your Foot and Turn the Corner': Amiri Baraka, the Black Arts Movement, and the Poetics of a Popular Avant-Garde," *African American Review* 37, nos. 2–3 (2003): 268–69.

43. Ingrid Monson, *Freedom Sounds: Civil Rights Call Out to Jazz and Africa* (Oxford: Oxford University Press, 2007), 263.

44. "SINCLAIR Jr., John Alexander," Personal File, ID No 244886, Detroit Police Department, folder "Legal and prison files, Red Squad and police files, Detroit police files, primarily 1966–1970," box 46, JLSP.

45. John Sinclair, "The Coatpuller," *Fifth Estate* 1, no. 15 (October 1–15, 1966): 2.

46. Franklin Bach, "Bach on Rock," *Fifth Estate* 1, no. 16 (October 16–31, 1966): 12. The extent to which the MC5's interest in jazz preceded their acquaintance with Sinclair is a matter of debate. Tyner's claim is supported by his name, which he had already changed from Bob Derminer in tribute to pianist McCoy Tyner of the Coltrane quartet, and Kramer claims that Tyner was interested in jazz and blues as early as 1963 (Carson, *Grit, Noise, and Revolution*, 99; Smethurst, "Pat Your Foot and Turn the Corner," 268; Kramer, *Hard Stuff*, 40, 60). In a 1969 interview, Wayne Kramer stated that the band was listening to Coltrane and Sun Ra before meeting Sinclair (Jonathan Kundra, "MC5," *Circus* 4, no. 11 [September 1969]: 37, 61). During the same year, however, Fred Smith told an interviewer that "we didn't get into listening to jazz until we met John (Sinclair) just a couple of years ago," and years later Dennis Thompson recalled that "when we were introduced to John Sinclair's Free Jazz collection—boom. We'd hit the motherlode: dynamics, propulsion, players who listened to each other" (David Walley, "MC5," *Jazz and Pop*, no. 9 [July 1969]: 16; Nick Hasted, "Search and Destroy," *Uncut*, no. 96 [May 2005]: 83). In his autobiography, Kramer remembers that it was at Sinclair's home that he "first heard the wondrous sounds of Sun Ra, Albert Ayler, Archie Shepp, and so many others" (Kramer, *Hard Stuff*, 75). In an interview with the author, Kramer confirmed this, although he explained that he was aware of modern jazz guitarists such as Jim Hall, Barney Kessel, and Mundell Lowe before meeting Sinclair (Kramer, interview with the author, March 28, 2019). Brett Callwood is likely correct in claiming that although Sinclair did not introduce the band to jazz, he "fueled their nascent interest considerably" (Callwood, *Sonically Speaking*, 27).

47. John Sinclair, "The Coatpuller," *Fifth Estate* 1, no. 17 (November 1–15, 1966): 2. As Steve Waksman points out, "energy," a term that Sinclair emphasizes, "was the keyword within the Five's program—an energy born from sound, and energy that reorganized the senses." Waksman argues that the MC5's notion of energy was both embodied and technological, "represent[ing] the ways in which sound acts upon the body, or more precisely, the ways in which sound and body act upon each other, and the process through which the sensual experience of a single individual and a single body might be communicated to other individuals and other bodies" (Waksman, *Instruments of Desire*, 229–30). In 1969, Kramer explained that "we met John Sinclair, and he helped us to the whole concept of energy which is essentially, man, if you take everything in the universe, take everything that the mind can conceive of, anything, everything, and break it down, you can only go so far as energy.... In other words, energy is freedom. Energy is real, as opposed to a fantasy that exists only in somebody's head" (Walley, "MC5," 15).

48. John Sinclair, "Interview: Rob Tyner Lead Singer MC5," *Sun* (Detroit), no. 3 [May 1967]: 7. Wayne Kramer equates the music of Chuck Berry with that of Albert Ayler and Pharoah Sanders in an interview with Denise Sullivan (Sullivan, *Keep on Pushing: Black Power Music from Blues to Hip-Hop* [Chicago: Lawrence Hill, 2011], 63).

49. John Sinclair, "Rock and Roll Dope," *Fifth Estate* 3, no. 3 (June 4–18, 1968): 15. Sinclair's first list, which includes names normally associated with jazz, comprises Black musicians, while his second, with the exception of Hendrix, includes only white musicians. Don McLeese points out that "ironically for an era that prided itself on such progressivism, black music wasn't con-

sidered rock, with rare, 'superspade' exceptions such as Jimi Hendrix and Sly and the Family Stone" (McLeese, *Kick Out the Jams* [New York: Continuum, 2005], 16). Sinclair seems to be simultaneously reinforcing and undermining this viewpoint.

50. Joseph Jarman and the MC5 were among the acts at the "Blow Your Mind" concert/ dance at Cranbrook School on April 28, 1967 (John Sinclair, "The Coatpuller," *Fifth Estate* 2, no. 2 [April 15–30, 1967]: 2). Sun Ra and the MC5 shared a bill at Wayne State University on June 18, 1967, and again at the Grande Ballroom on May 16–18, 1969; both were also featured at the Detroit Rock and Roll Revival at the Michigan State Fairgrounds on May 30–31, 1969 (John Sinclair, "The Coatpuller," *Fifth Estate* 2, no. 6 [June 15–30, 1967]: 2; advertisement, *Fifth Estate* 2, no. 6 [June 15–30, 1967]: 7; advertisement, *Fifth Estate* 4, no. 1 [May 15–28, 1969]: 10; Dave Sinclair, "Sun Ra," *Fifth Estate* 4, no. 1 [May 15–28, 1969]: 17; Ken Dabish, "Sun Ra," *Warren-Forest Sun* 1, no. 6 [May 28, 1969]: 12; advertisement, *Ann Arbor Argus* 1, no. 7 [May 24–June 9, 1969]: 18; Carson, *Grit, Noise, and Revolution*, 206; John F. Szwed, *Space Is the Place: The Life and Times of Sun Ra* [New York: Pantheon, 1997], 245, 275).

51. This film's source has been variously identified in secondary sources, but a clip available on YouTube begins with a handheld sign reading "DASPO CONUS," an acronym for "Department of the Army Special Photographic Office, Continental United States" ("MC5 DNC Chicago 1968," www.youtube.com/watch?v=C5sA6a0g31U, accessed May 18, 2016). Interviewed during the 1990s, Kramer suggested (but not confidently) that the band played "Starship" and perhaps "The Human Being Lawnmower" (McNeil and McCain, *Please Kill Me*, 43). In an interview with the author, Kramer also remembered playing "Starship" and suggested that the set probably comprised songs from *Kick Out the Jams* as well as a few "hip covers that not everybody was doing" (Wayne Kramer, interview with the author, March 28, 2019). Sources are also unclear on the length of the band's set. Abbie Hoffman claimed that "MC5 from Detroit played fantastic music for over an hour," while Dennis Thompson remembered that they "played about five or six songs" and Kramer believes it was a "forty- or fifty-minute set" (Hoffman, *Revolution for the Hell of It*, 124; McNeil and McCain, *Please Kill Me*, 44; Kramer, interview with the author, March 28, 2019).

52. Waksman, *Instruments of Desire*, 219.

53. "Programme for 'An Evening Recital of New Music' as Performed by Detroit's Own MC5 at the Grande Ballroom," May 10–11, 1968. This program is included in the Bell and Howell Underground Press Collection microfilm edition of the *Ann Arbor Sun* and reprinted in Eric Ehrmann, "MC5," *Rolling Stone*, no. 25 (January 4, 1969): 16–17. An undated press release confirms that "Slow Down" was Larry Williams's 1958 rock and roll classic, which had been covered by the Beatles in 1964 ("MC5," undated press release, Series I: Artist Files—MC5, Box AF8, folder 30, RRHOF). Wayne Kramer recalls that other R&B songs that the MC5 covered included "The Nitty Gritty" by Shirley Ellis, "Wang Dang Doodle" by Willie Dixon, and "Reach Out I'll Be There" and "Bernadette" by the Four Tops (Kramer, interview with the author, March 28, 2019). Although the Four Tops were Motown artists, Motown is conspicuous in its absence from the Grande Ballroom setlist, which is notable given that the MC5 were from Detroit. Stuart Cosgrove reports that Sinclair objected to what he saw as the label's exploitation of its musicians (Cosgrove, *Detroit 67: The Year That Changed Soul* [n.p.: Stuart Cosgrove, 2015]). Both Kramer and Davis, however, later cited Motown studio musicians such as bassists James Jamerson and Bob Babbitt as important influences (Davis, *I Brought Down the MC5*, 108; Kramer, *Hard Stuff*, 55; Sullivan, *Keep on Pushing*, 88). Clinton Heylin notes that soul and jazz covers played a less central role on the *Kick Out the Jams* album than in most of the MC5's live performances, "as if

the MC5 were unsure about the likely reception for songs overtly reflecting their rock/free-jazz fusion" (Heylin, *From the Velvets to the Voidoids: The Birth of American Punk Rock* [Chicago: Chicago Review Press, 2005], 35).

54. The bootleg is issued officially as *Starship: The MC5 Live at the Sturgis Armory June 27 1968* (Total Energy CD NER3018, 2002).

55. A. Freek, "MC5 'Live' at the Grande," *Fifth Estate* 3, no. 14 (November 14–27, 1968): 14. Only the latter two songs appear on the album.

56. Waksman, *Instruments of Desire*, 219.

57. Lillian Roxon, "Rock Frenzy Points a Way," *Sydney Morning Herald* (January 4, 1969).

58. In a 1970 concert review, *Billboard* described "guitarist Wayne Kramer, using the slide-step popularized by James Brown to move around the stage" ("Chicago's First Rock Fest Called Success; '71 Plans," *Billboard* 82, no. 32 [August 8, 1970]: 24). In 1992, Kramer told Fred Goodman that "our show was based on the dynamic of James's show" (Goodman, *The Mansion on the Hill: Dylan, Young, Geffen, Springsteen, and the Head-On Collision of Rock and Commerce* [New York: Times Books, 1997], 157). And in 2006, Kramer explained that "my idols of course are James Brown and Jackie Wilson and Tina Turner . . . people who really knew how to move on stage" (Bartkowiak, *MC5 and Social Change*, 127). Also see Kramer, *Hard Stuff*, 43–44.

59. Richard Goldstein, "Pop Eye," *Village Voice* (November 14, 1968).

60. Bob Rudnick and Dennis Frawley, "Kokaine Karma," *East Village Other* 4, no. 24 (May 14, 1969): 9.

61. Davis, *I Brought Down the MC5*, 85. Davis claims that Fred Smith, in contrast, "didn't want to be either black or white. His style was unique, something you just couldn't place. He gravitated toward all things hillbilly, but it was never obvious in anything he did" (85).

62. Eric Lott, *Love and Theft: Blackface Minstrelsy and the American Working Class* (New York: Oxford University Press, 1993), 84.

63. Lott, *Love and Theft*, 234.

64. Lott, *Love and Theft*, 148–50; also see Robert Cantwell, *When We Were Good: The Folk Revival* (Cambridge, MA: Harvard University Press, 1996), 57–59.

65. While the same might be said of the "Zip Coon" character popular in minstrelsy, "the very process of burlesquing this urban hustler entailed portraying him as an imposter. . . . He was, finally, only Sambo in the nineteenth-century version of a zoot suit" (Mel Watkins, *On the Real Side: Laughing, Lying, and Signifying—The Underground Tradition of African-American Humor that Transformed American Culture, from Slavery to Richard Pryor* [New York: Touchstone, 1994], 458).

66. Norman Mailer, *The White Negro* (San Francisco: City Lights Books, 1959), 5, 15. The essay originally appeared in the journal *Dissent* in 1957.

67. Mailer, *The White Negro*, 15, 22.

68. Ingrid Monson, "The Problem with White Hipness: Race, Gender, and Cultural Conceptions in Jazz Historical Discourse," *Journal of the American Musicological Society* 48, no. 3 (Fall 1995): 398.

69. Phil Ford, *Dig: Sound and Music in Hip Culture* (New York: Oxford University Press, 2013), 54. Elsewhere, Ford writes that "'The White Negro' . . . suggested that black men are criminals, psychopaths, and sex gangsters, and differed from a White Citizens' Council tract in supposing this to be a good thing" (Ford, *Dig*, 162).

70. Lott, *Love and Theft*, 6.

71. David R. Roediger, *The Wages of Whiteness: Race and the Making of the American Working Class* (London: Verso, 1991), 109, 118.

72. Mailer, *White Negro*, 8.

73. Monson, "Problem with White Hipness," 398.

74. An exception is David Roediger, who argues that "blackface performances tended to support proslavery and white supremacist politics" (Roediger, *Wages of Whiteness*, 124).

75. W. T. Lhamon Jr., *Raising Cain: Blackface Performance from Jim Crow to Hip Hop* (Cambridge, MA: Harvard University Press, 1998), 42; Lott, *Love and Theft*, 66.

76. Michael Rogin, *Blackface, White Noise: Jewish Immigrants in the Hollywood Melting Pot* (Berkeley: University of California Press 1996), 38.

77. Mailer, *White Negro*, 15.

78. John Leland, *Hip: The History* (New York: Ecco, 2004), 9.

79. Jack Hamilton points out that the "transhistoricism" of "the minstrelsy metaphor . . . leaves little room for *differences* between appropriations and exclusions, and it fails to reckon with the ever-changing character of both racial thought and expressive culture itself" (Hamilton, *Just around Midnight*, 10).

80. Ford, *Dig*, 115, 134.

81. Roediger, *Wages of Whiteness*, 119.

82. Constance Rourke, *American Humor: A Study of the National Character* (1931; repr., New York: New York Review Books, 2004), 100. Gayle Wald similarly describes Mezz Mezzrow's 1946 autobiography *Really the Blues*, which details the Jewish clarinetist's attempts to become Black, as a "deliberately and self-consciously self-mythologizing text," albeit one lacking "an inherently politically disruptive or subversive agency" (Wald, *Crossing the Line: Racial Passing in Twentieth-Century U.S. Literature and Culture* [Durham, NC: Duke University Press, 2000], 57, 60). Robert Cantwell argues that "the result" of blackface performance "is the audience's heightened self-consciousness about its own standing" (Cantwell, *When We Were Good*, 58).

83. John J. Sheinbaum, "'Think about What You're Trying to Do to Me': Rock Historiography and the Construction of a Raced-Based Dialectic," in *Rock over the Edge: Transformations in Popular Music Culture*, ed. Roger Beebe, Denise Fulbrook, and Ben Saunders (Durham, NC: Duke University Press, 2002), 111.

84. Abe Peck, *Uncovering the Sixties: The Life and Times of the Underground Press* (New York: Pantheon, 1985), 173.

85. Miller Francis Jr., "MC-5," *Great Speckled Bird* 2, no. 1 (March 17, 1969): 14.

86. John Lombardi, "MC-5," *Distant Drummer* (May 15, 1969): 10. Wayne Kramer explains that Crawford's introduction "was a great piece of performance poetry, combining elements of Danny Ray's great intro for James Brown, brother Dave Gardner's southern-fried stream-of-consciousness humor, White Panther militancy, and a dash of sanctified gospel revival meeting" (Kramer, *Hard Stuff*, 92; also see Davis, *I Brought Down the MC5*, 101). Crawford's political rhetoric mimicked that of Black Power activists, while his more philosophical musings, often linked to the White Panthers' invented religion "Zenta," borrowed from Sun Ra's interest in abstract "equations" (for example, Jesse Crawford, "Zenta Philosophy," ca. 1969, in *Music Is Revolution: From the John and Leni Sinclair Library*, CD produced and edited by Cary Loren, 2000). On Zenta, see Carson, *Grit, Noise, and Revolution*, 175; Kramer, *Hard Stuff*, 92; Plamondon, *Lost from the Ottawa*, 108. On Sun Ra and equations, see Szwed, *Space Is the Place*, 304–8.

87. Waksman, *Instruments of Desire*, 225.

88. Sumanth Gopinath, "Reich in Blackface: *Oh Dem Watermelons* and Radical Minstrelsy in the 1960s," *Journal of the Society for American Music* 5, no. 2 (2011): 139–93. Sinclair reviewed a Detroit performance of the Mime Troupe's *A Minstrel Show, or Civil Rights in a Cracker Barrel* in 1966, perhaps inadvertently revealing some of minstrelsy's ironies by describing the interracial cast as "spades acting like real spades, and not some middle-class white man's weird distortion of their reality" (John Sinclair, "The Coatpuller," *Fifth Estate* 1, no. 16 [October 16–31, 1966]: 2).

89. Gopinath, "Reich in Blackface," 140.

90. Note that Thomas Harroldson's article "The White Negro—Ten Years Later" appeared in the January 1–15, 1968, issue of *Fifth Estate*, which featured Sinclair as a columnist and regularly covered the MC5 (Thomas Harroldson, "The White Negro—Ten Years Later," *Fifth Estate* 2, no. 19 [January 1–15, 1968]: 12). In a 1977 interview, Sinclair claimed that he was a hipster before Mailer ever thought to write about it: "I was a White Negro in a purer sense. By the time that [book] came out, I was hangin' in the barbershops, in the pool rooms . . . [I was] doing it" (Hale, "Total Assault," 127). Kramer remembers that he and Rob Tyner read the work of critics such as Amiri Baraka and Eldridge Cleaver, although he is "not so sure the rest of the band cared all that much about it" (Wayne Kramer, interview with the author, March 28, 2019).

91. "Suggested Reading List from the White Panther Party," *Sun* [Ann Arbor] [July 8, 1969]: [4].

92. Amiri Baraka [LeRoi Jones], *Black Music* (New York: William Morrow, 1967); Eldridge Cleaver, *Soul on Ice* (New York: McGraw-Hill, 1968); Cleaver, *Eldridge Cleaver: Post-Prison Writings and Speeches*, ed. Robert Scheer (New York: Random House, 1969).

93. Cleaver, *Soul on Ice*, 81.

94. Ronald Radano, "Hot Fantasies: American Modernism and the Idea of Black Rhythm," in *Music and the Racial Imagination*, ed. Ronald M. Radano and Philip V. Bohlman (Chicago: University of Chicago Press, 2000), 459–80.

95. Cleaver, *Soul on Ice*, 81. Harold Cruse, in a review of Cleaver's 1969 book *Post-Prison Writings and Speeches*, argued similarly that "in the midst of this racial crisis, this deep conflict in cultural values, whites of all ages and classes sing the black people's music and dance to the black people's bodily rhythms, and there is no cultural history written and taught in the educational systems that explains why this is so, and is so American" (Cruse, "The Fire This Time?," *New York Review of Books* [May 8, 1969], in *The Essential Harold Cruse*, ed. William Jelani Cobb [New York: Palgrave, 2002], 115).

96. Cleaver, *Soul on Ice*, 204.

97. Cleaver, *Soul on Ice*, 203.

98. Baraka, *Black Music*, 13.

99. Baraka, *Black Music*, 124.

100. Cleaver, *Soul on Ice*, 80.

101. Baraka, *Black Music*, 180.

102. Baraka, *Black Music*, 205.

103. Baraka, *Black Music*, 206.

104. John Sinclair, "The Coatpuller," *Fifth Estate* 1, no. 18 (November 15–30, 1966): 2; Amiri Baraka [LeRoi Jones], "Leadbelly Gives an Autograph," *Trobar*, no. 5 (1964): 38–39.

105. Doggett, *There's a Riot Going On*, 229; John Sinclair, "White Panther Statement," *Sun* (Ann Arbor) [November 1968]: [1–3]; United States Government Memorandum from "SAC, Detroit (100–35879) P" to "Director, FBI," subject "'Sun' Internal Security—Miscellaneous," April 24, 1969, folder "Legal and prison files, FOIA documents, FOIA correspondence, 1975–1977," box 46, JLSP.

106. Doggett argues that Crawford's "verbal riff" was "lifted from Eldridge Cleaver, when the lives of the militant black community were at stake. In Detroit, however, it was no more than revolutionary chic, as meaningless as Crawford's gospel call to the audience: 'I want to know, are you ready to testify?'" (Doggett, *There's a Riot Going On*, 227). Sinclair's liner notes are reproduced in "Rock and Roll Dope," *Fifth Estate* 3, no. 22 (March 5-19, 1969): 17. "Feeling predicts intelligence" appears in Baraka, *Black Music*, 175.

107. Justin Schell points out that "one of the stylistic trademarks of Jones was his abbreviation of words such as 'could' as 'cd,' a technique emulated in much of Sinclair's own poetry" (Schell, "A Blacker Shade of White: The Cultural Dynamics of Oppositional Appropriation" [senior thesis, University of Wisconsin–Milwaukee, 2005], 50).

108. For critiques of Sinclair's sexism, see Robin Morgan, "Goodbye to All That" (1970), in *Counterculture and Revolution*, ed. David Horowitz, Michael Lerner, and Craig Pyes (New York: Random House, 1972), 93; Beth Bailey, "Sex as a Weapon: Underground Comix and the Paradox of Liberation," in *Imagine Nation: The American Counterculture of the 1960s and '70s*, ed. Peter Braunstein and Michael William Doyle (New York: Routledge, 2002), 311–12. In 1971, Sinclair apologized for the sexism of his earlier work and declared support for "the righteous women's movement" (John Sinclair, "Apology to My Sisters," *Chapter!*, no. 2 [1971], folder 29, box 17, JLSP; also see John Sinclair, "Dragon Teeth," *Ann Arbor Sun*, no. 7 [June 11–17, 1971]: 7, reprinted as "Free Our Sisters/Free Our Selves!" in John Sinclair, *Guitar Army: Street Writings/Prison Writings* [New York: Douglas, 1972], 295–99).

109. Sinclair, "White Panther Statement."

110. See, for example, Waksman, *Instruments of Desire*, 217–18; Doggett, *There's a Riot Going On*, 229.

111. "Grande Coltrane Memorial," *Fifth Estate* 2, no. 12 (September 15–30, 1967): 10. (This article is unsigned, but its prose style and promotional fervor point to Sinclair.)

112. John Sinclair, "Coat Puller," *Fifth Estate* 2, no. 20 (January 15–31, 1968): 14.

113. Sinclair, *Guitar Army*, 21.

114. Later scholars also have described the MC5 as "assimilat[ors] or interpret[ers]" of Black music (for example, Heylin, *Velvets to Voidoids*, 33; Schell, "Blacker Shade of White," 68). Ulrich Adelt and Michal Nanoru each employ the term "translate" in passing to describe white rock musicians' (Janis Joplin's and the Rolling Stones', respectively) borrowings from Black music during the 1960s (Adelt, *Blues Music in the Sixties: A Story in Black and White* [New Brunswick, NJ: Rutgers University Press, 2010], 111; Nanoru, "Here Be Dogs: Documenting the Visual Culture of the Czech Indie Scene," *Current Musicology*, no. 91 [Spring 2011]: 66).

115. MC5, *Back in the USA* (Atlantic SD8247, 1970).

116. Sue Cassidy Clark, interview with MC5, October 1, 1969, audiocassette, box 1, cassette 33, Sue Cassidy Clark Collection, RRHOF. Author's transcription. The MC5's third studio album, *High Time* (Atlantic SD 8285, 1971), includes a horn section arranged by jazz trumpeter Charles Moore (Kramer, *Hard Stuff*, 130).

117. Sue Cassidy Clark, interview with MC5, October 1, 1969, audiocassette, box 1, cassette 33, Sue Cassidy Clark Collection, RRHOF. Author's transcription. Jon Landau, the producer of *Back in the USA*, told *Creem* that "we try and retain some of the spirit of [older rock and roll], but to transpose or make more contemporary the notion of rock and roll" ("MC5 on the Cusp," *Creem* 2, no. 4 [August 31, 1969], 17). In 2005, bassist Michael Davis used similar rhetoric, claiming that "we were trying to channel the rock'n'roll thing through the principles of jazz players" (Hasted, "Search and Destroy," 83). Note that Kramer's comments here refer to race only in pass-

ing. Today, Kramer argues that "notes don't have an ethnic history" and asserts that the validity of white performances of music stemming from the "African American experience" "has more to do with *how* you're playing and what your intentions are than whoever wrote that phrase first" (Wayne Kramer, interview with the author, March 28, 2019). Although the MC5 during their White Panther period seem to have been invested in blackness as such, this 1969 interview may more closely mirror Kramer's current viewpoint.

118. Pharoah Sanders, *Tauhid* (Impulse! AS-9138, 1967).

119. The MC5's repertoire and imagery drew on the work of each of these musicians. Their song "Ice Pick Slim," recorded live at the Grande Ballroom in May 1968 (and subtitled "5 for Shepp" in a concert program in apparent tribute to Archie Shepp's album *Four for Trane*), is built loosely around the bass line of one section of Shepp's "Hambone" (MC5, *Ice Pick Slim: Live 1968* [Alive Records CD0008, 1997]; Archie Shepp, *Fire Music* [Impulse! AS-86, 1965]; "Programme for 'An Evening Recital of New Music'"; John Sinclair, "A Letter from Prison, Another Side of the MC5 Story, and [Incidentally] the End of an Era," *Creem* 2, no. 8 [November 28, 1969]). "Starship" (from *Kick Out the Jams*) includes Tyner's recitation of a Sun Ra poem printed on the cover of *The Heliocentric Worlds of Sun Ra, Vol. II* (Szwed, *Space Is the Place*, 244). A cut-and-pasted photo of Coltrane appears on the cover of the MC5's first record, the single "Looking at You" (A-Square Records A2-333, 1968), and the band covered his composition "Tunji" (see above).

120. Jonathan Kundra, "MC5: Muscle Music and Politics," *Circus* 6, no. 1 (October 1969): 19; Walley, "MC5," 17.

121. "Programme for 'An Evening Recital of New Music.'"

122. Bob Rudnick and Dennis Frawley, "'show me your love and i'll show you mine . . .'" *East Village Other* 3, no. 23 (May 10, 1968): 9. Rudnick and Frawley also claim that the MC5 is working on versions of Archie Shepp's "Mama Too Tight" and "Hambone." Sinclair reports that "Upper and Lower Egypt" was part of the MC5's set at the Grosse Pointe Hideout on June 1, 1968 (John Sinclair, "Rock and Roll Dope," *Fifth Estate* 3, no. 4 [June 19–July 1, 1968]: 7).

123. Richard C. Walls, review of *Karma* by Pharoah Sanders, *Creem* 2, no. 4 (August 31, 1969): 21; "MC5 Begin Recording," *Fifth Estate* 4, no. 4 (June 26–July 9, 1968): 12; "MC5 to Commence Recording First Atlantic Album in Detroit," press release issued by White Panther News Service and Trans-Love Energies, June 7, 1969. (This press release is included in the Bell and Howell Underground Press Collection microfilm edition of the *Ann Arbor Sun.*)

124. *Starship: The MC5 Live at the Sturgis Armory.*

125. John Sinclair, "Rock and Roll Dope," *Fifth Estate* 3, no. 20 (February 6–19, 1969): 9. In advocating the MC5's amplified "machinery," Sinclair may have been arguing against jazz critic Frank Kofsky, who wrote in 1968 that *Tauhid* "should be of more than passing interest to rock guitarists for the playing of . . . Sonny Sharrock, who demonstrates that it is eminently possible to play 'free' on the guitar without resorting to fuzztone, wah-wah pedals, feedback, and grotesquely high volume levels" (Frank Kofsky, "Three Jazz Reviews," *Fifth Estate* 2, no. 26 [April 16–30, 1968]: 13). As early as 1966, Tyner argued that "soundwise, we're forcing more of the guitar than would have seemed possible five years ago. I can't speak technically about this because I'm not a guitar player, but Wayne Kramer, our lead guitar, is getting into his instrument and away from it at the same time, because he's getting away from the note pattern thing and into exploration of the basic sound that his guitar can produce" (Bach, "Bach on Rock," 12).

126. Waksman, *Instruments of Desire*, 222.

127. The poor quality of this bootleg recording makes it difficult to determine whether the distorted guitar chord includes a C♯. Wayne Kramer suggests that the chord is probably an A minor 7th (Kramer, interview with the author, March 28, 2019).

128. Kramer, interview with the author, March 28, 2019.

129. Kramer, interview with the author, March 28, 2019.

130. Kramer, interview with the author, March 28, 2019. Kramer is likely describing May 16, 1969, when Sun Ra and the MC5 began three nights together at the Grande Ballroom. Ken Dabish, reviewing the opening night for the *Sun*, wrote that the audience "had no kind of idea what Sun Ra was all about but they all walked out of the clip joint with some kind of glassy look on their faces and it wasn't the pot and it wasn't the acid. Sun Ra literally mesmerized the kids. Me too" (Dabish, "Sun Ra," 12).

131. For a consideration of the influence on punk of MC5's approach to the blues, see Evan Rapport, "Hearing Punk as Blues," *Popular Music* 33, no. 1 (January 2014): 42–47.

132. "Programme for 'An Evening Recital of New Music.'"

133. Sue Cassidy Clark, interview with MC5, October 1, 1969, audiocassette, box 1, cassette 33, Sue Cassidy Clark Collection, RRHOF. Author's transcription.

134. "WABX/Creem Magazine Rock & Roll News," *Creem* 2, no. 3 (July 28, 1969): 3.

135. See, for example, Ulrich Adelt on Eric Clapton's romantic "equation of blackness and uninhibited male sexuality," which Adelt argues "was reminiscent of the colonialist fantasies of other White Negroes like Norman Mailer and Jack Kerouac" (Adelt, *Blues Music in the Sixties*, 62). Susan McClary argues that for British Invasion musicians, "blues seemed to offer an experience of sexuality that was unambiguously masculine" (McClary, *Conventional Wisdom: The Content of Musical Form* [Berkeley: University of California Press, 2000], 55).

136. Adelt, *Blues Music in the Sixties*, 7; also see Nadya Zimmerman, *Counterculture Kaleidoscope: Musical and Cultural Perspectives on Late Sixties San Francisco* (Ann Arbor: University of Michigan Press, 2008), 49–50; Ross Cole, "Mastery and Masquerade in the Transatlantic Blues Revival," *Journal of the Royal Musical Association* 143, no. 1 (2018): 186.

137. Amiri Baraka [LeRoi Jones], *Blues People: Negro Music in White America* (1963; repr., New York: Quill, 1999), 65; John Sinclair, "Killer Blues," *Ann Arbor Argus* 1, no. 10 ([August] 1969), reprinted in Sinclair, *Guitar Army*, 158.

138. Sinclair, "Killer Blues," 157.

139. Sinclair, "Killer Blues," 156. Nick Bromell, citing the MC5 as an example, argues similarly that white teenagers during the 1960s related to blues because they experienced their own form of the double consciousness described by W. E. B. Du Bois, although he adds the important caveat that "obviously, my life as a white kid in the '50s was worlds apart from that of a black sharecropper in the '20s or a black steelworker in the '50s" (Bromell, *Tomorrow Never Knows: Rock and Psychedelics in the 1960s* [Chicago: University of Chicago Press, 2000], 48–57).

140. Charles Shaar Murray, *Boogie Man: The Adventures of John Lee Hooker in the American Twentieth Century* (London: Viking, 1999), 342–43; also see Hubert G. Locke, *The Detroit Riot of 1967* (Detroit: Wayne State University Press, 1969).

141. Murray, *Boogie Man*, 344.

142. Murray, *Boogie Man*, 344.

143. Peter Werbe, "'Get the Big Stuff,'" *Fifth Estate* 2, no. 9 (August 1–15, 1967): 1; "Jailed Residents Describe Experiences," *Fifth Estate* 2, no. 9 (August 1–15, 1967): 12; Carson, *Grit, Noise, and Revolution*, 122–23; Hale, "Total Assault," 135–36; "Dope-o-Scope," *Warren Forest Sun* [September 1967]: [20]; Steve Miller, *Detroit Rock City: The Uncensored History of Rock 'n' Roll in American's Loudest City* (Boston: Da Capo, 2013), 56–58; Waksman, *Instruments of Desire*, 220–21.

144. John Sinclair, "The Coatpuller," *Fifth Estate* 2, no. 9 [August 1–15, 1967]: 3; Callwood, *Sonically Speaking*, 46. For retrospective accounts of the events by former White Panthers, see Kramer, *Hard Stuff*, 69–74; Plamondon, *Lost from the Ottawa*, 73–91.

145. Cosgrove, *Detroit 67*, 320.

146. Schell, "Blacker Shade of White," 80.

147. Tyner himself fled Detroit during the uprising after "my parents demanded that we leave the city," although he remembered seeing "whole neighborhoods going up" as he drove away (Bartkowiak, *MC5 and Social Change*, 47).

148. Schell, "Blacker Shade of White," 80–81. Although the song's composition is "officially attributed to former Vee Jay executive Al Smith," Hooker's biographer Charles Shaar Murray reports that Hooker actually wrote it (Murray, *Boogie Man*, 345, 354).

149. Schell, "Blacker Shade of White," 81–82. A *Time* magazine report on the MC5's 1968 Fillmore East performance (see chapter 4) of "Motor City Is Burning" quotes a different line: "All the cities will burn . . . You are the people who will build up the ashes" ("The Revolutionary Hype," *Time* 93, no. 1 [January 3, 1969]: 49).

150. The MC5's revision of Hooker recalls Dave Headlam's discussion of Cream's "blues transformations," in which he argues that the "procedure of extracting or arranging motivic figures or riffs from blues songs and using them repeatedly within a simplified and regularized harmonic and metric framework is characteristic of Cream and other rock bands" (Dave Headlam, "Blues Transformations in the Music of Cream," in *Understanding Rock: Essays in Musical Analysis*, ed. John Covach and Graeme M. Boone [New York: Oxford University Press, 1997], 71); also see Schell, "Blacker Shade of White," 80.

151. John Sinclair, liner notes to MC5, *Power Trip* (Alive Records CD 0005, 1994).

152. Sinclair, liner notes to MC5, *Power Trip*.

153. Justin Schell argues more skeptically that the song reflects "the White Negro in one of its uglier guises": "most of the . . . lyrics . . . do not really portray solidarity with the [Black] Panthers; rather, they inscribe the same narrative of the body as primitively sensuous and free from the problems of modernity," "an appeal to the idealized African-American male" (Schell, "Blacker Shade of White," 76–77).

154. Mike Bourne, "Sonny Sharrock's Story," *Down Beat* 37, no. 12 (June 11, 1970): 18.

155. Ingrid Monson, *Saying Something: Jazz Improvisation and Interaction* (Chicago: University of Chicago Press, 1996), 97.

156. Robert Gold, "Gold Slams MC5, Fowley," *Los Angeles Free Press* 6, no. 244 (March 21, 1969): 30.

157. Goldstein, "Pop Eye."

158. Sandy Pearlman, "Riffs," *Village Voice*, January 2, 1969. In a 2004 interview, former Sun Ra saxophonist Marshall Allen remembered that the MC5 "were good at what they were doing. It was sometimes so loud because they had that power. . . . They heard it [Sun Ra's music] and they could pick something out of it to help them" (Edwin Pouncey, "Invisible Jukebox: Marshall Allen," *Wire* 250 [December 2004]: 22; cited in Schell, "Blacker Shade of White," 73).

159. "In the Groove," *Daily Iowan*, undated clipping in box 10, folder 29, JLSP.

160. G C., "The MC5 Kick Out the Jams!," *OZ*, no. 18 (February 1969): 10.

161. Art Johnston, "MC-5 in San Francisco," *Fifth Estate* 3, no. 24 (April 3–16, 1969): 17, 21. Johnston added that "the only truly forward direction rock and roll can take—and one which will bring white youth into the revolutionary cadence of black militancy—is to confront and attempt to understand, and even assimilate, the black experience as it is being reflected in the atonal, explorative shriek of jazz artists like Sonny Rollins."

162. Jerry Rubin, *We Are Everywhere. Written in Cook County Jail* (New York: Harper and Row, 1971), 168.

163. McNeil and McCain, *Please Kill Me*, 49. In his autobiography, Kramer claims to have felt sincere veneration for the Black Panthers: "I admired the vanguard players in the revolution, the Black Panther Party, and saw them as a beacon lighting the way forward. I believed we were all involved in the same struggle" (Kramer, *Hard Stuff*, 90).

164. William Spencer Leach, "The White Left—Serious or Not?," *Fifth Estate* 3, no. 18 (January 9–22, 1969): 7; also see Waksman, *Instruments of Desire*, 215; Carson, *Grit, Noise, and Revolution*, 182. A letter to the editor in the same issue asserts that "if I were black, I'd want nothing to do with them . . . regardless of what that idiot Sinclair says, they are not 'bad.' They're just a disorganized crew of shitheads" (John Tidyman, "Letters," *Fifth Estate* 3, no. 18 [January 9–22, 1969]: 17). As Scott Saul observes, the Black Panthers' notion of freedom was linked to "collective power and self-determination for the black community," in contrast to Sinclair's emphasis on "the realm of commodities and individual freedom of choice" (Saul, *Freedom Is*, 300).

165. "Prison Interview" (Bobby Seale, ca. 1970), in *Music Is Revolution* CD; also see Sullivan, *Keep on Pushing*, 79. In 1971, Seale spoke at the John Sinclair Freedom Rally at the University of Michigan that preceded Sinclair's release from prison (Carson, *Grit, Noise, and Revolution*, 266). For a detailed comparison of the White Panther and Black Panther programs, see "Panthers Black and White," *Chicago Seed* 3, no. 5 (January 10–24, 1969): 4, 10.

166. Ishmael Reed, review of *Snaps* by Victor Hernandez Cruz, *East Village Other* 4, no. 16 (March 19, 1969): 18.

167. John Sinclair, "Rock and Roll Dope," *Fifth Estate* 3, no. 19 (January 23–February 5, 1969): 16.

168. Leni Sinclair, interview with the author, March 22, 2019. The archive reveals some collaboration between White Panthers and Black political groups. In November 1968, John Sinclair reported that the Up, another Trans-Love band, had performed at "rallies for the Black Panthers in Ypsilanti" (John Sinclair, "Rock and Roll Dope," *Fifth Estate* 3, no. 15 [November 28–December 11, 1968]: 17). Eric Ehrmann claimed in 1969 that Sinclair helped broker a pact between "white and black radicals" in Detroit during the spring of 1968, and that the MC5 played benefits for "Black UAW workers" (Ehrmann, "MC5," 16). On June 3, 1969, police spotted Sinclair leaving a meeting at Detroit's BPP headquarters ("Confidential," report signed by Roy Chlopan, Detective Inspector, Special Investigation Services [Detroit Police Department], folder "Legal and prison files, Red Squad and police files, MI state police files (1 of 2)," box 46, JLSP). On August 11, 1969, a press conference at Trans-Love Energies in Ann Arbor announced "the formation of a working coalition of the White Panther Party, the God's Children motorcycle club, the Black Berets, Sunnygoode Street commune, and the Congolean Maulers" to combat police harassment and a recent rise in dealing of "smack and speed" ("Street People Get It Together," *Fifth Estate* 4, no. 8 [August 21–September 3, 1969]: 21).

169. Hale, "Total Assault," 142; "Music Is a Revolutionary Force," in *Music Is Revolution* CD. This track is an excerpt from Cassette I:2 (White Panther Central Committee [June 1969]), box 28a, JLSP.

170. Saul, *Freedom Is*, 301.

Chapter 2

1. The performance, which also includes the song "Lather," also from *Crown of Creation*, appears on the DVD *Fly Jefferson Airplane*, produced and directed by Bob Sarles and Christina Keating (Eagle Rock Entertainment EV 30065–9, 2004).

2. Front cover, *TeenSet* 5, no. 1 (January 1969). This issue includes a brief profile of Slick that mentions the blackface performance, as well as an interview with Hendrix in which he expresses support for the Black Panthers (Jerry Hopkins, "Grace Slick Is an Attention Getting Device," 34–35, 59–60; Jacoba Atlas, "Jimi Hendrix, Black Power and Money," 22–5, 58–59).

3. Barbara Rowes, *Grace Slick: The Biography* (Garden City, NY: Doubleday, 1980), 147; Jeff Tamarkin, *Got a Revolution! The Turbulent Flight of Jefferson Airplane* (New York: Atria, 2003), 210; Grace Slick with Andrea Cagan, *Somebody to Love? A Rock-and-Roll Memoir* (New York: Warner, 1998), 189. This is one of several Slick performances that seem intended to outrage the audience with anti-Semitic implications: see also the references to "Jewish broads" and "Meadowlands" later in this chapter.

4. Rowes, *Grace Slick*, 122–23.

5. Peter Doggett, *There's a Riot Going On: Revolutionaries, Rock Stars, and the Rise and Fall of the '60s* (Edinburgh: Canongate, 2007), 209. Doggett also asserts: "the myth also insists that [Slick] ended the performance of 'Crown of Creation' with her own black power salute. But it was hidden beneath the flamboyant sleeves of her dazzlingly white dress" (209). While it is true that Slick was wearing a white dress with "flamboyant sleeves," her raised hand, on which she wears a black glove, is clearly visible in the video of the performance.

6. Rogers, Cowan & Brenner, press release, November 12, 1968, Series III, box 4, folder 19, Sue Cassidy Clark Collection, Library and Archives, Rock and Roll Hall of Fame and Museum [collection cited hereafter as SCC]. The press release is quoted or paraphrased in: "Random Notes," *Rolling Stone* 24 (December 21, 1968): 8; "Press Release," *Rat Subterranean News* 1, no. 23 (December 13, 1968–January 2, 1969): 23; "New Airplane Flick Flight," *Fifth Estate* 3, no. 15 (November 28–December 11, 1968): 14; Hopkins, "Grace Slick Is an Attention Getting Device"; "It Happened in 1968," *Rolling Stone*, no. 26 (February 1, 1969): 18. The Smothers Brothers, widely regarded as hip fellow-travelers of the counterculture, slyly acknowledged the blackface tradition during Slick's performance: as he introduced the band, Dick Smothers briefly lapsed into minstrel dialect, announcing "right now we're gwine [*sic*] to move right along to the Jefferson Airplane!" while his brother Tom looked on in mock confusion.

7. "Stones and Airplane," *Fusion*, no. 2 (November 15, 1968): 3. The article also claims that "Grace Slick has received favorable comment from her black friends for her appearance in black face [*sic*] on The Smothers Brothers television show." Other reports expanded on this explanation, with Slick explaining that "the whole thing started when I was watching TV and someone said that blacks look better on television in closeups, so I wandered around the house wearing blackface and flashing on myself in the mirror" (Hopkins, "Grace Slick Is An Attention Getting Device," 35; "It Happened in 1968," 18).

8. Tom Phillips, "Jefferson Airplane," *Jazz and Pop*, no. 8 (January 1969): 21.

9. Tamarkin, *Got a Revolution*, 177–78; Slick, *Somebody to Love*, 152.

10. Daphne A. Brooks, "'This Voice Which Is Not One': Amy Winehouse Sings the Ballad of Sonic Blue(s)face Culture," *Women and Performance: A Journal of Feminist Theory* 20, no. 1 (2010): 38. Brooks, citing Anne Anlin Cheng, is referring here to Sandra Bernhard's parodic performances as a "female racial masquerader too arrogant and obtuse to recognize her own spectacular absurdities" (38).

11. On the Olympic salute, see Terry H. Anderson, *The Movement and the Sixties* (New York: Oxford University Press, 1995), 230–31. Critic Ralph J. Gleason and the Airplane's manager Bill Thompson both state explicitly that Slick was making reference to the Olympic athletes (Ralph J.

Gleason, *The Jefferson Airplane and the San Francisco Sound* [New York: Ballantine, 1969], 79; Tamarkin, *Got a Revolution*, 177).

12. Doggett, *There's a Riot Going On*, 87.

13. "Jefferson Airplane Lands in City," *Fifth Estate* 2, no. 8 (July 15–31, 1967): 1.

14. Allan Katzman, "Poor Paranoid's," *East Village Other* 2, no. 17 (July–August 1967): 7; Abbie Hoffman, "Their Thing," unattributed clipping, Series III, box 4, folder 18, SCC.

15. Tamarkin, *Got a Revolution*, 169, 173.

16. "Jefferson Airplane Raps," *Chicago Kaleidoscope* 1, no. 2 (December 6–19, 1968): 4.

17. Jefferson Airplane, *Crown of Creation* (RCA Victor LSP-4058, 1968).

18. Paul Kantner, *A Guide through the Chaos (A Road to the Passion): The Spoken Word History of the Jefferson Airplane and Beyond* (MonsterSounds CD MSE-1017, 1996), disc 1, track 9.

19. Tamarkin, *Got a Revolution*, 168. The text borrowed by Kantner can be found in John Wyndham, *The Chrysalids* (London: Penguin, 1955), 153, 182–83, 196.

20. Craig Morrison, "Psychedelic Music in San Francisco: Style, Context, and Evolution" (PhD diss., Concordia University [Montreal], 2000), 224.

21. Doggett, *There's a Riot Going On*, 158.

22. Nadya Zimmerman, *Counterculture Kaleidoscope: Musical and Cultural Perspectives on Late Sixties San Francisco* (Ann Arbor: University of Michigan Press, 2008), 66–70.

23. Jefferson Airplane, *After Bathing at Baxter's* (RCA Victor LSO-1511, 1967).

24. See chapter 3.

25. Jefferson Airplane, *Volunteers* (RCA Victor LSP-4238, 1969).

26. Kantner, *Guide through the Chaos*, disc 1, track 10.

27. "We Are Outlaws!," *Berkeley Barb* 7, no. 16 (October 11–18, 1968): 13. An alternate version of this manifesto was previously published as "We Are Outlaws," *Rat Subterranean News* 1, no. 16 (September 6–19, 1968), 7, reprinted in Gavin Grindon, "Poetry Written in Gasoline: Black Mask and Up against the Wall Motherfucker," *Art History* 38, no. 1 (February 2015): 197; also see Caitlin Casey, "Up against the Wall Motherfucker: Ideology and Action in a 'Street Gang with an Analysis,'" in *Radical Gotham: Anarchism in New York City from Schwab's Saloon to Occupy Wall Street*, ed. Tom Goyens (Urbana: University of Illinois Press, 2017), 175–76. Kantner identifies the *Berkeley Barb* page as his source in a 1969 interview with Sue Cassidy Clark (Sue C. Clark, transcript of interview with Paul Kantner and Grace Slick, November 30, 1969, Series III, box 4, folder 20, SCC). Jon Savage reproduces the Motherfuckers' manifesto (as reprinted by 1960s British radical group King Mob) and points out its use on *Volunteers* (Savage, *England's Dreaming: Anarchy, Sex Pistols, Punk Rock, and Beyond* [New York: St. Martin's Griffin, 2001], 35). On UAW/MF, see chapter 4.

28. "Airplane Puts RCA Up Against Wall," *Rolling Stone*, no. 40 (August 23, 1969), 10; Tamarkin, *Got a Revolution*, 195.

29. Michael Hicks, *Sixties Rock: Garage, Psychedelic, and Other Satisfactions* (Urbana: University of Illinois Press, 1999), 33–35.

30. Kurt Vonnegut, *Slaughterhouse-Five: or, the Children's Crusade; A Duty-Dance with Death* (New York: Delacorte, 1969), 29.

31. Mezz Mezzrow and Bernard Wolfe, *Really the Blues* (1946, repr., New York: Citadel, 1990), 376.

32. Susan Vaneta Mason, *The San Francisco Mime Troupe Reader* (Ann Arbor: University of Michigan Press, 2005), 36, 39, 49; R. G. Davis, *The San Francisco Mime Troupe: The First Ten*

Years (Palo Alto, CA: Ramparts, 1975), 72–73. I thank Sumanth Gopinath for pointing out to me the Mime Troupe's use of "motherfucker."

33. Not every Black radical approved of the word, however. According to Bobby Seale of the Black Panther Party, he and Huey P. Newton objected to its use, while Eldridge Cleaver insisted that "if we have to use it . . . use it in reference to sadistic pigs who at least need cursing out for what they are: oppressors, murderers, rapers of justice and peace in our society" (Seale, *Seize the Time: The Story of the Black Panther Party and Huey P. Newton* [New York: Random House, 1970], 409).

34. LeRoi Jones [Amiri Baraka], "Black People!," *Evergreen Review* 50 (December 1967), 49. Baraka would certainly have been familiar with an earlier use of the phrase's opening, John Coltrane's "Up 'gainst the Wall," issued on the 1963 album *Impressions*. While Coltrane's biographer J. C. Thomas attributes Coltrane's title to a private musicians' joke, Ashley Kahn argues that it "had a definite law-enforcement ring to black listeners of the period" (J. C. Thomas, *Chasin' the Trane: The Music and Mystique of John Coltrane* [New York: Da Capo, 1976], 111; Ashley Kahn, *A Love Supreme: The Story of John Coltrane's Signature Album* [New York: Viking, 2002], 76).

35. Walter H. Waggoner, "LeRoi Jones Jailed for 2½ to 3 Years on Gun Charge," *New York Times*, January 5, 1968. The conviction was overturned in December 1968, with an appeals court finding that the judge's instructions to the jury had been "improper and prejudicial" (Walter H. Waggoner, "LeRoi Jones Wins Retrial in Jersey," *New York Times*, December 24, 1968).

36. Anderson, *Movement and the Sixties*, 195.

37. Dotson Rader, "Up Against the Wall!," in *The Radical Vision: Essays for the Seventies*, ed. Leo Hamalian and Frederick R. Karl (New York: Thomas Crowell, 1970), 199.

38. Osha Neumann, *Up against the Wall Motherf**ker: A Memoir of the '60s, with Notes for Next Time* (New York: Seven Stories Press, 2008), 53.

39. Or perhaps simply plagiarizing the byline: John Strausbaugh contends "that the Airplane had ripped it off and used it [the Motherfuckers' phrase], in effect, as an advertising slogan for a gold-selling Top 10 album was an irony largely lost on their primary market at the time" (Strausbaugh, *Rock 'til You Drop: The Decline from Rebellion to Nostalgia* [New York: Verso, 2001], 102).

40. Youth International Party New Service, "Dope Sheet: Yippie Communique No. 1," [1970], box 17, folder 29, John and Leni Sinclair Papers, Bentley Historical Library, University of Michigan.

41. MC5, *Kick Out the Jams* (Elektra EKS 74042, 1969). Note also that David Peel and the Lower East Side's debut album *Have a Marijuana* (1968) included "Up Against the Wall," a song whose only lyric is "Up against the wall, motherfucker" (Elektra EKS-74032, 1968).

42. John Sinclair, "Rock and Roll Dope," *Fifth Estate* 3, no. 16 (December 12–25, 1968): 18; Dave Sinclair, "Pontiac's Speech to the White Man," *Fifth Estate* 3, no. 12 (October 17–30, 1968): 13. It is unusual that Dave Sinclair uses the phrase in a romanticized Native American context rather than in relation to Black radicalism.

43. Steve Waksman, *Instruments of Desire: The Electric Guitar and the Shaping of Musical Experience* (Cambridge, MA: Harvard University Press, 1999), 235.

44. David A. Carson, *Grit, Noise, and Revolution: The Birth of Detroit Rock 'n' Roll* (Ann Arbor: University of Michigan Press, 2005), 188–89; Advertisement, *Ann Arbor Argus* 1, no. 2 (February 13, 1969): 17; Kramer, *Hard Stuff*, 103.

45. "MC-5 Kick Out Elektra," *Ann Arbor Argus* 1, no. 6 (May 8–22, 1969): 21.

46. Advertisement, *Fifth Estate* 3, no. 25 (April 17–30, 1969): 9. The MC5 had recorded a radio-friendly 45-RPM edit of the title song with "brothers and sisters" replacing the word

"motherfucker," which Elektra then used as the basis for a censored version of the LP without the band's consent (Carson, *Grit, Noise, and Revolution*, 188–89, 193–94).

47. Abbie Hoffman, *Woodstock Nation: A Talk-Rock Album* (New York: Vintage, 1969), 120.

48. Susan L. M. Huck, "Do Your Thing: Grace Slick, Acid-Rock, and the Airplane," *American Opinion* 13, no. 3 (March 1970), 18.

49. Benjamin DeMott, "The Age of Overkill," *New York Times*, May 19, 1968.

50. Francine Foskett, letter to the editor, *New York Times*, June 15, 1969; Nan Robertson, "Columbia Rebels Find Disruption Pays," *New York Times*, June 10, 1968.

51. Robertson, "Columbia Rebels."

52. Also see Seymour Krim, "Black English, or the Motherfucker Culture" (1969), in *Missing a Beat: The Rants and Regrets of Seymour Krim*, ed. Mark Cohen (Syracuse, NY: Syracuse University Press, 2010), 117–28.

53. Zimmerman, *Counterculture Kaleidoscope*, 29–30.

54. Zimmerman, *Counterculture Kaleidoscope*, 30.

55. Zimmerman, *Counterculture Kaleidoscope*, 33.

56. Michael Lydon, "Rock for Sale," in *Conversations with the New Reality*, ed. "the editors of *Ramparts*" (San Francisco: Canfield Colophon, 1971), 117. Nadya Zimmerman argues that Cleaver served as "the perfect outlaw role model for the counterculture" (Zimmerman, *Counterculture Kaleidoscope*, 32). Posters like the one Jefferson Airplane displayed were distributed in the underground press in late 1968 and early 1969. For example, see "Eldridge Cleaver Welcome Here," *Fifth Estate* 3, no. 17 (December 26, 1968–January 8, 1969): 3; "Eldridge Welcome Here," *Rat Subterranean News* 1, no. 26 (January 24–30, 1969): 10–11.

57. Sumanth Gopinath, "Reich in Blackface: *Oh Dem Watermelons* and Radical Minstrelsy in the 1960s," *Journal of the Society for American Music* 5, no. 2 (2011): 139–93.

58. Tamarkin, *Got a Revolution*, 32; Gleason, *Jefferson Airplane*, 128; Jorma Kaukonen, *Been So Long: My Life and Music* (New York: St. Martin's, 2018), 99–100.

59. Free [Abbie Hoffman], *Revolution for the Hell of It* (New York: Dial, 1968), 28; Jerry Farber, *The Student as Nigger: Essays and Stories* (New York: Pocket, 1970). For examples of Jefferson Airplane members using "spade" to refer to African Americans, see Gleason, *Jefferson Airplane*, 124, 129, 212. On the term's use in the San Francisco counterculture more generally, see Sarah Hill, *San Francisco and the Long 60s* (New York: Bloomsbury, 2016), 125–26.

60. Huck, "Do Your Thing," 18.

61. Zimmerman, *Counterculture Kaleidoscope*, 35.

62. Lydon, "Rock for Sale," 117.

63. Eric Lott, *Love and Theft: Blackface Minstrelsy and the American Working Class* (New York: Oxford University Press, 1993), 53. Baz Dreisinger, advocating more attention to women's role in the blackface tradition, argues that most critical accounts have been "steeped in the phallic posturing" of Mailer's "White Negro" (Dreisinger, *Near Black: White-to-Black Passing in American Culture* [Amherst: University of Massachusetts Press, 2008], 73). Daphne A. Brooks points out the presence of "a charged and complex history of white female racial mimicry that, until recently, has received far less critical attention" (Brooks, "This Voice Which Is Not One," 39).

64. Lori Harrison-Kahan, *The White Negress: Literature, Minstrelsy, and the Black-Jewish Imaginary* (New Brunswick, NJ: Rutgers University Press, 2011), 6–7.

65. Kathleen B. Casey, *The Prettiest Girl on Stage Is a Man: Race and Gender Benders in American Vaudeville* (Knoxville: University of Tennessee Press, 2015), 122–23.

66. M. Alison Kibler, *Rank Ladies: Gender and Cultural Hierarchy in American Vaudeville* (Chapel Hill: University of North Carolina Press, 1999), 112, 128.

67. Rowes, *Grace Slick*, 48, 100.

68. Slick, *Somebody to Love*, 153.

69. Kibler, *Rank Ladies*, 134. Slick's gesture anticipated another well-known image of "unruly womanhood": the cover of Tom Wolfe's *Radical Chic and Mau-Mauing the Flak Catchers* (1970), which "sports a satirical photograph of a well-coifed white woman on the lap of an African American man in an army fatigue jacket, both with black-gloved fists upraised" (Amy Abugo Ongiri, *Spectacular Blackness: The Cultural Politics of the Black Power Movement and the Search for a Black Aesthetic* [Charlottesville: University of Virginia Press, 2010], 58).

70. Daphne A. Brooks, *Bodies in Dissent: Spectacular Performances of Race and Freedom, 1850-1910* (Durham, NC: Duke University Press, 2006), 203.

71. Linda Mizejewski, *Ziegfeld Girl: Image and Icon in Culture and Cinema* (Durham, NC: Duke University Press, 1999), 131.

72. Zimmerman, *Counterculture Kaleidoscope*, 151.

73. Kibler, *Rank Ladies*, 112, 128.

74. Grace Halsell, *Soul Sister* (Greenwich, CT: Fawcett Crest, 1969), 221.

75. Halsell, *Soul Sister*, 19.

76. Halsell, *Soul Sister*, 83.

77. Dreisinger, *Near Black*, 80. For a more sympathetic account of Halsell's life and work, see Robin Kelley, "In Search of Grace Halsell," *Americans for Middle East Understanding*, vol. 47 (2014), http://www.ameu.org/Current-Issue/Current-Issue/2014-Volume-47/In-Search -of-Grace-Halsell.aspx, accessed April 26, 2018.

78. Robert Kanigher, Werner Roth, and Vince Colletta, "I Am Curious (Black)!," *Superman's Girl Friend Lois Lane*, no. 106 (DC Comics: November 1970), http://mutantstarr.blogspot.com/ 2012/01/they-really-made-that-into-comic.html, accessed October 30, 2017.

79. Larry Grathwohl and Frank Reagan, *Bringing Down America: An FBI Informer with the Weathermen* (New Rochelle, NY: Arlington House, 1976), 103; Slick, *Somebody to Love*, 41, 53.

80. Jeremy Varon, *Bringing the War Home: the Weather Underground, the Red Army Faction, and Revolutionary Violence in the Sixties and Seventies* (Berkeley: University of California Press, 2004), 163. Their privilege places Slick and Dohrn in a longer tradition that includes 1920s shipping heiress Nancy Cunard, who gained notoriety during the Harlem Renaissance for her engagement with Black culture (Carla Kaplan, *Miss Anne in Harlem: The White Women of the Black Renaissance* [New York: HarperCollins, 2013], 299).

81. John Leo, "Women Are Said to Be Infringing on Another Men's Prerogative: The Freedom to Curse," *New York Times*, October 20, 1968.

82. "It Happened in 1968," 18; Hopkins, "Grace Slick Is An Attention Getting Device," 35.

83. Grathwohl and Reagan, *Bringing Down America*, 103.

84. Susan Stern, *With the Weathermen: The Personal Journal of a Revolutionary Woman* (New York: Doubleday, 1975), 39.

85. Stern, *With the Weathermen*, 143.

86. Tamarkin, *Got a Revolution*, 129; Slick, *Somebody to Love*, 77; Rowes, *Grace Slick*, 25.

87. Gillian G. Gaar, *She's a Rebel: The History of Women in Rock and Roll* (London: Blandford, 1993), 103.

88. Tom Hayden, *Trial* (New York: Holt, Rinehart and Winston, 1970), 109.

89. Bernardine Dohrn, "White Mother Country Radicals," *New Left Notes* 3, no. 24 (July 29, 1968): 5; Grathwohl and Reagan, *Bringing Down America*, 103.

90. Varon, *Bringing the War Home*, 164.

91. Varon, *Bringing the War Home*, 159.

92. Dohrn, "White Mother Country Radicals," 1.

93. Dan Berger, *Outlaws of America: The Weather Underground and the Politics of Solidarity* (Oakland, CA: AK Press, 2006), 85.

94. Dohrn, "White Mother Country Radicals," 5.

95. Varon, *Bringing the War Home*, 81. Varon glosses "Custeristic" as "suicidal," and the term also suggests that the Weathermen resemble white imperialists.

96. Elaine Brown, *A Taste of Power: A Black Woman's Story* (New York: Anchor, 1994), 198; David Hilliard and Lewis Cole, *This Side of Glory: The Autobiography of David Hilliard and the Story of the Black Panther Party* (Boston: Little, Brown, 1993), 257–58.

97. Hilliard and Cole, *This Side of Glory*, 279–80.

98. Berger, *Outlaws of America*, 108, 118–22.

99. Casey, *Prettiest Girl*, 117; also see Armond Fields, *Sophie Tucker: First Lady of Show Business* (Jefferson, NC: McFarland, 2003), 25.

100. Casey, *Prettiest Girl*, 128.

101. Laura Joplin, *Love, Janis* (Petaluma, CA: Acid Test Productions, 1999), 124.

102. Joplin, *Love, Janis*, 259.

103. Myra Friedman, *Buried Alive: The Biography of Janis Joplin* (New York: Harmony, 1992), 107.

104. Gayle Wald, "One of the Boys? Whiteness, Gender, and Popular Music Studies," in *Whiteness: A Critical Reader*, ed. Mike Hill (New York: New York University Press, 1997), 156.

105. Friedman, *Buried Alive*, 265; also see Zimmerman, *Counterculture Kaleidoscope*, 41; Ulrich Adelt, *Blues Music in the Sixties: A Story in Black and White* (New Brunswick, NJ: Rutgers University Press, 2010), 103.

106. Big Brother and the Holding Company, *Cheap Thrills* (Columbia KCS9700, 1968). Ulrich Adelt dismisses Crumb's cover art as "highly offensive" in contrast to other Crumb works that are more "complex and contradictory," but one might also read Crumb as critiquing the offensive aspects of Joplin's own racial mimicry (Adelt, *Blues Music in the Sixties*, 107).

107. William Kloman, "Rock: The 50's Come Back," *New York Times*, September 1, 1968; Pat Thomas, *Listen, Whitey! The Sights and Sounds of Black Power 1965–1975* (Seattle: Fantagraphics, 2012), 107.

108. Michael Awkward, *Soul Covers: Rhythm and Blues Remakes and the Struggle for Artistic Identity* (Durham, NC: Duke University Press, 2007), 145; also see Hamilton, *Just around Midnight*, 186–92.

109. Joplin, *Love, Janis*, 225. Slick, in a more playful spirit, argued that "makeup is pretty silly anyway" ("It Happened in 1968," 18).

110. Slick, *Somebody to Love*, 152.

111. Slick, *Somebody to Love*, 57–58.

112. Slick, *Somebody to Love*, 58.

113. Slick, *Somebody to Love*, 70–71. In Barbara Rowes's account, the song was "It Ain't Necessarily So," but the outcome was the same (Rowes, *Grace Slick*, 19).

114. "Fly Jefferson Airplane with Drummer Spencer Dryden," *Hit Parader* 27, no. 43 (January 1968): 26–27; Gleason, *Jefferson Airplane*, 213–14.

115. Gleason, *Jefferson Airplane*, 107, 126; Tamarkin, *Got a Revolution*, 29; Kaukonen, *Been So Long*, 58, 134.

116. "There Is No San Francisco Sound," *Hit Parader* 26, no. 36 (June 1967): 49–50.

117. Gleason, *Jefferson Airplane*, 200; Tamarkin, *Got a Revolution*, 49.

118. Jim [Delehant] and Don [Paulsen], "Tempo: Rock Meets Jazz, Chapter 2," *Hit Parader* 26, no. 39 (September 1967): 60.

119. Although these influences are not obvious, the driving quarter notes of Kantner's opening guitar riff recall Berry's rhythm guitar in "Memphis," while the riff shares its emphasis on the flat-third scale degree with Hubert Sumlin's guitar line in Howlin' Wolf's 1960 recording of "Spoonful."

120. Jim Delehant, "Jefferson Airplane: After Bathing at Baxter's," *Hit Parader* 27, no. 44 (February 1968): 18.

121. James Lichtenberg, "Flock You," *East Village Other* 4, no. 43 ([September 24], 1969): 8.

122. Zimmerman, *Counterculture Kaleidoscope*, 39, 44.

123. Gleason, *Jefferson Airplane*, 212.

124. Gleason, *Jefferson Airplane*, 97.

125. Ray Lang, "Crown of Creation: Jefferson Airplane," *Daily Californian* (October 2, 1968): 9.

126. Casady and Kaukonen recorded Davis's "Death Don't Have No Mercy" with their band Hot Tuna in 1970 (*Hot Tuna*, RCA Victor LSP-4353), as did the Grateful Dead on *Live/Dead* (Warner Brothers-Seven Arts 2WS-1830, 1969).

127. Jimmie Strothers, "The Blood-Stained Banders" (1936), reissued on *A Treasury of Library of Congress Field Recordings*, selected and annotated by Stephen Wade (Rounder CD 1500, 1997); Kaukonen, *Been So Long*, 132–33.

128. Zimmerman, *Counterculture Kaleidoscope*, 6.

129. Gleason, *Jefferson Airplane*, 188.

130. Slick, *Somebody to Love*, 141.

131. Gleason, *Jefferson Airplane*, 87, 92–93, 108, 113, 181–82, 218, 245. Kaukonen praises "the vina player in the Nonesuch 'Music of Southern India' records" (113), which refers to Balachander. I speculate that the band's references to Bulgarian music refer to another Nonesuch recording, *Music of Bulgaria* by the Ensemble of the Bulgarian Republic, released in 1966.

132. Gleason, *Jefferson Airplane*, 161.

133. Slick, *Somebody to Love*, 107; Zimmerman, *Counterculture Kaleidoscope*, 66–70. A similar orientalism appears in "rejoyce," in which "a sinewy melody, ripe with augmented seconds, played by a wind instrument. . . . is meant to mimic what in American vaudeville shows and cinema had become characteristic sounds of a Middle Eastern snake charmer" (Zimmerman, *Counterculture Kaleidoscope*, 145). Frank Kofsky argues that these "*Arabian Nights* figurations" reflect the influence of John Coltrane's soprano saxophone style (Kofsky, *Black Nationalism and the Revolution in Music* [New York: Pathfinder, 1970], 192); also see Tamarkin, *Got a Revolution*, 153.

134. Bulgarian choral music often involves shifting, sometimes dissonant harmonies over a drone, an approach also heard in the final moments of "Crown of Creation" (Timothy Rice, *Music in Bulgaria: Experiencing Music, Expressing Culture* [Oxford: Oxford University Press, 2004], 58, 65).

135. Tamarkin, *Got a Revolution*, 199.

136. Tamarkin, *Got a Revolution*, 204.

137. Miller Francis Jr., "Jefferson Airplane: '. . . it's time for you and me,'" *Los Angeles Free Press* 6, no. 83 (December 19, 1969): 54.

138. Critic Dave Marsh noted in 1969 that "Grace Slick's 'Up against the wall motherfucker'

is far more sonorous than the MC5 or David Peel" (Dave Marsh, review of *Volunteers*, *Creem* 2, no. 7 [1969]: 19).

139. Vince Martin and Fred Neil, *Tear Down the Walls* (Elektra EKS 7248, 1964); Anderson, *Movement and the Sixties*, 197; Tamarkin, *Got a Revolution*, 194.

140. J. Lawrence, "The Airplane and Folk-Rock," *Changes* 1, no. 11 (1969): 14–15.

141. Tamarkin, *Got a Revolution*, 194.

142. Tamarkin, *Got a Revolution*, 176; Patricia Kennealy [as Patricia Kennely], "Pop Talk," *Jazz and Pop* 7 (November 1968): 34; [Sue Cassidy Clark], letter to "Ralph, Mother and Penny," October 4, 1968, box 4, folder 20, SCC. "Filthy jewels" is from Tamarkin, who claims that "some misheard" the line "as 'filthy Jews'"; Clark, in a firsthand account, reports hearing "Jewish broads with your jewels."

143. Tamarkin, *Got a Revolution*, 200.

144. "Abbie and Anita Rap with Grace and Paul," *East Village Other* 5, no. 27 (June 2, 1970): 12–13, 17. Slick and Abbie Hoffman's most famous exploit took place on April 24, 1970, when Slick, invited to a formal tea at the White House along with other alumnae of Finch College, brought Hoffman along as part of what they later claimed was a plot to dose President Nixon's drink with LSD. The plot failed when the pair were banned as a security risk ("Abbie Hoffman Barred from White House Tea," *New York Times*, April 25, 1970; Rowes, *Grace Slick*, 161–65; Tamarkin, *Got a Revolution*, 218).

145. United States Department of Justice, Federal Bureau of Investigation, San Francisco, "Confidential: Grace W. Slick nee Grace Barnett Wing," August 14, 1970, vault.fbi.gov, accessed April 28, 2018; Strausbaugh, *Rock 'til You Drop*, 106.

146. On Jefferson Airplane's role as "part of the counterculture's move towards Romantic naturism," see David Ingram, "'Go to the Forest and Move': 1960s American Rock Music as Electronic Pastoral," *49th Parallel* 20 (winter 2006–2007): 5.

147. Gleason, *Jefferson Airplane*, 20.

148. Bill Boehlke, "Pop," *Distant Drummer* 60 (November 27, 1969).

149. James Lichtenberg, "The Nameless Terror: Rolling Knights in the Great Hall of Greed," *East Village Other* 5, no. 2 (December 17, 1969): 7.

150. Francis, "Jefferson Airplane," 54.

151. Miller Francis Jr., "Airplane," *Great Speckled Bird* 3, no. 35 (August 31, 1970): 13.

152. Thomas Frank, *The Conquest of Cool: Business Culture, Counterculture, and the Rise of Hip Consumerism* (Chicago: University of Chicago Press, 1997), 16.

153. Michael Quigley, "Mikey Music," *Georgia Straight* 5, no. 46 (January 27, 1971): 23.

154. Zimmerman, *Counterculture Kaleidoscope*, 60.

155. Thomas D'Antoni, "Airplane Concert—Bust for Some, Groove for Others," *Harry* 1, no. 11 (April 3, 1970): 17.

156. Ed Leimbacker, "The Crash of the Jefferson Airplane," in *Conversations with the New Reality*, ed. "the editors of *Ramparts*" (San Francisco: Canfield Colophon, 1971), 106.

157. "The Revolutionary Hype," *Time* 93, no. 1 (January 3, 1969): 49.

158. Lydon, "Rock for Sale," 117.

159. Strausbaugh, *Rock 'til You Drop*, 102.

160. Tamarkin, *Got a Revolution*, 197. Kaukonen's father worked at various times for the FBI, the Asia Foundation, and the US State Department (26–27).

161. Kantner, *Guide through the Chaos*, disc 1, track 10.

162. Kantner, *Guide through the Chaos*, disc 2, track 7.

163. Wayne Glausser, "Gotta Revolution, 1987: Grace Slick, Paul Kantner, and 'Volunteers of America,'" *Popular Music and Society* 12, no. 2 (1988): 46.

Chapter 3

1. My account of this incident is compiled from two firsthand reports: Joel Finler, "L'affaire Godard," *IT*, no. 46 (December 13–31, 1968): 24; and Martha Merrill, "Black Panthers in the New Wave," *Film Culture*, no. 53–54–55 (spring 1972): 134–45.

2. Finler, "L'affaire Godard," 24.

3. Merrill, "Black Panthers," 137.

4. The competition may not have been very fierce: according to Finler, the National Film Theatre actually supplied the electrical power for the Open Festival screening (Finler, "L'affaire Godard," 24).

5. Merrill, "Black Panthers," 137.

6. "The Times Diary: Frozen Still," London *Times*, November 30, 1968; "Godard Punches Producer for Change Made in Film," *New York Times*, December 2, 1968; "London and the Film," *North Carolina Anvil* 2, no. 85 (January 4, 1969): 8.

7. David Mairowitz, "Random Notes from England," *San Francisco Express Times* 1, no. 47 (December 11, 1968): 8.

8. One exception is critic Marc Cerisuelo, who regards *One Plus One* as "the best rock film to date in the history of the cinema" thanks to "the freedom and the responsibility the filmmaker gives the spectator to line up, connect or oppose the various elements presented" (Marc Cerisuelo, "Jean-Luc, Community, and Communication," in *A Companion to Jean-Luc Godard*, ed. Tom Conley and T. Jefferson Kline [Chichester: Wiley-Blackwell, 2014], 301). Kevin J. Hayes argues that reception of the film has been "overharsh" and that *One Plus One* actually "marks an important development in Godard's understanding of the processes of production, publication, and consumption" (Kevin J. Hayes, "The Book as Motif in *One Plus One*," *Studies in French Cinema* 4, no. 3 [2004]: 219).

9. Colin MacCabe, *Godard: A Portrait of the Artist at Seventy* (New York: Farrar, Straus & Giroux, 2003), 212.

10. Kaja Silverman and Harun Farocki, *Speaking about Godard* (New York: New York University Press, 1998), 120. It is beyond my scope here to fully contextualize *One Plus One* within Godard's large, complex body of work, but it is worth noting that *One Plus One*'s major themes are anticipated in some of the director's earlier films. The politics and economics of mass media, especially film and television, are essential subjects in much of Godard's work throughout his career. The specific interest in popular music and the recording studio displayed in *One Plus One* is presaged in such films as *Masculin féminin* (1966), whose central female character, a *yé-yé* singer played by Chantal Goya, is shown making a recording; *Made in U.S.A.* (1966), in which Marianne Faithfull sings the Jagger/Richards composition "As Tears Go By"; *La Chinoise* (1967), whose soundtrack features "Mao-Mao," a driving rock song by Claude Channes that celebrates (or perhaps satirizes) Maoism; and *Weekend* (1967), in which a militant faction of cannibalistic hippies play rock beats on a drum set incongruously situated in their wooded hideout. In *British Sounds* (1969), students at the London School of Economics write new lyrics about Mao and Ho Chi Minh for Beatles songs. Several of these films also include references to Black radicalism: *Masculin féminin* contains dialogue from Amiri Baraka's play *Dutchman*; in *La Chinoise*, Black leftist Omar Diop lectures on Marxist theory; and in *Weekend*, two workers, an African and an

Arab, make political speeches. For thorough overviews of Godard's life and work, including the films cited here, see MacCabe, *Godard*; and Richard Brody, *Everything Is Cinema: The Working Life of Jean-Luc Godard* (New York: Metropolitan, 2008).

11. Richard Roud, *Jean-Luc Godard*, 2nd ed. (Bloomington: Indiana University Press, 1970), 149; Richard Roud, "In the Picture: One Plus One," *Sight and Sound* 37, no. 4 (autumn 1968): 182.

12. Roud, *Jean-Luc Godard*, 148.

13. Ian Wright, "A Warning from Battersea," *Manchester Guardian Weekly*, August 1, 1968.

14. Guy Monreal, "Qui n'a pas son petit Godard?," *L'Express*, no. 888 (July 15–21, 1968): 37.

15. Roud, *Jean-Luc Godard*, 151.

16. Jan Dawson, "1968 London Festival: One Plus One," *Sight and Sound* 38, no. 1 (winter 1968/1969): 32.

17. *Sympathy for the Devil*, with Quarrier's modified ending, is reissued on Abkco DVD 1005-9. Times given in discussions of individual scenes refer to this DVD.

18. A useful discussion of the film's structure can be found in James Roy MacBean, *Film and Revolution* (Bloomington: Indiana University Press, 1975), 79–81. I have found no source that identifies the pornographic novel, which was likely written for the film; for a detailed discussion of its contents, see Hayes, "The Book as Motif," 220–21.

19. Contemporaneous discussions of Godard filming in London include Monreal, "Qui n'a pas," 37–38; Wright, "Warning from Battersea"; Roud, "In the Picture," 182–83. On the film's title, see Andrew Sarris, "Films in Focus," *Village Voice* (April 30, 1970): 61; Walter S. Ross, "Splicing Together Jean-Luc Godard," *Esquire* 72, no. 1 (July 1969): 72.

20. Author's transcription from *Voices* (dir. Richard Mordaunt, 1968), included in *Sympathy for the Devil* (Fabulous DVD FHED 1937, 2006). *Voices* is a documentary on the making of *One Plus One*.

21. Des O'Rawe, *Regarding the Real: Cinema, Documentary, and the Visual Arts* (Manchester: Manchester University Press, 2016), 124. David Fresko argues that "by leaving unarticulated the exact nature of the relation between the Rolling Stones and politics, *One Plus One* delineates not an equivalence, but a relation designed to foment thought by soliciting the active participation of the audience within an open signifying structure that asks spectators to choose this . . . and then that" (Fresko, "Magical Mystery Tours: Godard and Antonioni in America," in *The Global Sixties in Sound and Vision: Media, Counterculture, Revolt*, ed. Timothy Scott Brown and Andrew Lison [New York: Palgrave Macmillan, 2014], 58).

22. Quarrier explained that he included the complete version of the song as a "tidbit to the kids" ("London and the Film"). Godard's original ending is included alongside Quarrier's in *Sympathy for the Devil* (Fabulous DVD FHED 1937, 2006).

23. Godard himself said of the film: "One plus one does not mean one plus one equals two. It means just what it says: one plus one . . ." (Richard Roud, "Sympathy for the Devil," *Monthly Film Bulletin* 38 [April 1971]: 83). Nora M. Alter claims that the May '68 slogan "One Plus One" "sought to bring together the colors of the two political movements of the day: the Red and the Black," while the film "operates through fragmentation, incompleteness, openness, possibility" (Alter, "Composing in Fragments: Music in the Essay Films of Resnais and Godard," *SubStance* 41, no. 2 [2012]: 33–34).

24. In his autobiography, Keith Richards remembers (not quite accurately) that "the voice of Jimmy Miller can be heard on the film, complaining, 'Where's the groove?' on the earlier takes. There wasn't one" (Keith Richards with James Fox, *Life* [New York: Little, Brown, 2010], 252).

25. Steven Feld, "Aesthetics as Iconicity of Style (uptown title); or, (downtown title) 'Lift-up-over Sounding': Getting into the Kaluli Groove," in Charles Keil and Steven Feld, *Music Grooves: Essays and Dialogues* (Chicago: University of Chicago Press, 1994), 109. For a more technical consideration of groove, see Anne Danielsen, *Presence and Pleasure: The Funk Grooves of James Brown and Parliament* (Middletown, CT: Wesleyan University Press, 2006).

26. Feld, "Aesthetics as Iconicity of Style," 111.

27. Robert S. Gold, *A Jazz Lexicon* (New York: A. A. Knopf, 1964), 130–31.

28. Griselda, "One Plus One," *inter/VIEW* 1, no. 8 (1970): 12.

29. As several critics have pointed out, Godard's use of direct address and refusal of naturalism reflect the influence of Bertolt Brecht's theories of distance and estrangement. See William S. Pechter, "For and against Godard," *Commentary* 47, no. 4 (April 1, 1969): 59–63; Joel Schechter, "Brecht and Godard in Ten Scenes from *The Decline and Fall of Aristotle*," *Theater* 3, no. 1 (1970): 25–30; Jan Uhde, "Influence of Bertolt Brecht's Theory of Distanciation on the Contemporary Cinema, Particularly on Jean-Luc Godard," *Journal of the University Film Association* 26, no. 3 (1974): 28–30, 44.

30. Marc Cerisuelo, discussing *One Plus One*, argues that the Rolling Stones were "a group whose music—at that time—(thanks to Keith Richards) was (as it were) one of the accomplishments of the blues" (Cerisuelo, "Jean-Luc, Community, and Communication," 301–2).

31. LeRoi Jones [Amiri Baraka], *Blues People: Negro Music in White America* (1963; repr., New York: Quill, 1999), 81.

32. LeRoi Jones [Amiri Baraka], *Black Music* (New York: William Morrow, 1967), 205. The remark about "male hormones" reflects the macho heterosexism common in Baraka's work of the period. Also see Baraka's short play "Rockgroup," in which a group of "white fags" called "The Crackers" sing a song with the refrain "White shit / hocuspocus in the clouds all right" with their guitars plugged into a chained Black man's anus (Imamu Ameer Baraka [Amiri Baraka], "Rockgroup," *The Cricket* 1 [1969]: 41–43). The play is revealing of the ways in which Baraka's homophobia intersected with his Black nationalism.

33. Gary Elshaw, "One Plus One," elshaw.tripod.com/oneplusone.html, accessed April 30, 2018.

34. Merrill, "Black Panthers," 143.

35. The quoted text, which I have transcribed from the film, is from a speech that Carmichael delivered in Oakland, California, on February 17, 1968, at a benefit for imprisoned Black Panther Huey Newton. The version in the film compiles lines from various sections of the original speech (Stokely Carmichael, *Stokely Speaks: Black Power Back to Pan-Africanism* [New York: Random House, 1971], 121, 124).

36. Richard Dyer, *White* (London: Routledge, 1997), 45.

37. Alan Clayson reports that Jagger's line "Get down with it!" was derived from Little Richard's 1966 single of the same title (Clayson, *Legendary Sessions: The Rolling Stones: Beggars Banquet* [New York: Billboard, 2008], 182).

38. Jack Hamilton, *Just around Midnight: Rock and Roll and the Racial Imagination* (Cambridge, MA: Harvard University Press, 2016), 251.

39. Peter Doggett, *There's a Riot Going On: Revolutionaries, Rock Stars, and the Rise and Fall of the '60s* (Edinburgh: Canongate, 2007), 262. Hamilton, while acknowledging that "Brown Sugar" "boasts some of the most appalling lyrics ever written for a rock and roll song," argues that it also can be heard as an "unflinching exploration of racial and musical imagination" in which the Stones critique themselves (Hamilton, *Midnight*, 273).

40. Jonathan Eisen, *Altamont: Death of Innocence in the Woodstock Nation* (New York: Avon, 1970), 261.

41. Hamilton, *Just around Midnight*, 263.

42. "Howlin' Wolf on Shindig Broadcast Date May 20, 1965," https://www.youtube.com/watch?v=gWBS0GX1s9o, accessed April 30, 2018.

43. Stanley Booth, *The True Adventures of the Rolling Stones* (Chicago: A Cappella, 2000), 110.

44. Bill Flanagan, for example, writes that "the incense parted after *Their Satanic Majesties Request*, and the Stones entered their richest period—a time when they took their R&B roots into a fresh, personal, and eventually harrowing rock & roll style" (Flanagan, *Written in My Soul: Rock's Great Songwriters Talk about Creating Their Music* [Chicago: Contemporary, 1986], 149); Rolling Stones, *Beggars Banquet* (London LKX 57150, 1968).

45. Ritchie Yorke, "Stones' Producer Jimmy Miller," *Fusion*, no. 5 (January 29, 1969): 6. Miller also claims here that "Banquet is really watermelon country, with the real, lousy sounding guitar," but it is not clear to me from context whether he was intentionally invoking minstrel stereotypes.

46. Stephen Davis, *Old Gods Almost Dead: The 40-Year Odyssey of the Rolling Stones* (New York: Broadway, 2001), 241. On Dzidzornu, also see David Henderson, *'Scuse Me While I Kiss the Sky: Jimi Hendrix: Voodoo Child* (New York: Atria, 2008), 273. Dzidzornu appears in the studio sequences of *One Plus One* (beginning at 46:30).

47. The performance appears in *Rolling Stones: The Stones in the Park* (Collector's Edition DVD, 2004).

48. On the idea of "hot rhythm," see Ronald Radano, "Hot Fantasies: American Modernism and the Idea of Black Rhythm," in *Music and the Racial Imagination*, ed. Ronald Radano and Philip V. Bohlman (Chicago: University of Chicago Press, 2000), 459–80.

49. Sheila Whiteley, *The Space between the Notes: Rock and the Counter-culture* (London: Routledge, 1992), 100.

50. Doggett, *There's a Riot Going On*, 262.

51. Biographer Philip Norman writes that on "Sympathy for the Devil" Jagger's "Deep South impersonation has become so extreme as to be almost unrecognizable as such, but instead seems the unique dialect of Planet Jagger" (Norman, *Mick Jagger* [New York: Ecco, 2012], 293).

52. Alan Clayson, *The Rolling Stones: Beggars Banquet* (New York: Billboard, 2008), 197; Yorke, "Stones' Producer," 6.

53. Happy Jack, "Yummy! Yummy! Yummy!," *Ann Arbor Argus* 1, no. 1 (January 24–February 7, 1969): 8.

54. Baraka, *Black Music*, 123–24.

55. Baraka, *Black Music*, 205–6. This passage appears on the same page as the quotation beginning "Not only the Beatles" cited above and recited in the film: one wonders if Godard made a conscious decision not to include this perhaps-too-obvious reference to the Stones.

56. Eldridge Cleaver, *Soul on Ice* (New York: McGraw-Hill, 1968), 194, 199.

57. Obi Egbuna, *Destroy This Temple: The Voice of Black Power in Britain* (London: MacGibbon and Kee, 1971), 142.

58. Stanley Booth, *The True Adventures of the Rolling Stones* (Chicago: A Cappella, 2000), 142.

59. Jonathan Cott, "Jean-Luc Godard," *Rolling Stone*, no. 35 (June 14, 1969): 21–22.

60. Christopher Sandford, *Mick Jagger: Primitive Cool* (New York: Cooper Square, 1999), 122.

61. Booth, *True Adventures*, 146.

62. Booth, *True Adventures*, 269.

63. Booth, *True Adventures*, 203; Doggett, *There's a Riot Going On*, 263.

64. "Jagger Rap/Stoned Earful," *IT*, no. 59 (July 4–17, 1969): 15. It is unclear in context whether Jagger means that "black people" or "repressed white people" (mentioned earlier in the interview) are the "bourgeoisie." Richards flatly dismisses *One Plus One* as "a total load of crap" in his 2010 autobiography (Richards, *Life*, 252).

65. Marcus Collins, "Sucking in the Seventies? The Rolling Stones and the Aftermath of the Permissive Society," *Popular Music History* 7, no. 1 (2012): 11–12. Alessandro Bratus demonstrates that the underground press drew similar conclusions about the Stones' "liberation of the individual" as early as the 1970s (Bratus, "Scene through the Press: Rock Music and Underground Papers in London, 1966–1973," *Twentieth-Century Music* 8, no. 2 [September 2011]: 232–33).

66. Doggett, *There's a Riot Going On*, 169, 314.

67. Whiteley, *Space between the Notes*, 89.

68. Tim Barnes, "Loosen Up: The Rolling Stones Ring in the 1960s," in *Living Through Pop*, ed. Andrew Blake (London: Routledge, 1999), 28.

69. Davis, *Old Gods*, 238–39. David E. James points out that the song also "invokes black vernacular culture's intense preoccupation with the devil that produced, among so many other instances, Robert Johnson's 'Me and the Devil Blues'" (James, *Rock 'n' Film: Cinema's Dance with Popular Music* [New York: Oxford University Press, 2016], 270).

70. Ned Rorem, *Critical Affairs: A Composer's Journal* (New York: G. Braziller, 1970), 41.

71. Terry H. Anderson, *The Movement and the Sixties* (New York: Oxford University Press, 1995), 200–202.

72. Doggett, *There's a Riot Going On*, 168–70; Neil Nehring, "Sir Michael and the Origin and Reception of 'Street Fighting Man,'" *Rock Music Studies* 2, no. 1 (2015): 63.

73. On the radio ban, see John Platoff, "John Lennon, 'Revolution,' and the Politics of Musical Reception," *Journal of Musicology* 22, no. 2 (2005): 260–61.

74. Platoff, "'Revolution,'" 257–59; also see Doggett, *There's a Riot Going On*, 195–96; Gerald Carlin and Mark Jones, "'Helter Skelter' and Sixties Revisionism," in *Countercultures and Popular Music*, ed. Jedediah Sklower and Sheila Whiteley (London: Routledge, 2016), 95.

75. Doggett, *There's a Riot Going On*, 170.

76. Brian Henderson argues that "it is . . . possible . . . that Godard's editing here fulfills the classical function of montage—that of contrast or opposition: the commercial protest of the Stones v. the authenticity of black revolt, etc." (Henderson, "Toward a Non-Bourgeois Camera Style," *Film Quarterly* 24/2 [winter 1970/71]: 6).

77. the black shadow, "Seven Days and Seven Nights Making Twelve Days and Twelve Nights in All," *San Francisco Good Times* 2, no. 43 (November 6, 1969): 9.

78. Norman Silverstein, "Godard's Maoism," *Salmagundi*, no. 18 (winter 1972): 22. Silverstein leaves the interpretation of this contrast open.

79. Author's transcription from film.

80. Rosie Wild, "'Black Was the Colour of Our Fight': The Transnational Roots of British Black Power," in *The Other Special Relationship: Race, Rights, and Riots in Britain and the United States*, ed. Robin D. G. Kelley and Stephen Tuck (New York: Palgrave Macmillan, 2015), 26.

81. Dilip Hiro, *Black British, White British*, rev. ed. (New York: Monthly Review Press, 1973), 59; Wild, "Black Was the Colour," 26.

82. Egbuna, *Destroy This Temple*, 16. Carmichael opened his speech with a moment of silence for the recently deceased John Coltrane (Pat Thomas, *Listen, Whitey! The Sights and Sounds of Black Power 1965-1975* [Seattle: Fantagraphics, 2012], 91–92).

83. Hiro, *Black British,* 61; also see Wild, "Black Was the Colour," 38–39.

84. Anne-Marie Angelo, "The Black Panthers in London, 1967–1972: A Diasporic Struggle Navigates the Black Atlantic," *Radical History Review,* no. 103 (winter 2009): 22.

85. Chris Mullard, *On Being Black in Britain* (Washington, DC: Inscape, 1975), 60; Hiro, *Black British,* 241; Wild, "Black Was the Colour," 35–36.

86. "Three on Threat to Kill Charge," London *Times,* July 27, 1968; "2 Black Panther Men Guilty," London *Times,* December 11, 1968; Egbuna, *Destroy This Temple,* 10–28.

87. Cott, "Jean-Luc Godard," 21.

88. "La récitation représente une variation de la répétition sonore musicale" (Marina Roumenova Grozdanova, "From Stardust to Stones to Bad Seed: Vers une déconstruction du *rock doc*: Le corps de la *rock star* au coeur de l'oeuvre audiovisuelle hybride" [MA thesis, University of Montreal, 2017], 68).

89. Gary Elshaw, "The Depiction of Late 1960's Counter Culture in the 1968 Films of Jean-Luc Godard" (MA thesis, Victoria University of Wellington, New Zealand, 2000), "Conclusion," elshaw.tripod.com, accessed April 30, 2018.

90. Raymond Durgnat, "One Plus One," in *The Films of Jean-Luc Godard,* ed. Ian Cameron (New York: Praeger, 1969), 181. Nora M. Alter argues that "in many ways *One Plus One* functions as a linchpin to Godard's increasing skepticism about media culture" (Alter, "Composing in Fragments," 32).

91. "Half-Done Godard Film Fails to Irk Its Brit. Producer," *Variety* (July 10, 1968): 12. US actor Bernard Boston, who appears in the junkyard scene, is an exception.

92. On Ansah, see Manthia Diawara, *African Cinema: Politics and Culture* (Bloomington: Indiana University Press, 1992), 159; Alfred Tamakloe, "Celebration of Local Fabrics," *Djembe Magazine,* no. 28 (1999), www.djembe.dk/no/28/26colf.html, accessed April 28, 2009. On Daniels, see Harris M. Lentz III, *Obituaries in the Performing Arts, 2010* (Jefferson, NC: McFarland, 2011), 91. On Jones, see "Clifton Jones," www.imdb.com/name/nm0427790/, accessed April 30, 2018. On Patterson, see "Curator's Choice: Actor, Model and Self-Taught Painter Rudi Patterson's Visions in Color," *Culture 24* (April 22, 2014), http://www.culture24.org.uk/art/painting-and-drawing/art476986-Curator-Choice-Actor-model-self-taught-painter-Rudi-Patterson-Visions-Colour, accessed April 30, 2018. On Spencer, see "Did I Ever Tell You . . . ? Linbert Spencer OBE," https://www.youtube.com/watch?v=N3JECZZ2OHk, accessed June 13, 2020. On Stewart, see Gavin Gaughan, "Roy Stewart," *The Guardian* (February 3, 2009), https://www.theguardian.com/culture/2009/feb/04/roy-stewart-obituary, accessed June 13, 2020. On Forster-Jones, see "The Times Diary," London *Times,* April 3, 1969. Both Des O'Rawe and James S. Williams list Senegalese actor Omar Diop as part of the cast, although he does not appear in the film's credits (O'Rawe, *Regarding the Real,* 126; James S. Williams, *Encounters with Godard: Ethics, Aesthetics, Politics* [Albany: State University of New York Press, 2016], 39). Godard's casting does not reflect the significant role of Asian immigrants in the British Black Power Movement (see Wild, "Black Was the Colour," 29).

93. Durgnat, "One Plus One," 180.

94. Angelo, "Black Panthers in London," 21.

95. John Walker, "London Letter," *Other Scenes* 3, no. 17 (December 1, 1969): 3; *Some People,* dir. Clive Donner (1962; Network DVD, 2013).

96. "Ying-Yang Uprising," *International Times,* no. 20 (October 27–November 11, 1967): 8. According to Des O'Rawe, Godard originally intended to cast Michael X in *One Plus One* (O'Rawe, *Regarding the Real,* 131).

97. John L. Williams, *Michael X: A Life in Black and White* (London: Century, 2008), 152; O'Rawe, *Regarding the Real*, 119. Williams points out that Dymon's new pseudonym, Frankie Y, was "the kind of playful name that would have received short shrift from Elijah Muhammad and the real Nation of Islam" (152). Dymon played a role in running Michael X's Racial Adjustment Action Society while Michael X was in prison in 1967–1968 ("Michael X," *OZ*, no. 18 [February 1969]: [8]).

98. "FCO 95/792: The Black Power Movement in Great Britain" (1970): 18 (UK Government Files: Records of the Foreign and Commonwealth Office and Predecessors, National Archives [UK]), at *Popular Culture in Britain and America, 1950–1975*, http://www.rockandroll.amdigital .co.uk.libproxy.wustl.edu/Search/DocumentDetailsSearch.aspx?documentid=586832&prevPos =586832&vpath=searchresults&pi=1, accessed April 30, 2018. For examples of Dymon's rhetoric (from a June 1968 speech to the Revolutionary Socialist Students' Federation at the London School of Economics), see Stu Glauberman, "Report from Lunnon: Uptight Little Island," *Berkeley Barb* 6, no. 24 (June 21–27, 1968): 4; Frankie Y, "Revoltionary? [*sic*]," *IT*, no. 34 (June 28– July 11, 1968): [18].

99. "1+1+JLG: 2 or 3 Tapes of a Press Conference," *OZ*, no. 14 (July 1968): 43.

100. "Godard Turns Black," *IT*, no. 37 (August 9–22, 1968): 17.

101. Walker, "London Letter," 3; Jim Pines, "The Cultural Context of Black British Cinema," in *Black British Cultural Studies: A Reader*, ed. Houston A. Baker et al. (Chicago: University of Chicago Press, 1996), 188; *Death May Be Your Santa Claus*, dir. Frankie Dymon Jr. (1969), https:// www.youtube.com/watch?v=JUGr4_eMv68, accessed April 30, 2018.

102. Walker, "London Letter," 3.

103. The passage appears in Cleaver, *Soul on Ice*, 158–60.

104. Williams, *Encounters*, 43.

105. hm, "White Wo/Man Black," *Great Speckled Bird* (May 25, 1970): 8.

106. MacBean, *Film and Revolution*, 92–93.

107. Craig J. Peariso, "Representing Black Power: Handling a 'Revolution' in the Age of Mass Media," in *Media and Revolt: Strategies and Performances from the 1960s to the Present*, ed. Kathrin Fahlenbrach et al. (New York: Berghahn, 2014), 258.

108. Elshaw, "One Plus One."

109. Cleaver, *Soul on Ice*, 155, 164–65, 175.

110. Gary Elshaw argues that "rhetoric is used within *One Plus One* as a source of 'inspiration' to the majority of the characters who have become immobilised by it" (Elshaw, "One Plus One").

111. O'Rawe, *Regarding the Real*, 129.

112. Shaun Inouye, "Indicting Truth: Jean-Luc Godard's *Sympathy for the Devil* and 1960s Documentary Cinema," *Studies in Documentary Film* 7, no. 2 (2013): 148.

113. Roberta T. Ash, "Durkheim's 'Moral Education' Reconsidered: Toward the Creation of a Counterculture," *The School Review* 80, no. 1 (November 1971): 116.

114. R. Huffman et al., "Letters," *Great Speckled Bird* 3, no. 22 (June 1, 1970): 5.

115. Finler, "L'affaire Godard," 24; Merrill, "Black Panthers," 134–35.

116. *Black Panthers*, dir. Agnès Varda (1968; Arte Editions/Ciné-Tamaris DVD, 2012); *Black Panther*, aka *Off the Pig*, dir. California Newsreel (1969; California Newsreel DVD, 2004); *Eldridge Cleaver, Black Panther*, dir. William Klein (1970; https://www.youtube.com/watch?v= oveOiKSj7Jo, accessed May 1, 2018).

117. Charles J. Stewart, "The Evolution of a Revolution: Stokely Carmichael and the Rhetoric

of Black Power," *Quarterly Journal of Speech* 83, no. 4 (November 1997): 439; also see Robert L. Scott and Wayne Brockriede, *The Rhetoric of Black Power* (New York: Harper and Row, 1969).

118. Peariso, "Representing Black Power," 153; Craig J. Peariso, *Radical Theatrics: Put-Ons, Politics, and the Sixties* (Seattle: University of Washington Press, 2014), 128.

119. Peariso, *Radical Theatrics*, 162.

120. "1+1+JLG," 42–44.

121. Merrill, "Black Panthers," 143.

122. Michael Goodwin and Greil Marcus, *Double Feature: Movies and Politics* (New York: Outerbridge and Lazard, 1972), 17, 51.

123. Ken Mate et al., "Let's See Where We Are," *Velvet Light Trap* 9 (Summer 1973): 35.

124. Brody, *Everything Is Cinema*, 341.

125. On the left, see Judy Baston, "The Struggle against Racism," *People's World* 33, no. 15 (April 11, 1970): 11; "No More Sympathy for the Devil," *Rat* (June 19, 1970): 20. For more conservative views, see John Simon, "Jean-Luc Raves Again," *New Leader* 53, no. 10 (May 11, 1970): 32–33; John Weightman, "Whatever Happened to Godard?," *Encounter* 33, no. 3 (September 1969): 58–59.

126. Leo Hamalian, "Waiting for Godard," *Journal of Popular Culture* 4, no. 1 (summer 1970): 308–9. Another fan of *One Plus One* was future punk icon Patti Smith, who was living in Paris when it was released and remembered that "we'd come in the morning and watch it over and over and over again, for five days running" (Dave Marsh, "Patti Smith: Her Horses Got Wings, They Can Fly," *Rolling Stone* [January 1, 1976]).

127. Bill Rasch, "Sympathy for the Devil," *Daily Planet* 1, no. 16 (June 22, 1970): 17.

128. Lee Davidson, "No Sympathy for Godard," *Berkeley Tribe* 2, no. 31 (February 6–13, 1970): 18.

129. Brody, *Everything Is Cinema*, 342–43.

130. Brody, *Everything Is Cinema*, 342.

131. Fresko, "Magical Mystery Tours," 60.

132. Keith Beattie, *D. A. Pennebaker* (Urbana: University of Illinois Press, 2011), 71.

133. In *1 PM*'s opening credits, Pennebaker claims that "the Leroi Jones street mass was not meant as part of the film"; nonetheless, Godard is visible on camera during the performance (*1 PM* [1969], dir. Jean-Luc Godard, Richard Leacock, and D. A. Pennebaker [Intermedio DVD, 2008]. Timings in the text refer to this DVD).

134. Brody, *Everything Is Cinema*, 342; Williams, *Encounters*, 40. In her critique of the film, Jan Dawson writes "when Rip Torn denounces the manipulative techniques of big business to the black schoolchildren, we can also observe the manipulative techniques used by Godard to provoke 'spontaneous' revolution in the classroom; more poignantly perhaps, as LeRoi Jones leads a group of black street musicians in a strident chant 'We are your nightmare, white man . . . ,' the camera shows us Godard watching awkwardly from the sidelines" (Dawson, "One PM," *Monthly Film Bulletin* 38, no. 444 [1971]: 168). In her later career, Bellamy "served as a New York State Senator, the president of the New York City Council, director of the Peace Corps," and "executive director of UNICEF" (Frank Verano, "D. A. Pennebaker and the Politics and Aesthetics of Mature-Period Direct Cinema," [PhD diss., University of Sussex, 2015], 180).

135. Advertisement, *Berkeley Tribe* 1, no. 22 (December 5–11, 1969): 23; Verano, "D. A. Pennebaker," 178; Dawson, "One PM," 168; Beattie, *D. A. Pennebaker*, 68–73. For a detailed and thoughtful discussion of *1 PM*, see Verano, "D. A. Pennebaker," 138–81.

136. Jerry Rubin is visible in the room with Cleaver, although he does not speak.

137. "Enter: Ronnie Cleaver," *Berkeley Barb* 7, no. 21 (November 15–21, 1968): 11.

138. Author's transcription from *1 PM*.

139. G. Roy Levin, "D. A. Pennebaker" (1970), in *D. A. Pennebaker: Interviews*, ed. Keith Beattie and Trent Griffiths (Jackson: University Press of Mississippi, 2014), 14; Williams, *Encounters*, 40.

140. Goodwin and Marcus, *Double Feature*, 10–11.

141. Goodwin and Marcus, *Double Feature*, 65; Beattie, *D. A. Pennebaker*, 140; Brody, *Everything Is Cinema*, 342.

142. Barbara Rowes, *Grace Slick: The Biography* (Garden City, NY: Doubleday, 1980), 135. In a 1969 interview, Slick said that when the band met Godard, he "sat down and he didn't say a word for about 15 minutes. He just sat there, you know, like a toad, with his dark glasses on, not saying anything and just kind of looked around the room . . . I thought what he did that day was interesting. His 15 minutes of silence" (Diane Gardiner, interview with Grace Slick, July 1, 1969, typescript, box AF6, folder 18, Rolling Stone Records, Library and Archives, Rock and Roll Hall of Fame and Museum).

143. "Rip Torn, Prod. Heads Arrested on N.Y. Set of Godard Film for PBL," *Variety* 253, no. 1 (November 20, 1968): 64.

144. Grace Slick with Andrea Cagan, *Somebody to Love? A Rock-and-Roll Memoir* (New York: Warner, 1998), 179.

145. Renata Adler, "In Which a Filmmaker Discovers the Evil City," *New York Times*, November 20, 1968; "Airplane Shot Down," *Fifth Estate* 3, no. 17 (December 26–January 8, 1968): 4.

146. Slick, *Somebody to Love?*, 180. In a 1969 interview, Airplane drummer Spencer Dryden asserted that the band was the "comedy relief" of Godard's film ("Jefferson Airplane Raps," *Chicago Kaleidoscope* 1, no. 2 [December 6–19, 1968]: 4).

147. Goodwin and Marcus, *Double Feature*, 65.

148. "Statement of Jean Luc Godard," *Black Panther* 4, no. 21 (April 25, 1970): 4.

Chapter 4

1. "White Panthers Name Central Committee," *Sun* (Ann Arbor) (December 5, 1968): 1–2.

2. Richard Goldstein, "Why Do the Kids Dig Rock . . . ," *New York Times*, November 24, 1968.

3. Brett Callwood, *MC5: Sonically Speaking: A Tale of Revolution and Rock 'n' Roll* (Detroit: Wayne State University Press, 2010), 85; also see Michael Davis, *I Brought Down the MC5* (Los Angeles: Cleopatra, 2018), 123.

4. Fred Goodman, *The Mansion on the Hill: Dylan, Young, Geffen, Springsteen, and the Head-On Collision of Rock and Commerce* (New York: Times Books, 1997), 169–70; see also David A. Carson, *Grit, Noise, and Revolution: The Birth of Detroit Rock 'n' Roll* (Ann Arbor: University of Michigan Press, 2005), 183–85; David R. Ellis, "Uproar on Common Laid to N.Y. Group," *Boston Globe*, July 24, 1968. According to Ben Edmonds, one of the Motherfuckers also "launched into an incoherent diatribe about hair power: 'All that hair just builds up inside and *breaks out*, and that's what *we* gotta do!'" (Edmonds, "The Battle of New York," *MOJO*, no. 106 [September 2002], 73).

5. Wayne Kramer, *The Hard Stuff: Dope, Crime, the MC5 and My Life of Impossibilities* (New York: Da Capo, 2018), 97.

6. Edmonds, "Battle of New York," 74.

7. Ken Pitchford, "Is Nonviolence Ever Justified?," *Rat Subterranean News* 1, no. 24 (January 3–16, 1969): 7; Sandy Pearlman, "Riffs: Revolutionary Moments," *Village Voice* (January 2, 1969): 17; John Sinclair, "Rock and Roll Dope," *Fifth Estate* 3, no. 18 (January 9–22, 1969): 11.

8. Paul Nelson, "The Motherfuckers: Fillmore East vs. the East Village: The Full Report," *Rolling Stone*, no. 27 (February 15, 1969): 10; David Peel and the Lower East Side, *Have a Marijuana* (Elektra LP EKS-74032, 1968); MC5, *Kick Out the Jams* (Elektra LP EKS-74042, 1969).

9. Legs McNeil and Gillian McCain, *Please Kill Me: The Uncensored Oral History of Punk* (New York: Grove, 1996), 59.

10. Bob Rudnick and Dennis Frawley, "Kokaine Karma," *East Village Other* 4, no. 3 (December 20, 1968): 10. Rudnick and Frawley were affiliated with the White Panther Party. *Rolling Stone* reported that "the community . . . threatened (in a telephone call to Elektra's Bill Harvey) to burn the hall to the ground" unless they received free tickets. Morea denied the charge, albeit rather evasively: "We, as a group, didn't threaten to burn the theater down. *Somebody* might have" (Nelson, "The Motherfuckers," 10).

11. Pitchford, "Nonviolence," 7.

12. McNeil and McCain, *Please Kill Me*, 59.

13. Nelson, "The Motherfuckers," 10.

14. Goodman, *Mansion on the Hill*, 171.

15. Author's transcription from "MC5, John Sinclair, Bob Rudnick and Frawley WFMU in East Orange, New Jersey. 1968 December," audiocassette, box 61, John and Leni Sinclair Papers, Bentley Historical Library, University of Michigan [collection cited hereafter as JLSP]; also see Sinclair, "Rock and Roll Dope," 11.

16. Nelson, "The Motherfuckers," 10.

17. Nelson, "The Motherfuckers," 10.

18. Wayne Kramer, "Riots I Have Known and Loved," *Left of the Dial*, no. 4 (2002), http://makemyday.free.fr/wk1.htm, accessed December 15, 2016. Sinclair, more critically, wrote in 1969 that "I had insisted that people off the street be let in until all the seats were filled, and here was asshole Graham trying to stop people personally from coming in because he had something against them" (John Sinclair, "A Letter from Prison, Another Side of the MC5 Story, and (Incidentally) the End of an Era," *Creem* 2, no. 8 [November 28, 1969], 14, 27).

19. Osha Neumann, *Up Against the Wall Motherf**ker: A Memoir of the '60s, with Notes for Next Time* (New York: Seven Stories, 2008), 110; also see Kramer, *Hard Stuff*, 98. Neumann had previously been involved in the protests outside the Democratic National Convention in 1968 (David Farber, *Chicago '68* [Chicago: University of Chicago Press, 1988], 166, 197).

20. Nelson, "The Motherfuckers," 10.

21. Davis, *I Brought Down the MC5*, 123.

22. "Rock Sinks to a New Sexual Low as MC-5, David Peel Debut in N.Y.," *Variety* 253, no. 7 (January 1, 1969): 39; Ed Ochs, "Motor City 5 a Non-Stop, Driving Unit," *Billboard* 61, no. 2 (January 11, 1969): 10, 12. *Time* described the band's Fillmore East performance as "less revolutionary than revolting," although it is not clear whether the reporter was referring to the December 26 show ("The Revolutionary Hype," *Time* 93, no. 1 [January 3, 1969]: 49).

23. Davis, *I Brought Down the MC5*, 123.

24. Callwood, *Sonically Speaking*, 85.

25. Kramer, "Riots I Have Known and Loved."

26. McNeil and McCain, *Please Kill Me*, 60; also see Kramer, *Hard Stuff*, 99. Robert Gold later criticized the MC5 as "the revolutionary group who played the Fillmore East during its

recent imbroglio and remained neutral, 'we just came here to play'" (Gold, "Gold Slams MC5, Fowley," *Los Angeles Free Press* [March 21, 1969]: 30). In Sinclair's account, J. C. Crawford had introduced the band by asserting "that we were there to play the music and have a good time, which pissed a lot of neighborhood people off. And when Tyner repeated J.C.'s statement in the middle of the set they got pissed off even more" (Sinclair, "Rock and Roll Dope," 16).

27. Sinclair, "Letter from Prison," 27.

28. Pitchford, "Nonviolence," 7; "Fillmore East vs. the Motherfuckers," *East Village Other* 4, no. 5 (January 3, 1969): 2; Sinclair, "Rock and Roll Dope," 16.

29. Paul Gionfriddo, "Kicking Out the Jams at Fillmore East," *New Haven Register*, January 5, 1969. Another interpretation is that the MC5's inevitable failure to live up to the utopian promise of their rhetoric contributed to the violence. As Bruce Johnson and Martin Cloonan argue in their study of popular music and violence, "pop is implicitly and often explicitly about transcending [the] banal quotidian. Being so intensely a site of an emancipative imaginary, its failure to deliver brings to a point of angry focus the accumulated force of all those other promises that consumerism fails to deliver" (Bruce Johnson and Martin Cloonan, *Dark Side of the Tune: Popular Music and Violence* [Aldershot: Ashgate, 2008], 90).

30. Davis, *I Brought Down the MC5*, 124.

31. Nelson, "The Motherfuckers," 10.

32. McNeil and McCain, *Please Kill Me*, 60; also see Davis, *I Brought Down the MC5*, 124.

33. Kramer, "Riots I Have Known and Loved"; also see Don McLeese, *Kick Out the Jams* (New York: Continuum, 2005), 88–89; Kramer, *Hard Stuff*, 99; Sinclair, "Rock and Roll Dope," 16. In another account, Kramer remembered that the Motherfuckers were already infuriated because they had seen the MC5 arriving at the Fillmore in a limousine (Carson, *Grit, Noise, and Revolution*, 186).

34. Pitchford, "Nonviolence," 7.

35. McNeil and McCain, *Please Kill Me*, 60. In Fields's account, the MC5's limo was attacked as they arrived at the Fillmore, but other reports suggest that the attack took place as they were trying to leave. Fields's boss, Elektra president Jac Holzman, remembered the more-radical-than-thou tone of the dispute with amusement: "Here you have MC5, roaring out of a Detroit commune, guns stashed in their basement and obscenities on their album, billing themselves as dedicated to the overthrow of just about everything—and in the East Village they are trashed for being merely misdemeanor motherfuckers. Very late sixties" (Holzman and Gavan Daws, *Follow the Music: The Life and High Times of Elektra Records in the Great Years of American Pop Culture* [Santa Monica, CA: FirstMedia, 1998], 262).

36. Kramer, *Hard Stuff*, 100; Kramer, "Riots I Have Known and Loved"; also see Edmonds, "Battle of New York," 76. It is unclear which Motherfuckers rescued Kramer and why.

37. Davis, *I Brought Down the MC5*, 124.

38. McNeil and McCain, *Please Kill Me*, 61; Thompson gives a related account in Nick Hasted, "Search and Destroy," *Uncut*, no. 96 (May 2005), 84. For bassist Michael Davis's similar account of the escape, see Callwood, *MC5*, 85.

39. Terry H. Anderson, *The Movement and the Sixties* (New York: Oxford University Press, 1995), 246.

40. Ron Eyerman and Andrew Jamison, *Music and Social Movements: Mobilising Traditions in the Twentieth Century* (Cambridge: Cambridge University Press, 1998), 138–39.

41. Peter Wicke, *Rock Music: Culture, Aesthetics and Sociology*, trans. Rachel Fogg (Cambridge: Cambridge University Press, 1990), 105.

42. Simon Frith, *Sound Effects: Youth, Leisure, and the Politics of Rock 'n' Roll* (New York: Pantheon, 1981), 50; Frith, "'The Magic That Can Set You Free': The Ideology of Folk and the Myth of the Rock Community," *Popular Music* 1 (1981): 166.

43. John Gruen, *The New Bohemia* (1966; repr., Chicago: A Cappella, 1990); Christopher Mele, *Selling the Lower East Side: Culture, Real Estate, and Resistance in New York City* (Minneapolis: University of Minnesota Press, 2000), x–xii, 155.

44. Jon Panish, *The Color of Jazz: Race and Representation in Postwar American Culture* (Jackson: University Press of Mississippi, 1997), 30.

45. The Dom and Slug's are discussed in Charlotte Curtis, "The Affluent Set Invades the East Village," *New York Times*, November 29, 1964, but Curtis does not indicate whether either featured live music at that time. *Grove Music Online* ("Nightclubs: United States of America") states that Slug's "opened early in 1966," presumably referring to the date when it became a jazz club. The opening of the Electric Circus is advertised in *East Village Other* 2, no. 15 (July 1–15, 1967): 11. On the Anderson Theater, see Robert Shelton, "Moby Grape Rocks with Procol Harum in Pair of Concerts," *New York Times*, February 12, 1968. On the Fillmore East, see Richard Kostelanetz, *The Fillmore East: Recollections of Rock Theater* (New York: Schirmer, 1995); John Glatt, *Live at the Fillmore East and West: Getting Backstage and Personal with Rock's Greatest Legends* (Guilford, CT: Lyons, 2015).

46. Mele, *Selling the Lower East Side*, 161; Walter Bowart, "Fugs Fuzzbomb Fizzles," *East Village Other* 1, no. 19 (September 1–15, 1966): 9.

47. Ed Sanders, *Tales of Beatnik Glory* (New York: Thunder's Mouth, 2004), 240; also see Sanders, *Fug You: An Informal History of the Peace Eye Bookstore, the Fuck You Press, The Fugs, and Counterculture in the Lower East Side* ([Boston]: Da Capo, 2011), 44.

48. Mele, *Selling the Lower East Side*, 153.

49. Mele, *Selling the Lower East Side*, 70, 75.

50. Sanders, *Tales of Beatnik Glory*, 4–5.

51. Ed Sanders, email correspondence with the author, July 12, 2013.

52. Allan Katzman, "Other Editorial: Does an East Village Exist?," *East Village Other* 1, no. 6 (February 15–March 1, 1966): 2.

53. Lionel Mitchell, "Look at Down Here" (1967), in *Notes from the New Underground: An Anthology*, ed. Jesse Kornbluth (New York: Viking, 1968), 226.

54. Margie Stamberg, "upagainstthewallmotherfucker," *Rat Subterranean News* 1, no. 4 (April 5–18, 1968): 4.

55. "A High Time Was Had by All: Tompkins Square Smoke-In," *East Village Other* 2, no. 18 (August 5–17, 1967): 21.

56. Ed Sanders, email correspondence with the author, July 12, 2013.

57. Edward Sanders, *1968: A History in Verse* (Santa Rosa, CA: Black Sparrow Press, 1997), 151.

58. Ed Sanders, email correspondence with the author, July 12, 2013.

59. Mele, *Selling the Lower East Side*, 170.

60. Mele, *Selling the Lower East Side*, 171; see also the account in Paul Hofmann, "Hippies' Hangout Draws Tourists," *New York Times*, June 5, 1967.

61. Alfred E. Clark, "City Hall Talks on Hippies Held," *New York Times*, June 3, 1967.

62. Ronald Sukenick, *The Death of the Novel and Other Stories* (New York: Dial, 1969), 94; similar versions are given in "Anti-Hippies Disrupt Concert in Tompkins Sq. Park," *New York Times*, June 2, 1967; Don McNeill, *Moving through Here* (New York: Alfred A. Knopf, 1970), 100–101.

63. "Anti-Hippies Disrupt Concert."

64. Mele, *Selling the Lower East Side*, 175–76.

65. Emmett Grogan, *Ringolevio: A Life Played for Keeps* (1972; repr., New York: New York Review Books, 2008), 322.

66. Mele, *Selling the Lower East Side*, 153, 169–72; Peter Braunstein and Michael William Doyle, "Introduction: Historicizing the American Counterculture of the 1960s and 1970s," in *Imagine Nation: The American Counterculture of the 1960s and '70s*, ed. Peter Braunstein and Michael William Doyle (New York: Routledge, 2002), 12; also see Ronald Sukenick, *Down and In: Life in the Underground* (New York: Beech Tree/William Morrow, 1987), 196; Marci Reaven and Jeanne Houck, "A History of Tompkins Square Park," in Janet L. Abu-Lughod et al., *From Urban Village to East Village: The Battle for New York's Lower East Side* (Oxford: Blackwell, 1994), 94.

67. John Kifner, "Youth: Violence Pursues the Flower People," *New York Times*, October 15, 1967.

68. Grogan, *Ringolevio*, 323.

69. Lewis Yablonsky, *The Hippie Trip* (New York: Pegasus, 1968), 114–15.

70. Paul Hofmann, "Hippies Heighten East Side Tensions," *New York Times*, June 3, 1967.

71. For a full survey of Graham's life and career, see Bill Graham and Robert Greenfield, *Bill Graham Presents: My Life Inside Rock and Out*, 1st Da Capo Press ed. (Cambridge: Da Capo, 2004).

72. Graham and Greenfield, *Bill Graham Presents*, 143.

73. Charles Perry, *The Haight-Ashbury: A History* (New York: Wenner, 2005), 50.

74. Ralph J. Gleason, *The Jefferson Airplane and the San Francisco Sound* (New York: Ballantine, 1969), 51.

75. Gleason, *Jefferson Airplane*, 58.

76. Sarah Hill, *San Francisco and the Long 60s* (New York: Bloomsbury, 2016), 81.

77. Hill, *Long 60s*, 81.

78. John Glatt, *Rage and Roll: Bill Graham and the Selling of Rock* (New York: Birch Lane, 1993), 65.

79. Graham and Greenfield, *Bill Graham Presents*, 180.

80. On "hip capitalism," see Michael J. Kramer, *The Republic of Rock: Music and Citizenship in the Sixties Counterculture* (New York: Oxford University Press, 2013), 13–14.

81. Hunter S. Thompson, "The 'Hashbury' Is the Capital of the Hippies," *New York Times*, May 14, 1967.

82. Graham and Greenfield, *Bill Graham Presents*, 149.

83. Glatt, *Rage and Roll*, 66.

84. Allan Katzman, "Poor Paranoid's Almanac," *East Village Other* 3, no. 14 (March 8–14, 1968): 2. Roger Euster was the owner of the Village Theater ("Loew's Theatres Sells Former Commodore House," *Boxoffice* 88, no. 11 [January 3, 1966]: E-4).

85. Jules Freemond, "Pop Rock & Jelly," *East Village Other* 3, no. 18 (April 5–11, 1968): 6.

86. Michael Lydon, "The Producer of the New Rock," *New York Times*, December 15, 1968.

87. Advertisement, *East Village Other* 3, [no. 23?] ([May 10?], 1968): 13; Lita Eliscu, "Black Theatre?," *East Village Other* 3, no. 25 (May 24, 1968): 10; Lennox Raphael, "Waiting for Marlon Brando," *East Village Other* 3, no. 25 (May 24, 1968): 11, 21; Peter Sutheim, "Black Eye for Black Theater," *Rat Subterranean News* 1, no. 8 (June 1–14, 1968): 5, 10.

88. In a 2006 interview, Ben Morea remembers that "amongst ourselves we were The Family, which might sound weird now because of the association of that name with Charles Manson

with whom we had no connection and nothing in common with" (Iain McIntyre, "Up Against the Wall Motherfucker!—Interview with Ben Morea" [2006], http://libcom.org/history/against -wall-motherfucker-interview-ben-morea, accessed June 14, 2020). In 1971, Ben Sidran posited a connection between radical visions of "family" and Black music: "I would suggest, for example, that the ability of black music to generate an extended family has been applied. The interest in black music among almost all young people today—and not just a passing interest but an intense identification—is the natural tendency of youth to gravitate toward where the warmth and the light and the heat are. White affinity groups are known by their members as 'families'; black music is one of the strongest bonds in this new family structure" (Ben Sidran, *Black Talk* [New York: Holt, Rinehart and Winston, 1971], 157–58).

89. Caitlin Casey, "Up against the Wall Motherfucker: Ideology and Action in a 'Street Gang with an Analysis,'" in *Radical Gotham: Anarchism in New York City from Schwab's Saloon to Occupy Wall Street*, ed. Tom Goyens (Urbana: University of Illinois Press, 2017), 165; Gavin Grindon, "Poetry Written in Gasoline: Black Mask and Up against the Wall Motherfucker," *Art History* 38, no. 1 (February 2015): 194.

90. Grindon, "Poetry Written in Gasoline," 182, 187.

91. Neumann, *Up Against the Wall*, 88; Thomas R. Brooks, "Metamorphosis in S.D.S.: The New Left Is Showing Its Age," *New York Times*, June 15, 1969.

92. Neumann, *Up Against the Wall*, 57. Caitlin Casey reports that "the Motherfuckers never had more than twenty members" (Casey, "Up Against the Wall," 161).

93. Neumann, *Up Against the Wall*, 66, 76.

94. On Morea, see Neumann, *Up Against the Wall*, 53–54; "Flower Power?," *King Mob* 3 (1969), reprinted in *King Mob Echo: English Section of the Situationist International* (Edinburgh: Dark Star, 2000), 104. Morea discusses Dada in his essay "Art and Revolution," *Black Mask*, no. 3 (January 1967): 3; on Dada's influence on UAW/MF, see Conor Hannan, "'We Have Our Own Struggle': Up Against the Wall Motherfucker and the Avant-Garde of Community Action, the Lower East Side, 1968," *The Sixties* 9, no. 1 (2016): 122–23. Black Mask anticipated the Mother-fuckers by engaging in a series of theatrical demonstrations that were designed to shock afflu-ent New Yorkers out of their bourgeois complacency. On October 10, 1966, for example, the group marched on the Museum of Modern Art to demand that it be closed, and on February 10, 1967, they marched on Wall Street in black masks while carrying skull replicas on stakes and declaring that Wall Street was now "War Street" ("A New Spirit Is Rising," *Black Mask*, no. 1 [November 1966]: 1; Neumann, *Up Against the Wall*, 55; "Revolution: Now and Forever," *Black Mask*, no. 4 [February–March 1967]: 2). For a discussion of UAW/MF's connection to anarchist groups in West Germany and Britain, see Timothy Scott Brown, "The Sixties in the City: Avant-Gardes and Urban Rebels in New York, London, and West Berlin," *Journal of Social History* 46, no. 4 (summer 2013): 817–42. For discussions of Black Mask and UAW/MF's role within the New York avant-garde, see Grindon, "Poetry Written in Gasoline"; Hannan, "We Have Our Own Struggle."

95. Ron Hahne, Ben Morea, et al., *Black Mask & Up Against the Wall Motherfucker: The In-complete Works of Ron Hahne, Ben Morea and the Black Mask Group* (London: Unpopular Books and Sabotage Editions, 1993), 75; Allan Katzman, "Poor Paranoid's Almanac," *East Village Other* 3, no. 10 (February 9–15, 1968): 10; Hannan, "We Have Our Own Struggle," 115–16. Newsreel's short film *Garbage* (1968) documents this action ("Garbage NY Newsreel/Motherfuckers, 1968," https://www.youtube.com/watch?v=KtX8IEWabTY, accessed March 21, 2019).

96. Neumann, *Up Against the Wall*, 99.

97. "Self-Defense," *Rat Subterranean News* 1, no. 13 (August 9–22, 1968): 10; Grindon, "Poetry Written in Gasoline," 204.

98. Hannan, "We Have Our Own Struggle," 116.

99. Neumann, *Up Against the Wall*, 53.

100. Neumann, *Up Against the Wall*, 53.

101. Neumann, *Up Against the Wall*, 97.

102. Ben Morea, "From Revolt to Revolution," *Black Mask*, no. 10 (April–May [1968]): 3.

103. Hahne, Morea, et al., *Black Mask*, 81.

104. Casey, "Up Against the Wall," 168.

105. Neumann, *Up Against the Wall*, 97.

106. "Cleaver Interview," *Berkeley Barb* 7, no. 8 (August 23–29, 1968): 8.

107. Grindon, "Poetry Written in Gasoline," 187.

108. My argument here is influenced by Bernard Gendron's work on the "Dixieland war" of the 1940s, in which he demonstrates that "diametrically opposed aesthetic views . . . nonetheless belonged to the same discursive world" (Gendron, "'Moldy Figs' and Modernists: Jazz at War (1942–1946)," in *Jazz among the Discourses*, ed. Krin Gabbard [Durham, NC: Duke University Press, 1995], 50).

109. "The Reclaiming Project," *Rat Subterranean News* 1, no. 24 (January 3–16, 1969): 4.

110. "The Reclaiming Project," 4.

111. "From the Old Reality Comes the New," *Rat Subterranean News* 2, no. 1 (March 14–21, 1969): 20.

112. "The Myth Killer," *Rat Subterranean News* 1, no. 21 (November 15–28, 1968): 16.

113. "Hip Survival Bulletin," *Rat Subterranean News* 1, no. 26 (January 24–30, 1969): 5.

114. Hannan, "We Have Our Own Struggle," 124.

115. Casey, "Up Against the Wall," 165.

116. "Armed Love," *Rat Subterranean News* 1, no. 31 (March 1–6, 1969): 8.

117. "Self-Defense," 10; Casey, "Up Against the Wall," 168.

118. Amiri Baraka [LeRoi Jones], *Black Music* (New York: William Morrow, 1967), 18.

119. "We are a new people," *Rat Subterranean News* 1, no. 29 (February 14–20, 1969): 8.

120. Frith, *Sound Effects*, 51.

121. Nelson, "The Motherfuckers," 8.

122. Hahne, Morea, et al., *Black Mask*, 132.

123. Baraka, *Black Music*, 205–7.

124. "We are a new people," 8.

125. Pitchford, "Nonviolence," 7.

126. Caitlin Casey claims that the Motherfuckers "were an all-white group working within a primarily white community," which assumes the community of bohemians rather than the Lower East Side as a whole (Casey, "Up Against the Wall," 168).

127. Baraka, *Black Music*, 205–6.

128. Jeff Shero, "Bill Graham: Part I," *Rat Subterranean News* 1, no. 19 (October 18–31, 1968): 20.

129. Shero, "Bill Graham: Part I," 20–21.

130. Lydon, "Producer of the New Rock."

131. Nelson, "The Motherfuckers," 10. Reflecting on the Motherfuckers years after the fact, Elektra's Danny Fields had a similar impression: "my favorite word, the 'Community.' They wanted to cook meals in there and have their babies make doody on the seats. These were really

disgusting people. They were bearded and fat and Earth motherish and angry and belligerent and old and ugly and losers. And they were hard" (McNeil and McCain, *Please Kill Me*, 59).

132. Graham and Greenfield, *Bill Graham Presents*, 256.

133. Graham and Greenfield, *Bill Graham Presents*, 257.

134. Howard Smith, *The Smith Tapes: Lost Interviews with Rock Stars and Icons 1969–1972*, ed. Ezra Bookstein (New York: Princeton Architectural Press, 2015), 77.

135. Jonathan Moore, "Space Energy Revolution," *Rat Subterranean News* 1, no. 22 (November 29–December 12, 1968): 3; Bob Rudnick and Dennis Frawley, "Kokaine Karma," *East Village Other* 4, no. 1 (December 13, 1968): 12.

136. Lydon, "Producer of the New Rock."

137. Bill Graham, "Scrooge McDuck?," *New York Times*, January 19, 1969.

138. Shero, "Bill Graham: Part I," 20; [Jeff Shero], "Graham on Graham," *Rat Subterranean News* 1, no. 20 (November 1–14, 1968): 22.

139. "Bill Graham Fights Off the N.Y. Motherfuckers 'Liberation' Attempt," *Rolling Stone*, no. 23 (December 7, 1968): 4.

140. Nelson, "The Motherfuckers," 8.

141. "Reclaiming Project."

142. Graham and Greenfield, *Bill Graham Presents*, 254.

143. Neumann, *Up Against the Wall*, 104–5; McIntyre, "Up Against the Wall." *East Village Other* writer Claudia Dreifus recalls a meeting at the paper's office, after the Motherfuckers "said they were going to bomb the Fillmore" and the paper expressed support, at which Graham "started ranting for hours on end about having to escape Nazi Germany for this kind of ingratitude," although it is not clear whether this was the same incident (Kostelanetz, *Fillmore East*, unpaginated).

144. Advertisement, *Rat Subterranean News* 1, no. 18 (October 4–17, 1968): 22.

145. "Reclaiming Project," 4; Moore, "Space Energy Revolution," 3.

146. "Lower East Side: Motherfuckers Hit The Fillmore East," *Rolling Stone*, no. 26 (February 1, 1969): 4. Fillmore East manager Kip Cohen gave *Rolling Stone* a different version of events, claiming that the Motherfuckers' radio broadcasts and pamphlets preceded their initial meeting with Graham, which Cohen stated took place in late October. Morea, in turn, asserted that "*none* of the Motherfuckers were *ever* on WBAI . . . But there *were* other groups involved" (Nelson, "The Motherfuckers," 8).

147. Advertisement, *Rat Subterranean News* 1, no. 18 (October 4–17, 1968): 21; Advertisement, *East Village Other* 3, no. 46 (October 18, 1968): 20. In his autobiography, Graham claims erroneously that the Living Theatre benefit took place "six months after the free Wednesday nights stopped" (Graham and Greenfield, *Bill Graham Presents*, 255).

148. "Reclaiming Project," 4; Advertisement, *Rat Subterranean News* 1, no. 18 (October 4–17, 1968): 21; Baby Jerry, "Sprockets," *East Village Other* 3, no. 45 (October 11, 1968): 4. Morea was arrested in Boston on July 23, 1968, and charged with stabbing two servicemen; he was acquitted in January 1969 ("Ben Morea Free," *Rat Subterranean News* 1, no. 26 [January 24–30, 1969]: 5).

149. "Bill Graham Fights Off," 4.

150. Richard Goldstein, "The Theater of Cruelty Comes to Second Avenue," *Village Voice* (October 31, 1968): 46.

151. Goldstein, "Theater of Cruelty," 46; Emanuel Perlmutter, "Hippie Threats Win a Theater," *New York Times*, October 24, 1968; "Graham Is Crackers or Try to Find the Wall," *Helix* 5, no. 3 (October 31, 1968): 2.

152. For a detailed account of the Living Theatre's performance, see Goldstein, "Theater of Cruelty," 46–47.

153. Neumann, *Up Against the Wall*, 105.

154. Perlmutter, "Hippie Threats." The entire text of the leaflet is given in "Graham Is Crackers," 2; also see "Fillmore Free Theater Leaflets," in *BAMN (By Any Means Necessary): Outlaw Manifestos and Ephemera 1965–70*, ed. Peter Stansill and David Zane Mairowitz (Middlesex: Penguin, 1971), 162.

155. Perlmutter, "Hippie Threats."

156. Lita Eliscu, "Up Against the Wall, Bill Graham!," *East Village Other* 3, no. 47 (October 25, 1968): 9.

157. Sidney Bernard, *This Way to the Apocalypse: The '6os* (New York: Smith, 1969), 17.

158. Goldstein, "Theater of Cruelty," 46; Eliscu, "Up Against the Wall," 9. John Glatt claims that Graham was "quickly overpowered" when he confronted the Motherfuckers, and was then "tied to a chair on the stage, where he remained for nearly six hours, arguing and screaming at the rioters" (Glatt, *Rage and Roll*, 111). Contemporaneous sources, however, do not mention this, and Osha Neumann responds, "I am quite sure he was not tied to a chair" (Neumann, *Up Against the Wall*, 218).

159. Neumann, *Up Against the Wall*, 106.

160. Neumann, *Up Against the Wall*, 107; Goldstein, "Theater of Cruelty," 47. A slightly different version of this leaflet is given in "Graham Is Crackers," 2.

161. Peter Doggett, *There's a Riot Going On: Revolutionaries, Rock Stars, and the Rise and Fall of the '6os* (Edinburgh: Canongate, 2007), 223; Curtis J. Austin, *Up Against the Wall: Violence in the Making and Unmaking of the Black Panther Party* (Fayetteville: University of Arkansas Press, 2006), 115.

162. "Bill Graham Fights Off," 4; "Reclaiming Project," 4; Moore, "Space Energy Revolution," 3; Dan McCauslin, "Fillmore East: Round II," *Rat Subterranean News* 1, no. 20 (November 1–14, 1968): 22; "Thing-Doing Costs Hippies Free Use of 2d Ave. Theater," *New York Times*, October 31, 1968; Nelson, "The Motherfuckers," 8. On the Group Image, see Stephen A. O. Golden, "'Warmth Day,' Cool Happening with Group Image," *New York Times*, May 15, 1967; McNeill, *Moving through Here*, 86–91.

163. Neumann, *Up Against the Wall*, 107–8.

164. "Reclaiming Project," 4.

165. Graham and Greenfield, *Bill Graham Presents*, 255.

166. Nelson, "The Motherfuckers," 8.

167. Moore, "Space Energy Revolution," 3.

168. Moore, "Space Energy Revolution," 3.

169. Moore, "Space Energy Revolution," 3.

170. Moore, "Space Energy Revolution," 3.

171. Wolfe Lowenthal, "Common Ground," *Rat Subterranean News* 1, no. 23 (December 13, 1968–January 2, 1969): 7.

172. Casey, "Up Against the Wall," 173.

173. Austin, *Up Against the Wall*, 356. The contrast between the Black Panthers and the Motherfuckers recalls that between the disciplined Sun Ra and the freewheeling White Panther Party. When Sun Ra stayed with the White Panthers in Ann Arbor in 1969, he "was shocked by their hippie lifestyle—their language, drugs, their state of undress, and the police surveillance which followed them" (John F. Szwed, *Space Is the Place: The Life and Times of Sun Ra* [New York: Pantheon, 1997], 245).

174. Douglas Kellner, *Herbert Marcuse and the Crisis of Marxism* (Berkeley: University of California Press, 1984), 154–96; David Greenham, *The Resurrection of the Body: The Work of Norman O. Brown* (Lanham, MD: Lexington, 2006), 77–84. Although Osha Neumann claims that in his "corner" of the New Left "we read next to nothing," the Motherfuckers were certainly familiar with these thinkers: Marcuse was Neumann's stepfather, and historian of the Frankfurt School Stuart Jeffries argues that "in a sense the Motherfuckers were counter-culturally resisting what Marcuse had called one-dimensional society." One of the Motherfuckers' slogans, "MY UTOPIA IS AN ENVIRONMENT THAT WORKS SO WELL THAT WE CAN RUN WILD IN IT," was an unattributed quotation from Brown's 1968 essay-poem "The Return of the Repressed" (Neumann, *Up Against the Wall*, 169; Stuart Jeffries, *Grand Hotel Abyss: The Lives of the Frankfurt School* [London: Verso, 2016], 313; "We Demand," *Rat Subterranean News* 1, no. 11 [July 13–28, 1968]: 6; Norman O. Brown, "The Return of the Repressed," *King Mob Echo*, no. 1 [April 1968]: 4).

175. Hahne, Morea, et al., *Black Mask*, 132.

176. Neumann, *Up Against the Wall*, 120.

177. Moore, "Space Energy Revolution," 10; Bob Rudnick and Dennis Frawley, "Kokaine Karma," *East Village Other* 4, no. 1 (December 13, 1968), 12; Allan Katzman, "Poor Paranoids," *East Village Other* 3, no. 52 (November 29, 1968): 14. On Sirocco, see Paul Samberg, "Blues and Folk," *Rat Subterranean News* 2, no. 1 (March 14–21, 1969): 19. On Children of God, see Jules Freemond, "Pop Rock and Jelly," *East Village Other* 3, no. 18 (April 5–11, 1968): 6.

178. Nelson, "The Motherfuckers," 10.

179. Neumann, *Up Against the Wall*, 108; "Lower East Side: Motherfuckers Hit the Fillmore East," 4. In another version of events, those arriving at the auditorium were surprised to find locked doors with Graham's letter posted on them (Pitchford, "Nonviolence," 7; also see Neumann, *Up Against the Wall*, 109).

180. Pitchford, "Nonviolence," 7. Neumann quotes from a flyer with similar wording, but claims that it was issued before the December 23 lockout (Neumann, *Up Against the Wall*, 108–9).

181. Pitchford, "Nonviolence," 7.

182. "Armed Love," *Rat Subterranean News* 1, no. 26 (January 24–30, 1969): 13.

183. Graham and Greenfield, *Bill Graham Presents*, 256.

184. Jeff A. Hale, "The White Panthers' 'Total Assault on the Culture,'" in *Imagine Nation: The American Counterculture of the 1960s and '70s*, ed. Peter Braunstein and Michael William Doyle (New York: Routledge, 2002), 143–44; also see Mathew J. Bartkowiak, *The MC5 and Social Change: A Study in Rock and Revolution* (Jefferson, NC: McFarland, 2009), 71–72; Scott Saul, *Freedom Is, Freedom Ain't: Jazz and the Making of the Sixties* (Cambridge, MA: Harvard University Press, 2003), 299.

185. Pearlman, "Riffs: Revolutionary Moments," 29.

186. Pitchford, "Nonviolence," 7.

187. Pitchford, "Nonviolence," 7.

188. Casey, "Up Against the Wall," 173.

189. Dan McCauslin, "Fillmore East Round II," *Rat Subterranean News* 1, no. 20 (November 1–14, 1968): 22.

190. Pitchford, "Nonviolence," 7.

191. Nelson, "The Motherfuckers," 6.

192. Dean Latimer, "Up Against the Mother, Fucker," *East Village Other* 4, no. 6 (January 10, 1969): 7.

193. L.A.M.F., "Barracudas Know," *East Village Other* 4, no. 8 (January 24, 1969): 2.

194. "There Is a Great Deal to Be Silent About," *IT*, no. 54 (April 11–24, 1969): 19.

195. "Zappa," *Ann Arbor Argus* 1, no. 8 (June 19–July 3, 1969): 13.

196. Patricia Kennealy [as Patricia Kennely], "Pop Talk," *Jazz and Pop* 7, no. 12 (December 1968): 34.

197. [Allan Katzman], "Editorial: Fillmore East vs. the Motherfuckers," *East Village Other* 4, no. 5 (January 3, 1969): 2.

198. L.A.M.F., "Barracudas Know," 2. The Motherfuckers' outrage may have reflected their real, if slight, relationship to the Puerto Rican community. Conor Hannan reports that "the group's flyers often included Spanish translations . . . and demonstrations were frequently organized to protest police beatings of black and Puerto Rican residents" (Hannan, "We Have Our Own Struggle," 129). Osha Neumann recalls that the group included Alfonso Texidor (aka Alfonso Motherfucker), "a soft-spoken Puerto Rican poet," and their "fellow travelers" included "a group of Puerto Rican street kids," one of whom was Bill Graham's assailant (Osha Neumann, "Motherfuckers Then and Now: My Sixties Problem," in *Cultural Politics and Social Movements*, ed. Marcy Darnovsky et al. [Philadelphia: Temple University Press, 1995], 61; Neumann, *Up against the Wall*, 117, 57, 110). Otherwise, however, "we were all white" (Neumann, "Motherfuckers Then and Now," 61). Yippie Stew Albert wrote, perhaps skeptically, in 1969 that "the Mother Fuckers hang out on street corners, give out shabby creative leaflets and try to relate to the Puerto Ricans" (Albert, "For Madmen Always," *Berkeley Barb* 8, no. 1 [January 3–9, 1969]: 10).

199. Pat Henry, letter to the editor, *East Village Other* 4, no. 10 (February 7, 1969): 4.

200. Pitchford, "Nonviolence," 7.

201. Latimer, "Up Against the Mother," 16.

202. Maxene Fabe, "Crazies Are Fascists," *Rat Subterranean News* 2, no. 2 (March 21, 1969): 2. The Crazies were a New York radical group whose membership overlapped with that of the Motherfuckers (Brooks, "Metamorphosis in S.D.S."); Fabe addresses her letter to both groups. Grindon describes the Crazies as "a 1968–70 New York hybrid imitation of the Motherfuckers and the Yippies . . . led by 'Prince Crazy' George Demmerle—actually an FBI-paid provocateur and informant" (Grindon, "Poetry Written in Gasoline," 204).

203. San Francisco's Fillmore West, Graham's successor to the original Fillmore, faced similar challenges. In October 1968, Black community group Mama Bear Productions employed claims about community and culture in protesting Graham: "Mama Bear people say they view art as expression deeply rooted in the community . . . 'Latin music is buried in San Francisco, and black music has been raped all over the United States,' [member Julio] Ramirez said." Graham snapped back in his typically acerbic style: "I'm fucking sick and tired of people telling me what I should do" (Walter F. Rice, "Clash of Words as Graham Lets Old Fillmore Go," *Berkeley Barb* 7/16 [October 11–18, 1968]: 5).

204. Glatt, *Rage and Roll*, 140.

205. Neumann, *Up Against the Wall*, 111.

206. Nelson, "The Motherfuckers," 10.

207. Ellen Sander, "The Future After the Fillmores," *Saturday Review* 54, no. 22 (May 29, 1971): 56.

208. Kramer, *Hard Stuff*, 101.

209. McNeil and McCain, *Please Kill Me*, 61. Ben Edmonds reports that "when I spoke with him 15 years later, Graham still clung to the irrational belief that the MC5 were somehow responsible for the assault" (Edmonds, "Battle of New York," 75). Dennis Thompson believes that Graham's assailant was actually "a guy who had an Afro that looked like Rob" (Thompson, "The

MC5: Berlin and NYC," http://www.machinegunthompson.com/2009/08/mc5-berlin-nyc.html, accessed June 1, 2010). On Graham's refusal to allow the MC5 to play at the Fillmore West, see John Sinclair, "The Story of the MC5 on the West Coast in March Part One," *Ann Arbor Argus* 1, no. 4 (March 28–April 11, 1969): 11; Bob Rudnick and Dennis Frawley, "Kokaine Karma," *East Village Other* 4, no. 16 (March 19, 1969): 13. Sinclair later claimed that Graham "very properly got smashed in the face during the course of the evening, and he deserved it for being such a lying punk and a fool" (Sinclair, "Letter from Prison," 27).

210. Michael D. Cary, "The Rise and Fall of the MC5: Rock Music and Counterculture Politics in the Sixties" (DA diss., Lehigh University, 1985), 139; see, for example, Bruce Alpert, letter to the editor, *Rolling Stone*, no. 27 (February 15, 1969): 3.

211. "Reclaiming Project," 4; L.A.M.F., "Barracudas Know," 2.

212. "Pull Out the Plugs," *Fifth Estate* 3, no. 18 (January 9–22, 1969): 5; Carson, *Grit, Noise, and Revolution*, 188–89, 193–94. Although the page does not explicitly mention UAW/MF, it is signed "Total Assault on Culture (IWWC)," which stands for "International Werewolf Conspiracy," a frequent pseudonym of the Motherfuckers, and *Fifth Estate* editor Peter Werbe believes that Detroit artist Allen Van Newkirk, an associate of the Motherfuckers, was involved in its production (Peter Werbe, conversation with the author, February 6, 2020). Wayne Kramer remembers an argument with Van Newkirk over his "brutal" criticism of the MC5 as a "capitalist rock band," which likely refers to this page (Cary Loren, "Guerrilla: Weapon of Culture Warfare: or Blazing Poets, Paleocybernetics and Voices on the Trans-Love Flame-out of Allen Van Newkirk" [2005], http://www.detroitartistsworkshop.com/guerrilla-weapon-of-cultural -warfare/, accessed February 17, 2020; Peter Werbe, "Surreal Life," *Detroit Metro Times*, January 5, 2005, https://www.metrotimes.com/detroit/surreal-life/Content?oid=2180445, accessed June 14, 2020).

213. Marilyn Lowen Fletcher, letter to John Sinclair, January 16, 1969, folder 33, box 2, JLSP.

214. Sinclair, "Letter from Prison," 14.

215. On the MC5's split with Sinclair and the White Panthers, see "MC5 on the Cusp," *Creem* 2, no. 4 (August 31, 1969), 16–17; Sinclair, "Letter from Prison."

216. Davis, *I Brought Down the MC5*, 125.

Chapter 5

1. Jeff A. Hale, "The White Panthers' 'Total Assault on the Culture,'" in *Imagine Nation: The American Counterculture of the 1960s and '70s*, ed. Peter Braunstein and Michael William Doyle (New York: Routledge, 2002), 147.

2. David A. Carson, *Grit, Noise, and Revolution: The Birth of Detroit Rock 'n' Roll* (Ann Arbor: University of Michigan Press, 2005), 214; Wayne Kramer, *The Hard Stuff: Dope, Crime, the MC5 and My Life of Impossibilities* (New York: Da Capo, 2018), 110–12. Kramer recalls that "the MC5 played benefits and raised funds for [Sinclair's] legal defense, but we could not keep up any regular payments. We were broke ourselves. The MC5 was left without a business structure to manage our financial affairs" (118).

3. Leni [Sinclair], letter to John [Sinclair], August 20, 1969, folder 36, box 2, John and Leni Sinclair Papers, Bentley Historical Library, University of Michigan [collection cited hereafter as JLSP].

4. Carson, *Grit, Noise, and Revolution*, 213; Leni Sinclair, interview with the author, March 22, 2019.

5. Pun [Plamondon], letter to Brother John [Sinclair], August 13, 1969, folder 36, box 2, JLSP.

6. Jim, "Tim Leary Meets the Motherfuckers," *Rat Subterranean News* 1, no. 32 (March 7–13, 1969): 3, 11; Bob Rudnick and Dennis Frawley, "Kokaine Karma," *Ann Arbor Argus* 1, no. 3 (March 13–27, 1969): 10; Lita Eliscu, "Pot Conference at Buffalo [*sic*] (or was it Detroit . . .)," *East Village Other* 4, no. 15 (March 14, 1969): 3; John Sinclair, "The Story of the MC5 on the West Coast in March Part One," *Ann Arbor Argus* 1, no. 4 (March 28–April 11, 1969): 11; Art Johnston, "MC-5 in San Francisco," *Fifth Estate* 3, no. 24 (April 3, 1969): 17; Lita Eliscu, "Thlm," *East Village Other* 4, no. 23 ([May 7], 1969): 13; David Walley, "MC5," *Jazz and Pop*, no. 9 (July 1969): 15.

7. Pun [Plamondon], letter to Brother John [Sinclair], August 13, 1969, folder 36, box 2, JLSP. In a September 1969 letter to Abbie Hoffman, Sinclair argued that "Ben [Morea] is a mad cultural nationalist and that's what we're all going to have to be now" (John Sinclair, letter to Abbott H. Hoffman, September 22, 1969, folder 40, box 2, JLSP). Leni Sinclair explains that Pun Plamondon, who had a "little adventurist streak himself," was "friends with the Motherfuckers," but that she and other White Panthers felt that the Motherfuckers were "too weird—to me, they were out to destroy what we were building up" (Leni Sinclair, interview with the author, March 22, 2019).

8. Joel Makower, *Woodstock: The Oral History*, 40th anniversary ed. (Albany, NY: Excelsior, 2009), 106.

9. Michael Lang with Holly George-Warren, *The Road to Woodstock* (New York: Ecco, 2009), 92.

10. Lang, *Road to Woodstock*, 93–94; Makower, *Woodstock*, 107–11; Bob Spitz, *Barefoot in Babylon: The Creation of the Woodstock Music Festival, 1969*, new ed. (New York: W. W. Norton, 1989), 167.

11. Lang, *Road to Woodstock*, 97–98.

12. Abbie Hoffman, *Woodstock Nation: A Talk-Rock Album* (New York: Vintage, 1969), 75–77; Jonah Raskin, *For the Hell of It: The Life and Time of Abbie Hoffman* (Berkeley: University of California Press, 1996), 194–95; "Woodstock 69 Program Guide—Abbie Hoffman on the Chicago Seven," http://www.celticguitarmusic.com/programhoffman.htm, accessed March 26, 2019.

13. Tom Smucker, "The Politics of Rock: Movement vs. Groovement," *Fusion*, no. 19 (October 17, 1969): 32.

14. Makower, *Woodstock*, 155.

15. Smucker, "Politics of Rock," 32. Filmmaker Roz Payne claims that after the festival the printing press and field hospital were donated to the Black Panther Party (Lang, *Road to Woodstock*, 244).

16. Spitz, *Barefoot in Babylon*, 346.

17. Makower, *Woodstock*, 152–54; Lang, *Road to Woodstock*, 155–56.

18. Caitlin Casey, "Up against the Wall Motherfucker: Ideology and Action in a 'Street Gang with an Analysis,'" in *Radical Gotham: Anarchism in New York City from Schwab's Saloon to Occupy Wall Street*, ed. Tom Goyens (Urbana: University of Illinois Press, 2017), 170; also see *Woodstock: Three Days That Rocked the World*, ed. Mike Evans and Paul Kingsbury (New York: Sterling, 2009), 81.

19. Lang, *Road to Woodstock*, 226; Spitz, *Barefoot in Babylon*, 451–52. Other radical groups were probably involved as well. Production coordinator John Morris remembers "Tom Newman and the Crazies" as the group who threatened the stands (Elliott Landy, *Woodstock Vision: The Spirit of a Generation*, rev. ed. [New York: Backbeat, 2009], 147). *East Village Other* reporter Allen Asnen complained that "Walter Teague (the capitalist, fascist revolutionary) and his Support

the NLF group. . . . wanted to 'liberate' everything from the cruddy bologna sandwiches to the Hog Farm's free food" (Asnen, "In the two years . . . ," *East Village Other* 4, no. 38 [August 20, 1969]: 10).

20. Casey, "Up against the Wall," 170.

21. Makower, *Woodstock*, 207.

22. Leni Sinclair, interview with the author, March 22, 2019. A map of the Woodstock grounds confirms that woods separated the main stage area from Movement City, which was adjacent to food concessions and medical services (Makower, *Woodstock*, 186).

23. Joyce Good Times, "The Woodstock Nation," *Fifth Estate* 4, no. 9 (September 4–17, 1969), 18.

24. Pun Plamondon, *Lost from the Ottawa: The Story of the Journey Back* (Victoria, BC: Trafford, 2004), 138–40.

25. Darlene [Pond], letter to John Sinclair, August 18, 1969, folder 36, box 2, JLSP.

26. Magdalene [Leni] Sinclair, letter to John Sinclair, August 19, 1969, folder 36, box 2, JLSP.

27. Carson, *Grit, Noise, and Revolution*, 213–14; Plamondon, *Lost from the Ottawa*, 140. My account here may be too maudlin; Leni Sinclair remembers of her jail time in New Jersey that "actually, it was kind of fun. I got to sew a dress for my daughter while I was there, and I was only there for one night" (Leni Sinclair, interview with the author, March 22, 2019).

28. Magdalene [Leni] Sinclair, letter to John Sinclair, August 19, 1969, folder 36, box 2, JLSP.

29. The recording is included in The Who, *Thirty Years of Maximum R&B* (Polydor CD 521 751-2, 1994).

30. Makower, *Woodstock*, 155, 235; Lang, *Road to Woodstock*, 203–4.

31. Makower, *Woodstock*, 236.

32. Leni Sinclair, interview with the author, March 22, 2019.

33. Peter Doggett, *There's a Riot Going On: Revolutionaries, Rock Stars, and the Rise and Fall of the '60s* (Edinburgh: Canongate, 2007), 274.

34. Ellen Willis, *Beginning to See the Light: Sex, Hope, and Rock and Roll* (Hanover, NH: Wesleyan University Press, 1992), 50.

35. Thomas M. Kitts, "Documenting, Creating, and Interpreting Moments of Definition: *Monterey Pop, Woodstock*, and *Gimme Shelter*," *Journal of Popular Culture* 42, no. 4 (2009): 721.

36. Lang, *Road to Woodstock*, 221.

37. Craig Werner, *A Change Is Gonna Come: Music, Race & the Soul of America* (Ann Arbor: University of Michigan Press, 2006), 93.

38. Ralph Marvin Abee, "Symbolism of Bethel," *New York Times*, September 3, 1969.

39. Smucker, "Politics of Rock," 32. Gina Arnold points out that from Woodstock to the present "the majority of festivals have never seriously courted or embraced black audiences" (Arnold, *Half a Million Strong: Crowds and Power from Woodstock to Coachella* [Iowa City: University of Iowa Press, 2018], 84).

40. Craig McGregor, "Woodstock: A Desperate Fear For the Future?," *New York Times*, April 19, 1970. Such arguments have largely been lost in later reflections on Woodstock. Arnold argues that "a . . . problematic absence in the discourse surrounding" Woodstock "is discussion of the fact Woodstock's audience was almost universally white" (Regina Arnold, "'Nobody's Army': Contradictory Cultural Rhetoric in *Woodstock* and *Gimme Shelter*," *Volume! La revue des musiques populaires* 9, no. 2 [2012]: 12).

41. On Hendrix's "Star-Spangled Banner" and its reception, see Mark Clague, "'This Is

America': Jimi Hendrix's Star Spangled Banner Journey as Psychedelic Citizenship," *Journal of the Society for American Music* 8, no. 4 (November 2014): 435–78.

42. David Henderson, *'Scuse Me While I Kiss the Sky: Jimi Hendrix: Voodoo Child* (New York: Atria, 2008), 302–7, 318–19.

43. Rickey Vincent, *Party Music: The Inside Story of the Black Panthers' Band and How Black Power Transformed Soul Music* (Chicago: Lawrence Hill, 2013), 56. On Sly Stone's ambivalence toward the Black Panthers, see Vincent, *Party Music*, 85–86. In addition to Havens, Hendrix, and Sly and the Family Stone, bands with Black members at Woodstock included Sweetwater, Santana, Janis Joplin's Kozmic Blues Band, the Paul Butterfield Blues Band, Sha Na Na, and Crosby, Stills, Nash & Young (backed by bassist Greg Reeves).

44. As historian Pete Fornatale points out, "Joan Baez's gentle proselytizing about draft resistance was acceptable and tolerated; Abbie Hoffman's rant about John Sinclair and the nation's marijuana laws was decidedly not" (Fornatale, *Back to the Garden: The Story of Woodstock* [New York: Touchstone, 2009], 36).

45. Gina Arnold points out that "at Woodstock, the gender proportion was only four women artists (Janis Joplin, Melanie, Joan Baez, and Grace Slick) out of hundreds of male musicians, and that proportion has held steady throughout the years" at later festivals (Arnold, *Half a Million Strong*, 120). Although a list of women musicians at Woodstock should also include Nancy Nevins (of Sweetwater), Licorice McKechnie and Rose Simpson (Incredible String Band), and Cynthia Robinson (Sly and the Family Stone), the vast majority of Woodstock's musicians were men.

46. Ulrich Adelt, *Blues Music in the Sixties: A Story in Black and White* (New Brunswick, NJ: Rutgers University Press, 2010), 1.

47. Adelt, *Blues Music in the Sixties*, 2.

48. Lang, *Road to Woodstock*, 232.

49. Jefferson Airplane, *The Woodstock Experience* (RCA Legacy CD 88697 48240 2, 2009).

50. Fito de la Parra with T. W. and Marlane McGarry, *Living the Blues: Canned Heat's Story of Music, Drugs, Death, Sex and Survival* (n.p.: Canned Heat Music, 2010), 10.

51. de la Parra, *Living the Blues*, 10.

52. de la Parra, *Living the Blues*, 92.

53. de la Parra, *Living the Blues*, 68.

54. de la Parra, *Living the Blues*, 73–74.

55. de la Parra, *Living the Blues*, 133.

56. Audio of the entire set is available at https://www.youtube.com/watch?v=RKsgXHuZaaY, accessed March 27, 2019.

57. The same groove forms the basis of "Fried Hockey Boogie," an eleven-minute jam from the 1968 album *Boogie with Canned Heat* (Liberty LST-7541, 1968). Hooker, assessing *Hooker 'n Heat*, asserted that Canned Heat "had my music *down*" and called Wilson a "genius," while Charles Shaar Murray writes that on the album Canned Heat showed "a blend of erudition and self-effacement unsurpassed among the plethora of blues legend/rockstar acolyte collaborations of the time" (Murray, *Boogie Man: The Adventures of John Lee Hooker in the American Twentieth Century* [London: Viking, 1999], 417–19).

58. de la Parra, *Living the Blues*, 60.

59. It is possible to read a subtext about draft dodging into "Going Up the Country" ("we might even leave the USA"), while "Sic 'em Pigs" (from *Hallelujah*, 1969) mocks the Los Angeles Police Department and includes provocative lines about bringing "guns" and "fire bombs to City Hall," but neither song advances a clear political position.

60. Ralph J. Gleason, "Perspectives: Believe in the Magic," *Rolling Stone*, no. 46 (November 15, 1969): 27.

61. Robert Christgau, "Consumer Guide (1)" (1969), in *Any Old Way You Choose It: Rock and Other Pop Music, 1967–1973*, expanded ed. (New York: Cooper Square Press, 2000), 90. The first track Christgau describes is "Down in the Gutter, But Free."

62. Alice Echols, *Scars of Sweet Paradise: The Life and Times of Janis Joplin* (New York: Metropolitan, 1999), 242–44.

63. J. P. Bean, *Joe Cocker: The Authorised Biography* (London: Virgin, 2003), 6, 34; also see Spitz, *Barefoot in Babylon*, 469.

64. Joe Cocker, *Live at Woodstock* (A&M 13316, 2009).

65. Jan Hodenfield, "It Was Like Balling for the First Time," *Rolling Stone*, no. 42 (September 20, 1969): 24, 26.

66. Advertisement, *Rolling Stone*, no. 48 (December 13, 1969): 13.

67. Ray Charles and David Ritz, *Brother Ray: Ray Charles' Own Story* (New York: Dial, 1978), 288–89.

68. Pat Thomas, *Listen, Whitey! The Sights and Sounds of Black Power 1965–1975* (Seattle: Fantagraphics, 2012), 40. Unlike Charles himself, Cosby argued that one "can't blame white people" for this problem, but rather Black audiences whom he claimed did not support Black musicians such as Charles.

69. John Street, "'This Is Your Woodstock': Popular Memories and Political Myths," in *Remembering Woodstock*, ed. Andy Bennett (Aldershot: Ashgate, 2004), 37.

70. On the Wild West Festival, see Michael J. Kramer, *The Republic of Rock: Music and Citizenship in the Sixties Counterculture* (New York: Oxford University Press, 2013), 94–129.

71. Jaakov Kohn, "Hirap," *East Village Other* 4, no. 38 (August 20, 1969): 2.

72. John Hilgerdt, "That Aquarian Exposition: 'We Are One . . . ,'" *East Village Other* 4, no. 38 (August 20, 1969): 9.

73. According to Leni Sinclair, she and Genie Plamondon were bailed out by the National Lawyers Guild, although the White Panther men remained in jail for three weeks before being released (Sinclair, interview with the author, March 22, 2019). Pun Plamondon claims instead that Leni was bailed out by Prentice Hall Publishing, which had signed John Sinclair to a contract for his forthcoming book *Guitar Army* (Plamondon, *Lost from the Ottawa*, 140). *Guitar Army* was published by Douglas Book Corporation in 1972.

74. Leni Sinclair, letter to John Sinclair, August 25, 1969, folder 37, box 2, JLSP. John Sinclair lays out the three-point program in "On Youth Culture: Proposal to the Central Comm.," typescript dated "Jan & Feb 1970," folder 19, box 17, JLSP.

75. Leni [Sinclair], letter to John [Sinclair], August 30, 1969, folder 37, box 2, JLSP.

76. Abbie [Hoffman], letter to John [Sinclair], [September 1969], folder 38, box 2, JLSP.

77. John Sinclair, letter to Abbott H. Hoffman, September 22, 1969, folder 40, box 2, JLSP. This letter was published as "Dear Abbie: John Sinclair Writes from Prison," *NOLA Express*, no. 46 (January 9, 1970): 5, 8.

78. John Sinclair, letter to Abbott H. Hoffman, September 22, 1969, folder 40, box 2, JLSP.

79. John Sinclair, letter to Abraham Peck, September 23, 1969, folder 40, box 2, JLSP.

80. John Sinclair, letter to Magdalene Sinclair, September 25, 1969, folder 40, box 2, JLSP; on Jerry Rubin's involvement in the merger of the White Panthers and the Yippies, see Pat Thomas, *Did It! From Yippie to Yuppie: Jerry Rubin, an American Revolutionary* (Seattle: Fantagraphics, 2017), 59.

81. Ken Kelley and Pun Plamondon, letter to "Sisters & Brothers," September 24, 1969, folder

26, box 17, JLSP; also see "Free Sinclair!," *Ann Arbor Argus* 1, no. 12 (September 17–October 2, 1969): 15.

82. Lawrence Lipton, "Radio Free America," *Los Angeles Free Press* 6, no. 271 (September 26, 1969): 4; Abe Peck, "Woodstock Nation," *The Seed* (Chicago) 4, no. 7 (October 1, 1969): 13.

83. Hoffman, *Woodstock Nation*, 63.

84. Sinclair, "On Youth Culture," 27.

85. Sinclair, "On Youth Culture," 31.

86. Letter from skip [Taube] to brother john [Sinclair], September 4, 1969, folder 38, box 2, JLSP.

87. Sinclair, "On Youth Culture," 13–14.

88. Plamondon, *Lost from the Ottawa*, 246.

89. Philip J. Deloria, *Playing Indian* (New Haven, CT: Yale University Press, 1998), 158, 161. Deloria argues that "similar dynamics" underlay white countercultural interest in Native Americans and in African Americans (164). For a more sympathetic account of how "more politically oriented hippies and elements of the New Left eventually came to a more sophisticated understanding of the issues at stake for Native Americans," see Sherry L. Smith, *Hippies, Indians, and the Fight for Red Power* (Oxford: Oxford University Press, 2012), 8.

90. John Sinclair, letter to Abbott H. Hoffman, September 22, 1969, folder 40, box 2, JLSP.

91. Hoffman, *Woodstock Nation*, 111.

92. Raskin, *For the Hell of It*, 109–10.

93. "Testimony of Abbie Hoffman (from Chicago Trial)," in *Counterculture and Revolution*, ed. David Horowitz, Michael Lerner, and Craig Pyes (New York: Random House, 1972), 28.

94. Kramer, *Republic of Rock*, 211.

95. Hoffman, *Woodstock Nation*, 24–28.

96. Hoffman, *Woodstock Nation*, 128–30. Elsewhere, however, he calls the Motherfuckers "gutsy" and quotes their "To love we must survive . . ." slogan (112, 127).

97. Hoffman, *Woodstock Nation*, 133.

98. Hoffman, *Woodstock Nation*, 5.

99. Hoffman, *Woodstock Nation*, 123–25. Hoffman's reference to Hitler was probably intended to refer not to Townshend, but to Who singer Roger Daltrey, who praised Hitler as a strong leader in a 1969 interview (Doggett, *There's a Riot Going On*, 263).

100. Hoffman, *Woodstock Nation*, 120.

101. Hoffman, *Woodstock Nation*, 120.

102. Sinclair, "On Youth Culture," 12–13.

103. Biographer Marty Jezer argues that *Woodstock Nation* was Hoffman's attempt to compensate for his "failure to politicize the festival itself" (*Abbie Hoffman: American Rebel* [New Brunswick, NJ: Rutgers University Press, 1992]: 190).

104. Sinclair, "On Youth Culture," 11.

105. Sinclair, "On Youth Culture," 15.

106. John Sinclair, "Message to the People of Woodstock Nation (2)," *Sun/Dance*, no. 2 (October 1970): 6–7.

107. Sinclair, "Message to the People," 16.

108. John Sinclair, letter to Abraham Peck, September 23 [1969], folder 40, box 2, JLSP.

109. Franklin Bach, "Rock for Our People," *Sun/Dance* [no. 1] [July 4, 1970]: 11; also see "Up the White Panther Party," *Sun/Dance* [no. 1] [July 4, 1970]: 25.

110. Program for "the UP at the Jackson Armory," March 20, 1970, folder 27, box 17, JLSP.

Studio recordings of "Hassan I Sabbah" and "Just Like an Aborigine" are included in *Killer Up (1969–1972)* (Total Energy CD NER3002).

111. Although note that an April 18, 1970, Up program includes a reference to the Black Panthers' motto "Seize the Time" (program for "Up at the Diag," April 18, 1970, folder 35, box 15, JLSP).

112. Abbie Hoffman, *Woodstock Nation*, Pocket Book ed. (New York: Pocket, 1971), 157.

113. Hoffman, *Woodstock Nation*, Pocket Book ed., 159.

114. Hoffman, *Woodstock Nation*, Pocket Book ed., 163.

115. John Sinclair, "Draft Statement for the Movement," manuscript, April 12, 1971, folder 20, box 17, JLSP. During his time underground, Plamondon was assisted by both Kathleen Cleaver and the Motherfuckers, and eventually made his way to Algeria, where he met Eldridge Cleaver, also a fugitive. Plamondon was placed on the FBI's Ten Most Wanted List early in 1970. White Panthers Skip Taube and Jack Forrest were arrested alongside Plamondon and charged with harboring a fugitive (Hale, "Total Assault," 147–48; Plamondon, *Lost from the Ottawa*, 151, 190, 198).

116. Plamondon, *Lost from the Ottawa*, 246. Leni Sinclair remembers that she also disliked the name "Woodstock People's Party" "because of what happened to us at Woodstock" (Sinclair, interview with the author, March 22, 2019).

117. John Sinclair, "We Are a People!," *Ann Arbor Sun*, no. 23 (January 17–30, 1972): supplement, p. 2. This essay is a revised version of Sinclair's 1970 "Message to the People of Woodstock Nation," which proposes Woodstock as a national symbol (see above).

118. Arnold, *Half a Million Strong*, 52–54.

119. Leni Sinclair, interview with the author, March 22, 2019.

120. "Statement of the Central Committee, Rainbow People's Party," *Ann Arbor Sun*, no. 1 (April 30–May 6, 1971): 12.

121. Central Committee, Rainbow People's Party, and Huey P. Newton, "Two Statements on the Defection of Eldridge Cleaver from the BPP and the Defection of the BPP from the Black Community," *Ann Arbor Sun*, no. 6 (June 4, 1971): 6.

122. Leni Sinclair, interview with the author, March 22, 2019.

123. Hale, "Total Assault," 150.

124. Leni Sinclair, interview with the author, March 22, 2019. On the People's Ballroom, which hosted live music during 1972, see Mike Gould, "The People's Ballroom: Seeing the Light, Taking the Heat" (2006), http://mondodyne.com/a2observer/peoplesballroom.shtml, accessed March 24, 2019.

125. Carson, *Grit, Noise, and Revolution*, 268–69.

Epilogue

1. James McNally, "Azealia Banks's '212': Black Female Identity and the White Gaze in Contemporary Hip-Hop," *Journal of the Society for American Music* 10, no. 1 (February 2016): 74.

2. Vanessa Grigoriadis, "The Passion of Nicki Minaj," *New York Times Magazine*, October 7, 2015.

3. Macklemore & Ryan Lewis, "White Privilege II" (Macklemore & Ryan Lewis LLC, 2016).

4. Eminem, "Untouchable," *Revival* (Aftermath Entertainment, 2017).

5. Dave Sinclair, "A Memo from the Chief of Staff (for former members of the Rainbow People's Party)," in Pun Plamondon, *Lost from the Ottawa: The Story of the Journey Back* (Victoria, BC: Trafford, 2004), 317.

6. See Jonathan Eisen, *Altamont: Death of Innocence in the Woodstock Nation* (New York: Avon, 1970).

7. Robert Christgau, "The Rolling Stones: Can't Get No Satisfaction" (1972) in *Any Old Way You Choose It: Rock and Other Pop Music, 1967–1973* (New York: Cooper Square Press, 2000), 220.

8. Sol Stern, "Altamont: Pearl Harbor to Woodstock Nation," in *Counterculture and Revolution*, ed. David Horowitz, Michael Lerner, and Craig Pyes (New York: Random House, 1972), 118.

9. Ralph J. Gleason, "Who's Responsible for the Murder?," *San Francisco Chronicle*, December 8, 1969.

10. Joel Selvin, *Altamont: The Rolling Stones, the Hells Angels, and the Inside Story of Rock's Darkest Day* (New York: Dey St., 2016), 251. As Jack Hamilton points out, "the Rolling Stones' racial transgressions became absorbed into the figure of Hunter and the Altamont narrative, and Hunter's murder legitimized the idea that the violence found in the music of the Rolling Stones was in fact simply a 'surrogate' for a wider violence lingering about the culture that embraced the band" (Hamilton, *Just around Midnight: Rock and Roll and the Racial Imagination* [Cambridge, MA: Harvard University Press, 2016], 271).

11. Sandy Darlington, "Let It Bleed," *Great Speckled Bird* 3, no. 2 (January 12, 1970): 20.

12. *Blender*, for example, awarded Starship's 1985 hit "We Built This City" the #1 slot in its list of the "50 Worst Songs Ever," explaining that "Starship . . . spend the song carrying on as if they invented rock & roll rebellion, while churning out music that encapsulates all that was wrong with rock in the '80s: Sexless and corporate, it sounds less like a song than something built in a lab by a team of record-company executives" (John Aizlewood et al., "Run for Your Life! It's the 50 Worst Songs Ever!," www.blender.com/guide/articles.aspx?id=786, viewed December 14, 2008).

13. Stern, "Altamont," 121; Ralph J. Gleason, "Aquarius Wept," *Esquire* 74, no. 2a (August 1970): 92; Ralph "Sonny" Barger with Keith and Kent Zimmerman, *Hell's Angel: The Life and Times of Sonny Barger and the Hell's Angels Motorcycle Club* (New York: William Morrow, 2000), 162.

14. Darlington, "Let It Bleed," 20.

15. David A. Carson, *Grit, Noise, and Revolution: The Birth of Detroit Rock 'n' Roll* (Ann Arbor: University of Michigan Press, 2005), 266.

16. Rolling Stones, "Sweet Black Angel," *Exile on Main St* (Rolling Stones Records COC 2-2900, 1972).

17. On Rock against Racism, see *Reminiscences of RAR: Rocking against Racism 1976–1982*, ed. Roger Huddle and Red Saunders (London: Redwords, 2016); Daniel Rachel, *Walls Come Tumbling Down: The Music and Politics of Rock against Racism, 2 Tone and Red Wedge* (London: Picador, 2016).

18. On the reception of *Graceland*, see Louise Meintjes, "Paul Simon's 'Graceland,' South Africa, and the Mediation of Musical Meaning," *Ethnomusicology* 34, no. 1 (winter 1990): 37–73.

19. Rage against the Machine, "Wake Up," *Rage against the Machine* (Epic 472224 1, 1992).

20. Hamilton, *Just around Midnight*, 19.

21. Mark Kennedy, "John Mellencamp Takes a Knee for Black Lives Matter," AP News, February 2, 2018, https://www.apnews.com/b7dfda83e41b47cba4ba046f599d9108, accessed March 29, 2019; Jon Bernstein, "Rise Above: Will Donald Trump's America Trigger a Punk Protest Renaissance?," *The Guardian*, December 15, 2016, https://www.theguardian.com/music/2016/dec/15/protest-songs-hip-hop-punk-black-flag-trump, accessed March 29, 2019.

22. G'Ra Asim, "Punk Rock and Protest," *The Baffler*, July 7, 2016, https://thebaffler.com/latest/punk-rock-and-protest-asim, accessed March 29, 2019; https://girlslivingoutsidesocietysshit.bandcamp.com/track/fight, accessed June 10, 2020.

23. Bernstein, "Rise Above."

24. For insightful case studies, see *Black Lives Matter and Music: Protest, Intervention, Reflection*, ed. Fernando Orejuela and Stephanie Shonekan (Bloomington: Indiana University Press, 2018).

25. Kyra D. Gaunt, "YouTube, Twerking, and You: Context Collapse and the Handheld Co-Presence of Black Girls and Miley Cyrus," *Journal of Popular Music Studies* 27, no. 3 (September 2015): 245.

26. Gaunt, "YouTube, Twerking, and You," 256.

27. Gaunt, "YouTube, Twerking, and You," 256.

28. Grigoriadis, "Passion of Nicki Minaj."

29. Melvin L. Williams, "White Chicks with a Gangsta' Pitch: Gendered Whiteness in United States Rap Culture (1990–2017)," *Journal of Hip Hop Studies* 4, no. 1 (fall 2017): 67; McNally, "Azealia Banks's '212,'" 75.

30. McNally, "Azealia Banks's '212,'" 74.

31. McNally, "Azealia Banks's '212,'" 75–76.

32. Lanre Bakare, "'We Are Michael Brown's Family': How Rap and R&B Stars Responded to the Ferguson Protest," *The Guardian*, November 27, 2014, https://www.theguardian.com/music/2014/nov/27/michael-brown-rap-stars-responded-ferguson-protest, accessed March 25, 2019.

33. Alex Blue V, "'Hear What You Want': Sonic Politics, Blackness, and Racism-Canceling Headphones," *Current Musicology*, no. 99–100 (spring 2017): 104.

34. Brittney Cooper, "Iggy Azalea's Post-Racial Mess: America's Oldest Race Tale, Remixed," *Salon*, July 16, 2014, https://www.salon.com/2014/07/15/iggy_azaleas_post_racial_mess_americas_oldest_race_tale_remixed/, accessed March 17, 2019.

35. kris ex, "Macklemore's 'White Privilege II' Is a Mess, But We Should Talk About It," *Pitchfork*, January 22, 2016, https://pitchfork.com/thepitch/1003-macklemores-white-privilege-ii-is-a-mess-but-we-should-talk-about-it/, accessed March 29, 2019.

36. Critic Spencer Kornhaber compares "White Privilege II" to the work of Kendrick Lamar, but adds that "Lamar would never let anyone come away thinking the solution was as exciting as Macklemore makes it sound here. He probably wouldn't tack on the uplifting coda at the end of the song" (Kornhaber, "Sympathy for the Macklemore," *The Atlantic*, January 22, 2016, https://www.theatlantic.com/entertainment/archive/2016/01/macklemore-white-privilege-ii-review-admirable-unlistenable/426588/, accessed March 29, 2019).

37. Carl Hancock Rux, "Eminem: The New White Negro," in *Everything but the Burden: What White People Are Taking from Black Culture*, ed. Greg Tate (New York: Broadway, 2003), 21–22; also see Edward G. Armstrong, "Eminem's Construction of Authenticity," *Popular Music and Society* 27, no. 3 (October 2004): 344.

38. Loren Kajikawa, *Sounding Race in Rap Songs* (Oakland: University of California Press, 2015), 134–35.

39. Kajikawa, *Sounding Race*, 139.

40. Adele Platton, "5 Celebrity Reactions to Macklemore's 'White Privilege II,'" *Billboard*, February 4, 2016, https://www.billboard.com/articles/columns/hip-hop/6866892/macklemore-white-privilege-ii-celebrity-reactions, accessed March 29, 2019; Allison P. Davis, "Macklemore Is All of My Woke Ex-Boyfriends," *The Cut*, January 27, 2016, https://www.thecut.com/2016/

01/macklemore-is-all-of-my-woke-ex-boyfriends.html, accessed March 29, 2019. *Rolling Stone* critic Jonah Weiner was effusive, praising Macklemore's "smoldering earnestness and abiding sense of conscience" and pointing out that he "looped in a number of activists, musicians, intellectuals and academics, and rewrote it based on their feedback" (Weiner, "Why Macklemore Risked It All for 'White Privilege II,'" *Rolling Stone*, March 10, 2016, https://www.rolling stone.com/music/music-news/why-macklemore-risked-it-all-for-white-privilege-ii-235951/, accessed March 29, 2019).

41. Platton, "5 Celebrity Reactions."

42. Carl Lamarre, "Here Are Eminem's 'Untouchable' Lyrics Decoded," *Billboard*, December 8, 2017, https://www.billboard.com/articles/columns/hip-hop/8062711/eminem-untouchable-lyrics-decoded, accessed March 29, 2019.

43. Kornhaber, "Sympathy for the Macklemore." *Pitchfork* argues that throughout "White Privilege II" "he outs himself as a self-doubting ally in the war against racism, sits confounded as he's congratulated by unconscious racists, places himself in culture-vulture crosshairs, and finally, reveals himself as a knowing recipient of white privilege. But, at no point does he broach the possibility of this all being part of an elaborate white savior strategy." Reviewer kris ex adds that "this song puts Macklemore in the conversation about Black lives mattering and—due to [the] very same white privilege he's wrestling with in this song—he's going to get an inordinate amount of attention for speaking out" (kris ex, "Macklemore's 'White Privilege II'").

44. Jonathan Cunningham, "White Privilege II Showed Me What an Unruly Mess We're In," *Yes!,* February 1, 2016, https://www.yesmagazine.org/democracy/2016/02/01/white-privilege-ii -showed-me-what-an-unruly-mess-were-in/, accessed June 10, 2020.

45. Gene Demby, "I Guess We Gotta Talk About Macklemore's 'White Privilege' Song," *NPR*, January 29, 2016, https://www.npr.org/sections/codeswitch/2016/01/29/464752853/i-guess-we -gotta-talk-about-macklemores-white-privilege-song, accessed March 29, 2019.

46. Tshepo Mokoena, "Eminem's 'Untouchable' Is Another Entry-Level Musing on Whiteness," *Noisey*, December 8, 2017, https://noisey.vice.com/en_us/article/nedzzb/eminem -untouchable-whiteness-joyner-lucas-im-not-racist, accessed March 29, 2019.

47. Marc Hogan, "Eminem: 'Untouchable,'" *Pitchfork*, December 8, 2017, https://pitchfork .com/reviews/tracks/eminem-untouchable/, accessed March 29, 2019.

48. Cooper, "Iggy Azalea's Post-Racial Mess."

49. Davis, "Macklemore Is All of My Woke Ex-Boyfriends."

50. Gaunt, "YouTube, Twerking, and You," 256.

51. Michael Denning, *Noise Uprising: The Audiopolitics of a World Musical Revolution* (London: Verso, 2015), 167.

52. Denise Sullivan, *Keep on Pushing: Black Power Music from Blues to Hip-Hop* (Chicago: Lawrence Hill, 2011), 86; Howard Brick, *Age of Contradiction: American Thought and Culture in the 1960s* (New York: Twayne, 1998).

Index